Growing Old in Canada

Growing Old in Canada
Demographic and Geographic Perspectives

Eric G. Moore and Mark W. Rosenberg, with Donald McGuinness

Department of Geography
Queen's University

 Statistics Statistique
Canada Canada

Published in conjunction with

I(T)P® Nelson

an International Thomson Publishing company

Toronto • Albany • Bonn • Boston • Cincinnati • Detroit • London • Madrid • Melbourne
Mexico • New York • Pacific Grove • Paris • San Francisco • Singapore • Tokyo • Washington

I(T)P® **International Thomson Publishing**

The ITP logo is a trademark under licence

Published in 1997 by

I(T)P® **Nelson**

A division of Thomson Canada Limited, 1997

1120 Birchmount Road

Scarborough, Ontario M1K 5G4

Visit the ITP Nelson Web site at **http://www.nelson.com/nelson.html**

Published by authority of the Minister responsible for Statistics Canada

Canadian Cataloguing in Publication Data

Moore, Eric G.

　　Growing old in Canada

Issued also in French under title : Vieillir au Canada : les aspects démographique et géographique du vieillissement. "Part of the 1991 Census monograph series" — foreword. Includes bibliographical references and index.
ISBN 0-17-605633-5

1. Aged – Canada. 2. Aged – Canada – Statistics. 3. Aged – Services for – Canada. 4. Canada – Census, 1991. I. Rosenberg, Mark. II. McGuinness, Donald. III. Statistics Canada. IV. Title.

HQ1064.C2M64 1996　305.26'0971　C96-932168-6

Printed and bound in Canada
1 2 3 4　(BG)　00 99 98 97

DEDICATION

Edward Thomas Pryor, 1931–1992

This series of census analytical volumes is dedicated to the memory of Dr. Edward T. Pryor, a respected and internationally acclaimed sociologist, demographer and author. Dr. Pryor served as Director General of the Census and Demographic Statistics Branch of Statistics Canada and was affectionately known as "Mr. Census." His scholarship, vision, leadership and unfailing dedication to his profession served as inspiration and guidance in the conception and development of this series.

CONTENTS

LIST OF FIGURES

LIST OF TABLES

LIST OF TABLES

FOREWORD

Growing Old in Canada is the first in a series of eight monographs produced by Statistics Canada as part of the 1991 Census Analytic Program. The 1991 Census monographs continue a tradition in census analysis that began with the 1931 Census and was repeated in 1961 and 1971. Although several studies were conducted following the 1981 Census, there has not been a formal monograph program associated with the census since 1971. Many of the 1971 series are still used today in university programs and by the general public.

It has always been the purpose of census monographs to provide analysis of topics related to Canadian social and economic life. To this end, the current series deals with some major issues of Canadian life in the 1990s that will continue to have ramifications into the 21st century. These issues concern education, aging of the population, the changing Canadian labour market, families, immigrants, income distribution, women, and Aboriginal peoples. Using sophisticated analytic techniques, the monographs deal with the selected themes in a comprehensive way and complement the *Focus on Canada* series, which presents more general analyses.

I would like to express my appreciation to all the authors who contributed to this excellent series. I would also like to thank the staff of the Census Analytic Program of Statistics Canada, who so efficiently oversaw the program, as well as the Advisory Committee for their valuable expertise.

I hope the series will help Canadians understand the challenges our country faces as we approach the 21st century, and contribute to informed discussion of how to deal with them.

DR. IVAN FELLEGI
Chief Statistician, Statistics Canada

FOREWORD

Canada's aging population is a major social phenomenon that will continue well into the next century. Throughout the 20th century, the proportion of the population that is elderly has risen dramatically, reflecting the combined effects of declining fertility and increasing ages of survival for both men and women. What are the social and economic characteristics of this growing segment of Canadian society? Where do the elderly live, and in what kinds of accommodation? What are their needs, and are these needs likely to be met?

These questions are addressed in *Growing Old in Canada*. This census monograph provides detailed profiles of the elderly population in Canada, and it assesses the support and services available. The study includes a spatial analysis of where the elderly live, focusing on major migration trends. It also examines elderly people's income, health status, living arrangements and other characteristics. This emphasis on elderly people's needs and characteristics is accompanied by analysis focusing on the capacities of communities to provide the support and services the elderly need. The discussion on public policy issues alerts us to the challenges that inevitably arise from elderly people's social, economic and health needs, when juxtaposed against the existing social services targeted at the elderly.

Growing Old in Canada is part of the 1991 Census Monograph Series, which provides substantive, in-depth analyses of selected themes, and demonstrates the power and value of census data on their own and when analytically coupled with other data sources. Topics in the series include aging, income distribution, immigration, the family, education, the labour force, women, and Aboriginal peoples. The monographs are designed to be integrated into a variety of academic programs and to serve as background in formulating and developing public policy.

Planning and overseeing the 1991 Census monograph program was the responsibility of the Census Analysis Division of Statistics Canada. The program manager and those responsible within the division were assisted by the Advisory Committee, whose members reflect the broad interests and professional backgrounds of Canada's socio-economic research community. The committee provided advice on all aspects of the monograph program, including topic suggestions, methodology for competitions, assessment of proposals, and the process for peer review. In the Acknowledgements page of this volume, a listing is provided of Advisory Committee members as well as Statistics Canada personnel who gave generously of their time and effort to the monograph series.

The invitation to submit research proposals was extended by the Chief Statistician to all members of the Canadian research community, both new scholars and those with proven track records. Proposals were assessed on the basis of their relevance to socio-economic issues facing Canada, the scope of the analytical approach, the suitability of the analytical techniques and methodologies, and the importance of census data to the study. The authors selected represent the full spectrum of Canada's social science research community. They come from universities across Canada as well as from Statistics Canada.

By encouraging investigations of the trends and changes in Canadian society, the 1991 Census monograph program continues a valuable tradition in census analysis. As we approach the millennium, many social issues will persist and possibly intensify. Canada, and all Canadians, will benefit from insight provided by the 1991 Census Monograph Series. Persons interested in issues arising from the aging of Canada's population will find *Growing Old in Canada* an informative analysis of today's elderly and the support available to them.

DR. MONICA BOYD
Chair, Census Monographs Advisory Committee

PREFACE

For more than 20 years, demographers have tracked changes in Canadian society using analysis based on census data, and have linked those changes to their economic and social consequences. A lineage of work can be traced back to Kalbach and McVey (1971, 1979), whose summaries of key census findings, especially of the 1971 Census, set the stage for those who followed. Kalbach and McVey's work on the Canadian population including, most recently, McVey and Kalbach (1995) has been enlarged upon by Stone and Marceau (1977), Foot (1982), McDaniel (1986), Health and Welfare Canada (1989) and Beaujot (1991). The latter works have focused explicitly on the public policy implications of demographic trends. Clearly, these authors see the aging of the Canadian population as a major demographic issue. This monograph examines Canada's elderly population from demographic and geographic perspectives; it also considers the broader public policy implications of its findings.

Censuses every five years, post-censal surveys and special surveys provide researchers, policy makers and communities the opportunities to verify the trends and relationships identified in this study. Various recent national surveys (such as Statistics Canada's General Social Survey [GSS], Health and Activity Limitation Surveys [HALS] and Survey on Ageing and Independence [SAI]) as well as provincial surveys (such as the Ontario Health Survey) have illuminated the health status and behaviours of Canadians and provided rich sources of data. They have been reported in federal studies (such as Seniors Secretariat 1993; Statistics Canada 1987, 1990a, 1990b), but have remained underused sources for provincial and sub-provincial studies. This is particularly true of the 1986 HALS (Moore and Rosenberg 1992). The second cycle of the GSS dealing with health (GSS 6), the SAI, and the 1991 HALS are other sources of data for examining health status and its implications for health and social services. Without these sources of demographic, economic and social data, we could not continue to examine and understand the changing nature of Canada's elderly.

Study after study show strong links between health status and many key socioeconomic and demographic variables. These links form the basis of our discussion of individual aging and health status in Canada. Age and gender are well-documented variables, but education, income, marital status and household composition also have consistent links with health. Canadians who are better educated and better off economically are healthier (Wilkins, Adams and Brancker 1989), and married people report better health than singles (Stone and Fletcher 1986). Living alone also emerges as an important variable. Those who live alone tend to be more reliant on formal supports than those who live with others (Stone and Fletcher 1986; Moore 1992).

The role of health care institutions such as nursing homes and chronic care hospitals is significant to our discussion. Canada has a relatively high rate of institutionalization; approximately 8.1% of the population 65 and over lives in institutions. Since 98% of those in institutions are disabled (Dunn 1990), it is important to include them in any procedure for estimating the propensity to be disabled. We need to know more about what factors lead to institutionalization. We particularly need to know the degree to which people are institutionalized because their community lacks the supports to help them live independently rather than because they are in poor health (Gibson and Rowland 1984). The various HALS, which cover both households and institutions, bring together data on household composition and availability of family support with information on health status and service needs. This gives us a basis for assessing the pressures on both institutions and communities when different policies related to health care institutions are applied.

Moore, Burke and Rosenberg (1990), in a series of studies and papers, have already demonstrated the potential of using the 1986 HALS to examine health status and the implications for health care and social service delivery. In this book, knowledge from previous studies is used in conjunction with the GSS, the SAI and the HALS to provide a detailed analysis of the health status of elderly persons, and how such variables as gender, household structure and economic circumstances interact with health status.

Without these sources of demographic, economic and social data, we could not continue to examine and understand the changing nature of Canada's elderly.

ERIC G. MOORE
MARK W. ROSENBERG
Department of Geography
Queen's University

ACKNOWLEDGEMENTS

Statistics Canada and ITP Nelson wish to acknowledge the following for their excellent efforts on behalf of the Census Monograph Series:

For Statistics Canada
Gustave Goldmann, Manager, Census Analysis Division
Tom Caplan, Chief, Census Socio-economic Research and Analysis
Patty Paul, Senior Technical Consultant
Andy Siggner, Senior Analyst
Nicole Kelly, Research and Administrative Clerk
Gaye Ward, Head, English Writing/Editing Unit, Communications Division
Tom Vradenburg, English Editor
Nathalie Turcotte, Senior French Editor
Danielle Courchesne, French Editor
Sylvette Cadieux, Official Languages Division

Advisory Committee on Census Monographs
Monica Boyd, Carleton University, Chair
Tom Symons, Trent University
John Myles, Carleton University
Susan McDaniel, University of Alberta
Jacques Légaré, Université de Montréal
Allan Maslove, Carleton University
Paddy Fuller, Canada Mortgage and Housing Corporation
Derrick Thomas, Citizenship and Immigration Canada
Elizabeth Ruddick, Citizenship and Immigration Canada
Ramona MacDowell, Human Resources Development Canada
James Wetzel, United States Bureau of the Census
Réjean Lachapelle, Statistics Canada
Ian Macredie, Statistics Canada

For ITP Nelson
Michael Young, Team Leader and Publisher
Bob Kohlmeier and Marcia Miron, Production Editors
Angela Cluer, Art Director
Sylvia Vander Schee, Assistant Art Director
Brad Horning, Production Co-ordinator
Niche Electronic Publishing, Page Composition
Steve MacEachern, Interior Design
Telmet Design Associates, Cover Design

INTRODUCTION

Canada's population is aging. Collectively, the nation is entering an unprecedented period in its demographic history: The children born between the end of the Second World War and the early 1960s, who form the largest age group in Canadian history, will reach their golden years in the early part of the 21st century. The seniors of today and tomorrow are more numerous and constitute a larger portion of the population than any generation before them.

Taking a demographic perspective, this book explores older Canadians' lives today and tomorrow and the implications for the rest of the nation. It discusses in depth the separate but related issues of "individual aging" and "population aging." For individuals, the major aging issue is the long-term increase in life expectancy (see Nagnur 1986a), and the continuing but narrowing life-expectancy gap between women and men—now 25% at age 65.

Population aging occurs when the proportion of older people in the population in a given area rises. This changing age distribution can be measured in many ways, most simply by the proportion of the population that is 65 and over (McDaniel 1986). The prime cause of increases at the provincial and national levels in the proportion who are elderly has been declines in the fertility rate (Stone and Fletcher 1986), while at the local level, the prime cause has often been out-migration of younger people (McCarthy 1983).

Public debate on the aging population has focused mostly on national and, to some degree, provincial concerns. However, it is at the local level, the level of the municipality, health district or regional planning authority, that the consequences of larger societal changes are played out and must be accommodated in local planning and policies. Some authors, such as Denton and Spencer (1995), argue that the growing proportion of elderly will create a huge financial burden in the coming decades unless the health care system is substantially restructured. At the same time, we must be careful not to over-emphasize the relationship between aging and poor health. The overwhelming majority of younger elderly (those under 75, also called the "young old") enjoy good health and are active and independent. It is only in the 75-and-over population that we find sharp increases in the proportions of those who need substantial help with daily activities such as meal preparation, shopping or housework, or of those who cannot live independently and need to be institutionalized.

To answer many questions relating to the effective delivery of health care and social services, it is important to understand better the geographical dimensions of aging and health. There are basic questions concerning the changing spatial distribution of the elderly population. In absolute terms, has the elderly population continued to concentrate in the cores of Canada's largest cities, or has rapid urban expansion led to a growing suburban elderly population? In relative terms, has the elderly proportion of the rural population continued to grow faster than that of the urban population? Have smaller towns and cities been more prone to rapid aging than large metropolitan areas? How have those communities with dynamic local economies fared compared with less advantaged areas? The answer likely depends on the strength of the local economic base, how the socio-economic conditions of their elderly populations are perceived, and on the policy decisions made by higher levels of government. Among elderly people themselves, differences between those in rural, suburban and urban areas—differences in household structure, economic circumstances and availability of social supports—raise fundamental questions about ensuring equal access to health care and social services.

While it is beyond the scope of this study to measure services offered within communities, we conduct a limited amount of analysis on seniors' use of services in support of "activities of daily living" and "instrumental activities of daily living." We accept "living at home" as a working definition of independent living. The ability to remain in one's own home is a function of economic circumstances, health status and services one uses as disability increases with age. Looking at distinctions among different elderly age groups, we examine how health status changes. Specifically, we analyse how rates of illness and disability and severity of disability increase according to age, poverty status, gender and level of isolation—those living alone compared with those living with someone else. At the individual level, we are particularly concerned with identifying those segments of the elderly population which, because of economic circumstances, are particularly vulnerable—especially elderly women living alone.

But before discussing these questions in detail, we must first set the context. We describe the aging of the Canadian population in Chapter 1—the growth of the elderly population between 1951 and 1991, the longer life expectancy of women and their preponderance in the elderly population, and the relative importance of fertility, mortality and immigration as bases for population aging are explained. Population aging at the provincial scale and urban–rural differences are described. The size and basic characteristics of the elderly population in institutions are presented. Chapter 1 is also where the basic measures of the elderly population used throughout this book are introduced and defined.

Chapter 2 focuses on individual aging. Our emphasis is on the socio-demographic characteristics of elderly Canadians. In particular, we describe their marital status, living arrangements, level of poverty, employment status and education, drawing mainly on Statistics Canada's 1991 Public Use Micro-data File. Availability of social support is also explored as a characteristic of individual aging using the Survey on Ageing and Independence. This analysis leads us to a model of low-income status that confirms that increasing age, gender and living alone are most closely associated with the likelihood of elderly individuals living in poverty. Regional differences are also captured in this model.

In the second half of the chapter, we examine the roles of migration and mobility as adjustments, either in anticipation of future life course events or as a result of them. This leads to a multivariate model of individual migration behaviour distinguished by separate analyses of those between the ages of 55 to 64 (the pre-retirement stage), those between the ages of 65 and 74 (the "young" old) and those 75 and over. Migration is expressed as a function of the socio-economic and geographic differences among the elderly that appear to influence the frequency with which and the circumstances when they move.

In Chapter 3, we turn to a more geographically detailed analysis of where elderly Canadians lived in 1991, and their demographic characteristics. While in Chapters 1 and 2 provincial and regional differences are emphasized, in this chapter demographic patterns at the census division level are presented. Census divisions can be equated with counties, cantons, regional municipalities and districts across Canada (see Figure I.1). Canada's three largest metropolitan areas, Toronto, Montréal and Vancouver, are singled out for more detailed analysis.

In the second half of the chapter, the spatial distribution of the elderly population at the census division scale is decomposed into those who are staying where they are and growing old—or "aging in place"—and those who have moved into the area to retire—the migration component. This analysis shows that underlying population change at the local level is a complex mix of changes involving older and younger age groups. Here the dominance of aging in place emerges, emphasizing the power of the existing age structure in determining the rate of population aging. The second component of this analysis stresses the influence of the migration patterns of younger people on aging. The areas of Canada that have the strongest out-migration, particularly the Prairie and Atlantic provinces, age more rapidly, while in British Columbia and Ontario the flows of younger in-migrants significantly slow the aging rate.

The focus of Chapter 4 is elderly people's health status. Disability, defined as functional limitations on daily activities, is the main measure of health status in this analysis. Distinctions are made on the basis of type of disability, severity of disability, activities of daily living and instrumental activities of daily living. As well, satisfaction with health status and service utilization measures are presented in this chapter. By linking elderly people's health status to their socio-economic status, we create a multivariate model. We conclude the chapter by examining regional variations in the incidence of disability.

Chapter 5 examines the spatial distribution of the elderly population in the year 2011, using Statistics Canada's Projection Series No. 2 at the provincial level and the authors' own cohort (five-year age group) projection model at the census division scale. Paralleling Chapter 1, basic demographic measures at the national and provincial scales are presented. The second part of the chapter presents the future spatial distribution of the elderly population by census division; the third part examines a projected spatial distribution of disability among the elderly population in 2011.

In the concluding chapter, we return to the issues raised in this introduction, and discuss the insights Chapters 1 to 5 provide in a public policy context for the present and the future.

FIGURE I.1:   CENSUS DIVISIONS AND MAJOR METROPOLITAN AREAS OF
              CANADA, 1991

Source: Census of Canada, 1991

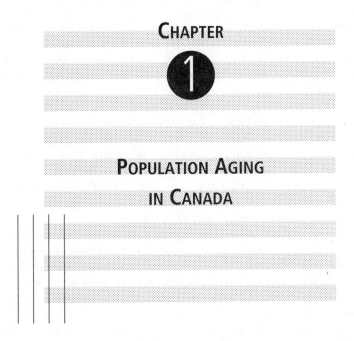

CHAPTER

1

POPULATION AGING
IN CANADA

Beyond Canadians' personal concerns as they grow older or watch loved ones grow older are a set of issues that beset communities and all levels of government. The two issues that have received most attention are income support and the cost of health care for an aging population. Well-publicized actuarial studies suggest that as the elderly population grows in the coming decades, the Canada and Quebec pension plans must be changed if they are to meet their obligations (Auditor General of Canada 1993).

The elderly population's role in generating health care costs has received enormous attention (Angus 1984; Barer, Evans, Hertzman and Lomas 1987; Barer, Evans and Hertzman 1995; Denton and Spencer 1995; Denton, Li and Spencer 1987; Evans 1987; Marshall 1994; McDaniel 1987). Closely connected to the debates on income and health care policies are debates on social support and housing within the community versus institutionalization. Should the costs be borne privately or publicly? If publicly, what level of government should fund and deliver services and housing? The issues, questions and suggested answers have raised public consciousness to the point where population aging is viewed as a "problem paradigm" (McDaniel 1987; Northcott 1994), although, as both McDaniel and Northcott indicate, to view aging as a problem per se misplaces the sources of many of our concerns.[1]

To solve the public policy problems that an aging population presents, we must first clearly understand the basic trends in Canada, the rate at which population aging is taking place and where Canada's population is aging. We will also use this chapter as an opportunity to define the basic concepts and measures used throughout this monograph.

Let's first discuss individual aging and population aging. Individual aging is linked to what demographers call the "life course." As one moves from youth to adolescence to adulthood and then old age, one goes through life experiences such as marriage, the birth of children, employment, unemployment, illness and death. There is no necessary sequence and, apart from death, each individual will not necessarily experience each life phase.

Life course events often lead to changes in other aspects of everyday life. Aging changes the likelihood of a range of events and conditions, including retirement, grandparenthood, chronic illness, disability, widowhood and death. The likelihood of these events happening changes over time, reflecting advances in medical knowledge and practice, changes in social values and shifts in societal affluence. Central to these changes in individual experiences has been the substantial increase in life expectancy over the last 40 years; this is particularly evident for life expectancy at age 65 (Adams 1990; Stone and Fletcher 1986). It changes both the time frame and the likelihood of other significant events in elderly people's lives. As people live to increasingly older ages, the death of a spouse, transition to a frail state and the inability to manage daily living without support will tend to occur later. And, as a result of longer life expectancy, there will be more of those older people.

Population aging refers specifically to the relative size and attributes of the elderly in the population as a whole. The age of 65 has been the significant dividing line between "young" and "old," largely because of its traditional and institutionalized links to retirement and the initiation of a range of social benefits. The proportion of the population 65 and over is the most common measure of population aging (McDaniel 1986), and is used extensively in this book. However, there is no necessary transition in the life of an individual at that age, and clearly the great majority of individuals 65 and over consider themselves active, healthy contributors to society (Stone and Fletcher 1986). As we show in Chapter 4, the sharp increase in the likelihood of major health problems, loss of independence and institutionalization comes much later, particularly after the age of 80. We therefore pay close attention to the variation in conditions and behaviours by age for those 65 and over, with particular emphasis on the contrasts between younger and older elderly.

Population aging is not just about the growing population 65 and over, but also about increases or decreases in the population under 65. In examining how to reduce the impact of a growing elderly population on health care and pension costs, Henripin (1994) illustrates this idea by exploring the relative merits of increasing women's lifetime employment, increasing the number of children born per woman and postponing retirement. He estimates that a 10% reduction in health costs is possible by increasing women's lifetime employment by 6.3 years, by adding 0.2 children per woman or by postponing women's retirement by 3.0 years. Two of the solutions, therefore, hinge on changes in characteristics of the young, not the old, while the third solution hinges on changing the threshold age at which people become "old." The relationships between the young and the old and the implications of those relationships for public policy are recurring themes throughout this chapter and the remainder of this book.

1.1   THE AGING CANADIAN POPULATION

A discussion of the geographic dimensions of aging should begin with a discussion of the country in question. Social values with respect to fertility and reproduction, advances in medical knowledge influencing mortality and morbidity, and controls over immigration, for example, are all influenced by forces at the national (or international) level.

Canada's population has grown at one of the fastest rates in the developed world since the end of the Second World War, fueled by the baby boom that lasted from the late 1940s to the early 1960s (Romaniuc 1994). The total population in 1951 was 14.0 million; by 1991 it was 27.1 million (see Table 1.1).[2] The peak annualized growth rate reached 2.8% a year during the height of the baby boom between 1951 and 1956 and declined steadily until the early 1980s, when it fell to just under 1.0% a year. However, with a marked increase in immigration levels and the halt in the free fall in fertility rates at the end of the 1980s, the annualized growth rate for the 1986-to-1991 period increased again to 1.5% a year.[3]

As in all other developed countries experiencing both declining fertility and mortality, the elderly population in Canada is growing at a considerably faster rate than the total population. In 1951 the population 65 years of age and over totalled 1.08 million, and was 7.8% of the total population. Of the population 65 years of age and over, 149,000 were 80 years of age and over and accounted for 1.1% of the population. By 1991, the population 65 years of age and over stood at nearly 3.2 million, or 11.7% of the total population. The population 80 and over had grown more than fourfold to 657,000, or 2.4% of the population. The population 65 and over grew by more than 3% a year for the entire 40 years, while the 80-plus population grew by close to 4% a year. Not only has the Canadian population been aging steadily, the internal composition of the 65-plus group has itself changed. It contains a progressively greater proportion of people 80 and over. This has many important public policy consequences.

1.1.1   Differences in aging by gender

The growth in the elderly population has had a gendered character (see Figure 1.1). The female elderly population grew steadily and rapidly during the postwar period, while the male population, particularly that 80 and over, saw a marked decline in the rate of growth in the middle decades and has only recently met or exceeded the female growth rates. Clearly, part of the reason for this are the relative changes in mortality of the groups (Stone and Fletcher 1986), but it also reflects the relative sizes of the aging cohorts. Those who turned 80 in the 1960s and 1970s were members of the cohort exposed to the high mortality of the First World War. Relatively smaller cohorts reaching old age decreases the overall rate of aging, while the converse is true for large cohorts.

TABLE 1.1: GROWTH OF THE CANADIAN POPULATION, 1951 TO 1991

('000)

YEAR	FEMALES Total population	FEMALES Population 65+	FEMALES Population 80+	MALES Total population	MALES Population 65+	MALES Population 80+	TOTAL POPULATION Total population	TOTAL POPULATION Population 65+	TOTAL POPULATION Population 80+
1951	6,921	535	81	7,089	551	69	14,009	1,086	149
1956	7,929	622	98	8,152	622	84	16,081	1,244	182
1961	9,019	717	123	9,219	674	104	18,238	1,391	228
1966	9,961	823	156	10,054	717	124	20,015	1,540	280
1971	10,773	963	201	10,795	782	140	21,568	1,744	342
1976	11,543	1,127	240	11,450	875	145	22,993	2,002	385
1981	12,275	1,350	292	12,068	1,011	159	24,343	2,361	451
1986	12,824	1,564	353	12,486	1,133	185	25,309	2,698	537
1991	13,730	1,834	432	13,344	1,327	226	27,073	3,161	657

YEAR	FEMALES Percentage 65+	FEMALES Percentage 80+	FEMALES Percentage 65+ who are 80+	MALES Percentage 65+	MALES Percentage 80+	MALES Percentage 65+ who are 80+	TOTAL Percentage 65+	TOTAL Percentage 80+	TOTAL Percentage 65+ who are 80+
1951	7.7	1.2	15.1	7.8	1.0	12.5	7.8	1.1	13.7
1956	7.8	1.2	15.8	7.6	1.0	13.4	7.7	1.1	14.6
1961	7.9	1.4	17.2	7.3	1.1	15.5	7.6	1.2	16.4
1966	8.3	1.6	19.0	7.1	1.2	17.3	7.7	1.4	18.2
1971	8.9	1.9	20.9	7.2	1.3	17.9	8.1	1.6	19.6
1976	9.8	2.1	21.3	7.6	1.3	16.6	8.7	1.7	19.2
1981	11.0	2.4	21.6	8.4	1.3	15.7	9.7	1.9	19.1
1986	12.2	2.7	22.5	9.1	1.5	16.3	10.7	2.1	19.9
1991	13.4	3.1	23.6	9.9	1.7	17.0	11.7	2.4	20.8

Source: Census of Canada, 1951–1991.

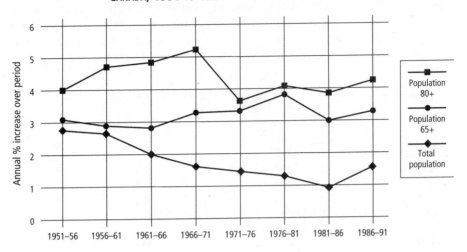

FIGURE 1.1A: ANNUALIZED GROWTH RATES FOR FEMALES, BY AGE, CANADA, 1951 TO 1991

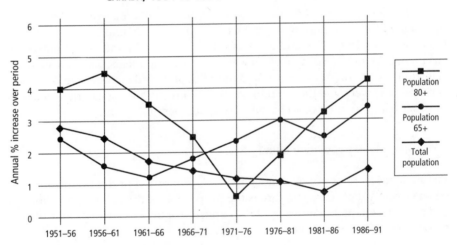

FIGURE 1.1B: ANNUALIZED GROWTH RATES FOR MALES, BY AGE, CANADA, 1951 TO 1991

Source: Census of Canada, 1951–1991.

Consequently, the ratio of men to women (the sex ratio) among the elderly has both decreased and become progressively more pronounced for older ages (see Table 1.2). While recent shifts both in life expectancy (see Figure 1.2) and the size of under-65 cohorts suggest some increase of the preponderance of women at older ages, the reduction in the sex ratios will be small and the dominance of women at older ages is expected to endure (Stone and Fletcher 1986).

TABLE 1.2: RATIO OF MALES PER 100 FEMALES, BY AGE, CANADA, 1951 TO 1991

	AGE GROUP			
Year	55–64	65–74	75–84	85+
1951	107.1	107.9	96.6	76.3
1956	103.7	103.7	96.5	76.6
1961	103.1	96.1	93.3	76.9
1966	101.0	89.8	85.1	72.2
1971	97.3	87.1	74.2	65.9
1976	93.1	86.0	67.8	57.2
1981	91.3	83.4	66.5	48.9
1986	93.3	81.1	65.8	43.6
1991	96.8	81.7	65.6	43.8

Source: Census of Canada, 1951–1991.

The gendered nature of Canada's aging population is a recurring theme of this book and of other authors who have examined its policy implications (Aronson 1994; Connidis 1994; Gee and McDaniel 1994; Rosenthal and Gladstone 1994). The preponderance of elderly women with health care problems, their concentration in institutional settings, their roles and the roles of their daughters and daughters-in-law as caregivers, and the continuing level of poverty among elderly women are all issues that have their roots in these basic demographic trends.

1.1.2 The rate of population aging

The basic measure of population aging is the proportion of the population aged 65 and over. A secondary measure is the proportion of the elderly population 80 and over, which offers a measure of the exposure of the elderly to a range of more serious conditions and events (see Table 1.1).

FIGURE 1.2A: CHANGE IN LIFE EXPECTANCY FOR FEMALES, BY AGE AND PERIOD, 1921 TO 1991

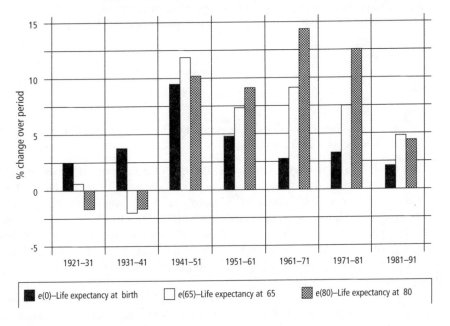

FIGURE 1.2B: CHANGE IN LIFE EXPECTANCY FOR MALES, BY AGE AND PERIOD, 1921 TO 1991

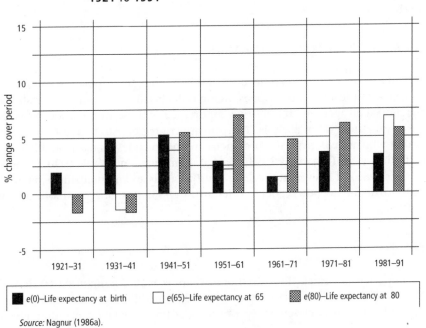

Source: Nagnur (1986a).

The rate of population aging has been changing and it is useful to establish a measure of the rate of population aging. For the population aged 65 and over (or any other specific age group), the proportion of males in an age group in a given time period compared with another time period can be shown thus:

$$C_{m,k}^{(t)} = \frac{P_{m,k}^{(t)}}{P_{m,k}^{(t-1)}}$$

where

C = the ratio
$P_{m,k}^{(t)}$ = the proportion of the male population in age group k at time t
$t-1$ = the previous time period

For both men and women 65 and over, the rate of aging peaked between 1971 and 1976, and remained close to that peak between 1986 and 1991 (see Figure 1.3). For the population aged 80 and over, women's rates of aging increased between 1951 and 1966, while men's decreased. After 1971, the rates begin to converge, and were very close to each other at about 15% for the five-year period 1986–1991. Figure 1.3 presents the ratios for men 65 and over ($C_{m,65+}^{(t)}$), women 65 and over ($C_{f,65+}^{(t)}$), men 80 and over ($C_{m,80+}^{(t)}$) and women 80 and over ($C_{f,80+}^{(t)}$) for five-year periods from 1951 to 1991.

The convergence in the rates of population aging should not, however, be misinterpreted. Since they are well above unity, the elderly population will continue to grow as the baby boomers—those born between the end of the Second World War and the early 1960s—pass 65 years of age, and the sex ratios of the elderly population will continue to be heavily skewed in favour of elderly women over elderly men.

1.2 SOURCES OF POPULATION AGING

The aging of the population reflects what is happening to population composition at all ages, not just the elderly ones. Aging reflects shifts in fertility, mortality and migration at all ages, and the relative importance of these three processes is itself sensitive to the level of analysis. The primary contributor to increases in the proportion who are elderly at the provincial and national levels has been changes in the fertility rate (Desjardins 1993; George, Romaniuc and Nault 1990; Stone and Fletcher 1986). However, at the level of urban areas and municipalities, migration tends to dominate other effects (McCarthy 1983; Rosenberg, Moore and Ball 1989).

1.2.1 Fertility

Declining fertility since the baby boom years is well documented (Wright and Maxim 1987). In relative terms, this means that, as the proportion of the population under 15 has declined, the proportion of the population of other ages has

FIGURE 1.3A: $C_{65+}{}^1$ BY SEX FOR CANADA, **1951** TO **1991**

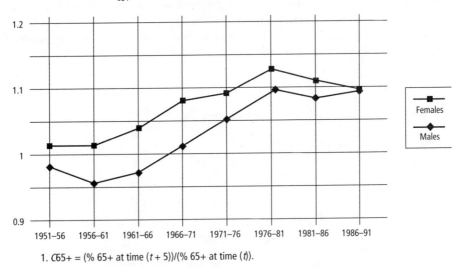

1. $C65+ = (\% \ 65+ \ \text{at time} \ (t+5))/(\% \ 65+ \ \text{at time} \ (t))$.

FIGURE 1.3B: $C_{80+}{}^2$ BY SEX FOR CANADA, **1951** TO **1991**

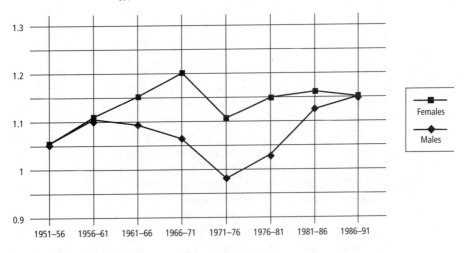

2. $C80+ = (\% \ 80+ \ \text{at time} \ (t+5))/(\% \ 80+ \ \text{at time} \ (t))$.

Source: Census of Canada, 1951–1991.

increased in relative terms. One of the clearest methods for illustrating the impact of fertility on the relative proportions of different age groups is provided by the components of the dependency ratio (Foot 1982).

The overall dependency ratio (DR) measures the relative size of the *dependent* populations of young and old to those in the labour force:

$$DR = \frac{P_{0-14} + P_{65+}}{P_{15-64}} * 100$$

DR can be decomposed into two components:

$$YDR = \frac{P_{0-14}}{P_{15-64}} * 100$$

and

$$ODR = \frac{P_{65+}}{P_{15-64}} * 100$$

where

$\qquad$ YDR = the young component of the dependency ratio
$\qquad$ ODR = the old component of the dependency ratio

From 1951 to 1976, the DR was dominated by the behaviour of the YDR (see Figure 1.4). First, increases in fertility pushed up the YDR between 1951 and 1961. After 1961, the slowing of the baby boom led to relative increases in the working-age population compared to the YDR and ODR. Since 1976, with the continuing decline in fertility rates and the maturing of the working-age population, the ODR has progressively offset the declining YDR. The ODR will come to equal the YDR early in the 21st century and then surpass it (Beaujot 1991).

The use of dependency ratios in this form is merely an indicator of the relative roles of the elderly and youth in the changing structure of the population. But what do they tell us about the concept of dependency? As Foot (1989) has pointed out, the concept of dependency cannot be accurately captured until certain measures can be refined, particularly the likelihood of different age groups being employed and the different costs of social programs (education, unemployment benefits, health care and old age benefits) associated with different ages.

Whether the relative growth of the elderly will lead to conflicts over intergenerational equity has only recently become an issue in Canada (Gee and McDaniel 1994). In one sense, this can be seen as an accounting problem. The limited resources of the society are allocated to different segments of the population in differing proportions, and any net outcome implies a transfer of resources from one segment to another. In simplistic terms, these transfers are sometimes viewed as the trade-off between education for the young and health care and social security for the elderly. More sophisticated arguments see the investment in human capital[4] among the young extending well beyond education. Children, especially disadvantaged children, benefit from health care spending, as well as from programs that enhance their social and emotional well-being. At the other end of the

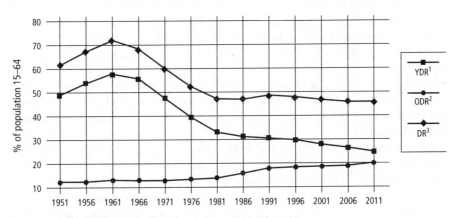

FIGURE 1.4: COMPONENTS OF THE DEPENDENCY RATIO, 1951 TO 2011

1. YDR = (population aged 0–14/population aged 15–64) × 100.
2. ODR = (population aged 65+/population aged 15–64) × 100.
3. DR = YDR + ODR.

Sources: Census of Canada, 1951–1991; Series 2 Population Projections, 1996–2011.

age spectrum lies the question of support for elderly who cannot otherwise maintain their independence. What types of support are needed and who should provide it? As Menken (1985) has shown so effectively, when such support focuses on the family, increases in life expectancy create greater pressures on the providers of care, who often must support both children and parents.

Some fear that, as the ODR increases relative to the YDR, the aging population will exert increasing pressure on the working-age population to support its needs, tilting the intergenerational equity balance towards older Canadians. Those concerned with increases in child poverty in Canada (e.g., Dooley 1994) would argue that the political power of the growing elderly population has already had the effect of reducing poverty among the elderly at the expense of children. A separate argument points to the growing costs of health care and the role that the aging population supposedly plays in generating these costs. As McDaniel (1987) and Gee and McDaniel (1994) argue, such a view is misleading, and the solutions proposed may generate their own social policy problems (see Chapter 6).

1.2.2 Mortality

The last 100 years have seen continual improvements in life expectancy (Nagnur 1986a, 1986b). In the first half of this century, the major reasons for these improvements were reductions in both infant mortality and death due to infectious diseases.

While life expectancy at birth ($e(0)$) has continued to increase (see Table 1.3 and Figure 1.2), the gains in life expectancy at older ages ($e(65)$ and $e(80)$) are becoming increasingly important (see also Stone 1986). This is particularly true for females. Life expectancy at birth has increased 33%, but since 1921 life expectancies for women 65 and over, and 80 and over, have increased 46% and 57% respectively. Only during the most recent period (1986 to 1991) have males' life expectancies started to increase at a faster rate than females', especially among men 65 and over. However, females' life expectancies are likely to remain above that for males for the foreseeable future, among both the population as a whole and the elderly.

In the longer run, the differences between males and females will decline only if the underlying patterns of cause of death change. The assumption made by most analysts is that we are in the third stage of the epidemiological transition (Omran 1971) in which diseases associated with chronic conditions have replaced infectious and parasitic illness as the dominant cause of death. (Without questioning the basic premise, we see the growth of antibiotic-resistant strains of bacteria as one of a few disturbing trends.)

Among chronic diseases, the primary contributor to death is ischemic heart disease, which is significantly more prevalent among men than women. This relationship is also strongly class based; men in blue-collar environments have particularly high propensities for this disease (Nathanson and Lopez 1987). Future declines in mortality differentials between males and females will depend on

TABLE 1.3: LIFE EXPECTANCY, BY AGE AND SEX, 1921 TO 1991

	FEMALES			MALES		
	Life expectancy at birth	Life expectancy at age 65	Life expectancy at age 80	Life expectancy at birth	Life expectancy at age 65	Life expectancy at age 80
Year	$e(0)$	$e(65)$	$e(80)$	$e(0)$	$e(65)$	$e(80)$
1921	60.6	13.6	6.0	58.8	13.0	5.7
1931	62.1	13.7	5.9	60.0	13.0	5.6
1941	64.6	13.4	5.8	63.0	12.8	5.5
1951	70.9	15.0	6.4	66.4	13.3	5.8
1961	74.3	16.1	7.0	68.4	13.6	6.2
1971	76.5	17.6	8.0	69.4	13.8	6.5
1981	79.1	18.9	9.0	71.9	14.6	6.9
1991	80.8	19.8	9.4	74.3	15.6	7.3

Source: Nagnur (1986a).

shifts in underlying behaviour, which contribute to differing propensities for diseases such as ischemic heart disease. At present, it is not clear what shifts are most likely to occur, but the growing rates of lung cancer among Canadian women should be cause for concern.

George et al. (1990) attempted to estimate the relative importance of mortality and fertility changes for the growth in the proportion of the population 65 and over. They conclude that during the period from 1961 to 1986 the primary impact on aging was the result of falling fertility. Mortality improvements only contributed 39% of the effect fertility did. For the 25 years after 1986, mortality will, however, contribute more than fertility to the changing proportion of the population 65 and over. This finding emphasizes the importance of better understanding the determinants of differentials in mortality rates.

1.2.3 Immigration

Immigration has contributed to population growth at varying levels during this century, although in both absolute and relative terms the peak numbers of 300,000 to 400,000 per year in the years 1911–1913 have never been surpassed. Immigration was equal to more than 2.5% of the total population in each year of that period.

In recent years, immigration has again assumed increasing importance. It has climbed from a low of 84,000 in 1985 to 249,000 in 1993—just less than 1% of the total population. Recent estimates indicate a decline in 1994 and 1995 to approximately 200,000 for 1995, when the national population was approaching 30 million.

There are often substantial social and economic costs when an individual migrates to another country, but these are clearly offset by the long-term gains. Viewed as an investment in human capital (Todaro 1969), it is to be expected that such migration is more likely to occur at younger ages, when the impact on lifetime earnings is greatest. Immigrants tend to be significantly younger than the resident population, concentrated in the younger adult years (20 to 39). They help slow down the aging of the population, both directly through their own age distribution (see Table 1.4) and through the children they bear after arriving. The direct effects are clearly illustrated in Figure 1.5, which shows the lower proportions of those 65 and over among immigrants.

The detailed age composition of the immigrant population is also affected by policies governing criteria for admission. In Canada, the role of family reunification policies has been key. The increased emphasis on family reunification after 1978 produced significant increases in the proportion of elderly, especially elderly women, among immigrants (Boyd 1989). This was sustained through the early 1980s.

In the latter part of the decade, a sharp change in immigration policy produced not only an increase in the number of immigrants, but also a tenfold increase in the number of economic/independent immigrants[5] between 1985 and 1988 (Stafford 1992). This wave of economic/independent immigrants effectively

		FEMALES			MALES		
		Percentage 5–14	Percentage 65+	Percentage 75+	Percentage 5–14	Percentage 65+	Percentage 75+
Non-immigrants	1981	16.0	11.1	4.0	17.2	8.7	2.8
in the last five	1986	14.8	12.2	4.4	16.1	9.5	3.0
years	1991	14.5	13.5	5.3	15.8	10.6	3.6
Immigrants to	1981	15.9	6.5	2.0	17.8	4.7	1.0
Canada in the last	1986	13.5	7.0	1.8	13.7	5.3	1.6
five years	1991	15.4	4.9	1.5	17.3	3.7	1.0

Source: Census of Canada, Public Use Micro-data Files, 1981–1991.

decreased the proportion of elderly immigrants (see Table 1.4). Although the differences in age profiles are marked, the overall impact of immigration on population aging is considerably less than the impact of fertility and mortality shifts in the population as a whole. Furthermore, because immigrants themselves age, immigration has very little effect on the long-run age structure of the population (Mitra 1992).

From a policy perspective, there may be various reasons why the federal and provincial governments might want to manipulate fertility, mortality and immigration trends, but it would take unprecedented changes in one or all of these trends to affect how Canada's elderly population will grow over the next 25 years. For example, Gee and McDaniel (1994)[6] estimate it would take immigration levels of 600,000 per year to affect significantly the age structure of the Canadian population. That would be triple the current level of immigration, and double the peak levels that occurred at the beginning of the century.

1.3 THE GEOGRAPHY OF AGING

Across Canada there is as much geographical diversity in both the distribution and rates of growth of the elderly population as there is in the topography or the climate. The main cause of the differences in distribution and rates of elderly growth are regional disparities in economic opportunity, which generate strongly age-selective migration flows (Shaw 1985).

Net migration is the net effect of migration on younger and older age groups. If the net in-migration rate is greater for the older than the younger population (or the net out-migration rate is less) then the population will age, or vice versa. The young are much more prone to migrate than are the elderly (see Figure 2.3). Therefore, generally, significant out-migration will increase the rate of aging, while substantial in-migration has the opposite effect. There is a secondary effect, which receives little attention, and that is the impact of migration decisions on fertility (MOORE 1993)."

FIGURE 1.5: PERCENTAGE OF IMMIGRANTS AND NON-IMMIGRANTS 65 AND OVER,
BY SEX, 1981 TO 1991

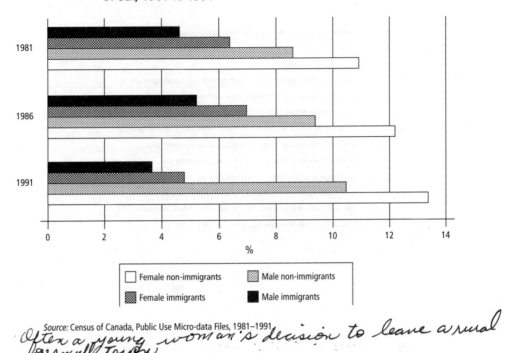

Source: Census of Canada, Public Use Micro-data Files, 1981–1991

Often a young woman's decision to leave a rural or small town.

environment to pursue postsecondary education or join the labour force elsewhere is also a decision to forego marriage and childbearing for many years. Spatially, this results in higher fertility in rural areas and a reduction in the rate of
aging there, although this reduction is offset by the much larger migration effect.

In this section, we examine the differences in population aging between provinces and between rural and urban areas. More detailed analysis of regional and
local variations in aging is in Chapter 3.

1.3.1 The provinces

The proportion of the population aged 65 and over varies substantially among the
provinces and territories (see Figure 1.6). In the Northwest Territories (2.7%) and
the Yukon (3.9%) relatively low proportions of the population were 65 and over
in 1991. Among the provinces, 7.9% of Alberta's male population was 65 and over,
while in Saskatchewan, at the other end of the spectrum, it was 12.6%. The proportion of females 65 and over was higher in every province, with Alberta (10.3%)
and Saskatchewan (15.7%) again anchoring the distribution. In the territories the
male–female gap among the elderly was narrower than in southern Canada,
although the proportions are much lower than in the rest of the country.

FIGURE 1.6A: PERCENTAGE 65 AND OVER, BY PROVINCE AND TERRITORY, AND BY SEX, 1991

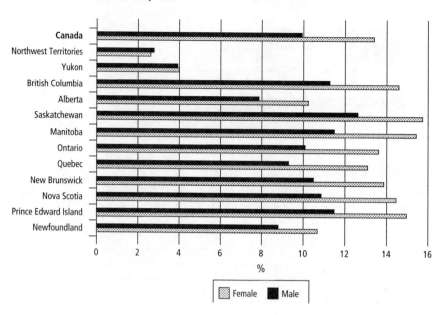

FIGURE 1.6B: PERCENTAGE 80 AND OVER, BY PROVINCE AND TERRITORY, AND BY SEX, 1991

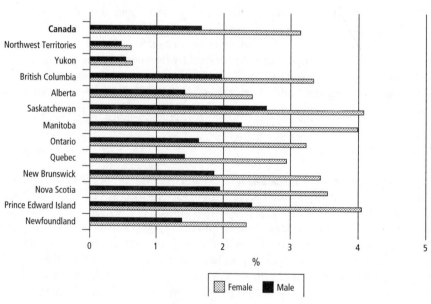

Source: Census of Canada, 1991.

The differentials tend to reflect the long-run patterns of age-selective migration away from rural and primary resource areas in the Atlantic and Prairie provinces and towards the urban regions of economic growth in Central and Western Canada. Alberta in particular received substantial in-migration of younger people during the 1970s; this is reflected in both low proportions of elderly and the low growth rate of this segment in that decade (see Figure 1.7). The trend in the 1980s, however, was towards a gradual convergence in the interprovincial proportions. The highest rates of aging tended to be in those provinces with the smallest proportions 65 and over (Quebec, Newfoundland and Alberta), which shows the importance of aging of the larger cohorts aged 55 to 64 in 1981 and who reached 65 during the decade from 1981 to 1991.

Interprovincial migration plays a complex role in the rate of aging of the provinces. As we've discussed, there have been steady streams of working-age people leaving rural, resource-based areas for better opportunities in growing urban areas in Central and Western Canada. However, those same migrants sometimes eventually return to the area where they grew up. This return migration phenomenon has received some attention in the literature (Newbold and Liaw 1990). It is older people who are more likely to return-migrate, particularly in those provinces where the strong out-migration streams of people of working age originated.

Superimposed on these return migration flows are the movements of retired people to regions whose physical amenities, particularly their climate and scenery, are highly attractive. British Columbia, Ontario and Prince Edward Island have been the primary destinations. The net result is that migration produces differential aging effects across the nation—the Atlantic provinces and British Columbia are the prime recipients of relative gains in the proportion who are elderly from these moves (see Table 1.5). The only major example of consistently higher proportions of elderly among out-migrants than in-migrants is Quebec. This net out-migration moderates what is now the highest rate of aging among the provinces (see Table 1.6).

Leaving migration aside, the other factor influencing population aging is aging in place,[7] the *net* effect of generalized births and deaths on an age group in a given time period. Generalized births within a given age group refers to those moving or "aging into" that age group from the next-younger age group. Generalized deaths combine actual deaths of people in the given age group plus those who age into the next higher age group.

FIGURE 1.7A: C_{65+} VALUES FOR MALES, BY PROVINCE, 1971 TO 1991

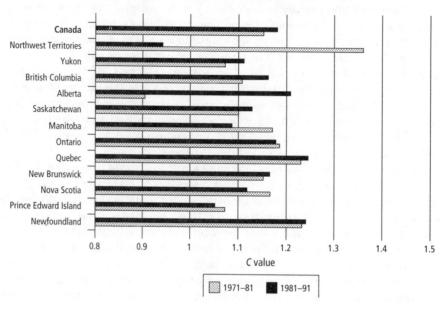

FIGURE 1.7B: C_{65+} VALUES FOR FEMALES, BY PROVINCE, 1971 TO 1991

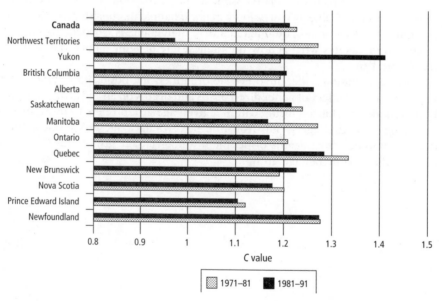

Source: Census of Canada, 1971–1991.

TABLE 1.5: IMPACT OF INTERPROVINCIAL MIGRATION ON POPULATION AGING, 1976 TO 1991

		Female	Male
Newfoundland	1976–1981	−	−
	1981–1986	+	0
	1986–1991	+	0
Prince Edward Island	1976–1981	NA	NA
	1981–1986	+	+ +
	1986–1991	0	+ +
Nova Scotia	1976–1981	0	+ +
	1981–1986	0	+
	1986–1991	−	+
New Brunswick	1976–1981	+ +	+
	1981–1986	+	+ +
	1986–1991	+	+
Quebec	1976–1981	− −	− −
	1981–1986	− −	− −
	1986–1991	− −	− −
Ontario	1976–1981	+ +	+
	1981–1986	+	−
	1986–1991	− −	−
Manitoba	1976–1981	−	+
	1981–1986	−	− −
	1986–1991	+	−
Saskatchewan	1976–1981	−	−
	1981–1986	−	− −
	1986–1991	+ +	+
Alberta	1976–1981	−	− −
	1981–1986	0	0
	1986–1991	+	0
British Columbia	1976–1981	0	+ +
	1981–1986	+ +	+ +
	1986–1991	+	+
Yukon/Northwest Territories	1976–1981	+	0
	1981–1986	− −	−
	1986–1991	0	+

++   > 2% difference between in- and out-migrants in proportion > 65
+   0.5% to 2.0% difference
0   −0.5% to 0.5% difference
−   −0.5% to −2.0% difference
− − > −2.0% difference

We can define α as the rate of aging attributable to aging in place and η as the rate of aging attributable to net migration, such that

$$C_{65} = 1 + \alpha + \eta$$

where

$A = 100\alpha$

$N = 100\eta$

A is the percentage increase in aging due to aging in place

N is the percentage increase in aging due to net migration

The values of C, A and N by province for the period 1986 to 1991 are given in Table 1.6. In all provinces except Prince Edward Island and Saskatchewan, aging in place was a significantly larger factor in population aging than was net migration. In the Atlantic and Prairie provinces, the positive net migration values are a function of the much larger volume of out-migration of the young, working-age cohorts compared with the out-migration of the elderly. In contrast, the negative net migration value for Quebec is the result of more out-migration of the elderly population relative to the working-age population. The negative values calculated for Ontario and British Columbia represent the attraction these provinces hold for working-age in-migrants rather than elderly in-migrants—although British Columbia is also a popular destination for retirees.

TABLE 1.6: POPULATION AGING DUE TO NET MIGRATION AND AGING IN PLACE

Province	RATIO OF PROPORTION 65+ IN 1991 TO PROPORTION 65+ IN 1986	RATIO OF PROPORTION 65+ IN POPULATION SURVIVING TO 1991 TO PROPORTION 65+ IN 1986	PERCENTAGE INCREASE IN POPULATION AGING DUE TO AGING IN PLACE	PERCENTAGE INCREASE IN POPULATION AGING DUE TO NET MIGRATION
	$C(65)$	$CS(65)$	$A(65)$	$N(65)$
Newfoundland	1.1	1.07	6.74	3.55
Prince Edward Island	1.04	1.01	1.21	2.96
Nova Scotia	1.06	1.04	4.44	1.51
New Brunswick	1.1	1.07	7.31	2.48
Quebec	1.13	1.14	13.76	−1.09
Ontario	1.09	1.12	12.07	−3.53
Manitoba	1.07	1.06	6.11	0.63
Saskatchewan	1.11	1.05	4.73	6.47
Alberta	1.12	1.1	9.98	2.43
British Columbia	1.07	1.11	10.66	−4.05
Yukon/Northwest Territories	1.01	1.07	7.04	−6.12
Canada	**1.1**	**1.11**	**10.86**	**−1.33**

Source: Census of Canada, 1986, 1991.

Even at the provincial level, these trends imply a tremendous geographic variation in the size of the elderly population and the underlying causes of its growth. The importance of aging in place is that the spatial distribution of the population aged 55 years and over today to a large degree tells us where the population aged 65 and over will be in 10 years. How the relative size of the elderly population will contract or expand therefore depends on the differential effects of net migration of the working-age people and the elderly.

1.3.2 Urban–rural contrasts

Migration from rural to urban areas has been a significant element of change in the distribution of population in Canada for the last 150 years (Shaw 1985). This movement has been highly age-selective. The implication is that less mobile older people tend to accumulate and increase the rate of population aging in those areas where out-migration is strong, while those areas receiving significant in-migrant flows will tend to maintain younger populations.

The urban fabric itself varies considerably according to size of centre. At one end of the spectrum are the metropolitan areas of Toronto, Montréal and Vancouver, collectively home to 38% of the Canadian population in 1991. At the other end are the thousands of small towns and villages, which are service and retail centres in essentially rural landscapes.

Migration affects aging differently in rural areas than in the largest cities. Rural environments are difficult places for an older person to live alone independently (see Grant and Rice 1983). Given the greater life expectancy of women, it is reasonable to expect that elderly widowed, divorced or single women are more likely to live in small centres with greater access to services and to social supports than in rural areas.

The structure of migration between urban areas of different sizes also suggests that the largest in-migrant streams head for the biggest cities, and that the size of the stream decreases with the size of the centre (Shaw 1985). This would suggest that aging may be slower in larger cities. Even among rural and small-town communities, those within reach of larger centres and their wider range of services would presumably be more attractive to the elderly than more remote locations.

This age selectivity in migration results in some clear aging and gender effects by size of settlement (see Figures 1.8 and 1.9). The smaller centres—those of between 1,000 and 10,000 inhabitants—have the highest measures of population aging. However, that population aging declines steadily with increasing size. Rural areas, in general, have younger populations than the villages and towns near them, although they are not as "young" as larger cities over 100,000.

The gender contrasts are just as strong. Since non-married women are less likely to live in rural than urban areas at older ages, there is a stark contrast in the ratios of men to women between rural areas and villages and towns. There is a general decrease in the number of males per 100 females as the size of settlement increases (see Figure 1.9); so it is in urban areas where the growth in demand for services by elderly women is particularly strong, and above all in the large

FIGURE 1.8A: PERCENTAGE OF MALES 65 AND OVER, BY SIZE OF PLACE,
1971 TO 1991

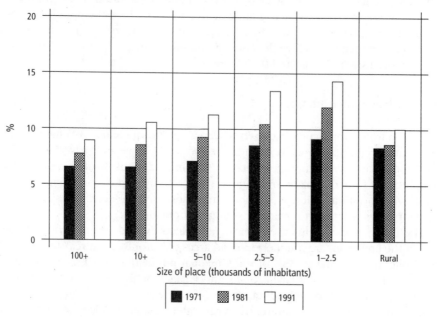

Size of place (thousands of inhabitants)

■ 1971　▨ 1981　□ 1991

FIGURE 1.8B: PERCENTAGE OF FEMALES 65 AND OVER, BY SIZE OF PLACE,
1971 TO 1991

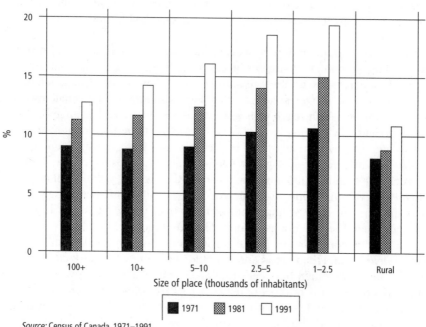

Size of place (thousands of inhabitants)

■ 1971　▨ 1981　□ 1991

Source: Census of Canada, 1971–1991.

FIGURE 1.9: MALES PER 100 FEMALES, BY SIZE OF URBAN PLACE, 1971 TO 1991

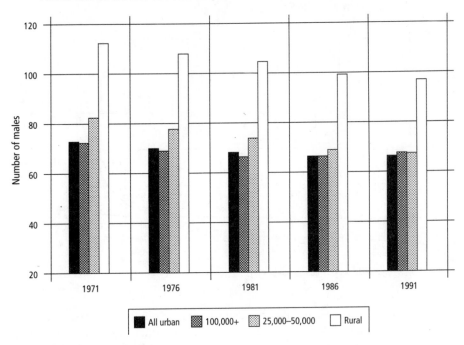

Source: Census of Canada, 1971–1991.

metropolitan areas. This is a function of the concentration of the population in the large cities as well as these reported ratios.

Age and geographic differentials in selective migration also cause a mismatch between where elderly people concentrate and where their daughters, sons and other relatives locate. The lack of geographically close family support networks only makes home care and informal care more difficult to provide, and further increases elderly people's demand for formal services.

1.4   THE ELDERLY IN HEALTH-RELATED INSTITUTIONS

As people get older, their ability to live independently, whether it is in a large city, small town or rural area, often declines, and they move to an institutional setting that provides a range of health services and social support. The likelihood of making this transfer from community to institutional living is a function not only of health status but also of the availability of social support in the community, particularly from kin. The propensity to live in an institution is one of the most strongly age-dependent conditions for both males and females, although the rates jump for women 75 and over (see Figure 1.10). Note also that the likelihood of being widowed is also much greater for women (Ram 1990).

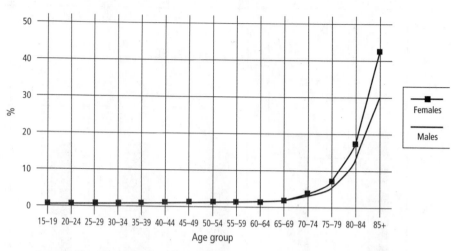

Source: Health and Activity Limitation Survey, 1991.

Although the age-specific likelihoods changed little between 1986 and 1991, there were substantial flows between the non-institutional and institutional populations. Recent research in the United States based on the Longitudinal Study of Aging[8] shows that the flows are by no means one-way. As many as 30% of the institutionalized population—particularly those who are not severely limited in their functional ability—might return to the community within two years of entering an institution (Crimmins and Saito 1990). Unfortunately, comparable data do not exist in Canada. However, we should be mindful that such flows are taking place in Canada, and that they have implications for the delivery of local services; we simply do not know their magnitude.

The lower bound for the proportion of an age group that became newly institutionalized between 1986 and 1991 can be estimated by the relation

$$NewI_k = I_k(t) - I_{k-1}(t-1)S_{k-1,k}$$

where

$NewI_k$ is the lower bound for age group
k, $I_k(t)$ is the number in age group k at time t who are institutionalized
$S_{k-1,k}$ is the five-year survival rate from age group $k-1$ to k.

$$P(newI)_{k-1} = \frac{NewI_k}{P_{k-1}(t-1)}$$

is the lower bound of the proportion of the population on age group $k-1$ who enter institutions between $t-1$ and t.

Using these relations, the following estimates of the lower bounds on the proportions of the each age group entering institutions between 1986 and 1991 were:

Females		Males	
65–69	1.6%	65–69	0.9%
70–74	3.1%	70–74	1.6%
75–79	5.5%	75–79	4.3%
80+	10.4%	80+	5.4%

The actual percentages will be higher for two reasons. First, a proportion of the institutional population returns to the community, and therefore the institutional population that survives the five years is overestimated. Second, we have used the population survival rates, which will be greater than the survival rates in institutions. This means that, again, the survived population is overestimated.

The implications of these figures are that, if the propensities to be institutionalized do not change, the pressure for institutional spaces will escalate rapidly as the size of the elderly population grows. The age-specific likelihoods of being institutionalized have changed little in the last decade. As well, they vary only in minor ways between provinces. However, neither of these considerations holds much predictive power; the actual level of institutionalization depends as well on health status, kin availability and the number of institutional spaces provided by both public and private agencies. While improvements in older people's health status will raise the age of entry to institutions, the lower fertility of the post-baby boom years will reduce the number of kin in the community who could supply support. The critical issue, however, will be how governments will treat institutional living in their strategies for supporting long-term care—specifically, the criteria they use to define eligibility and the number of spaces they make available in institutions.

There is an important reason for knowing the proportion of the population in institutions. Much of the analysis of health conditions and behaviours and their association with economic circumstances and living arrangements is based on large-sample surveys funded by Statistics Canada or other public agencies. These surveys focus on the population living in the community. Excluding the institutional population makes little difference to conclusions for younger populations, or even for the young elderly. However, given that 40% of women 85 and over lived in a health-related institution in 1991, one cannot make generalizations about the very old without surveying this population. In the following chapters, we will indicate whether statements refer to the total population or are restricted to the population living in the community (the non-institutionalized population).

1.5 CONCLUSION

This chapter has focused on population aging. At the time of the 1991 Census, Canada's elderly population stood at 3.2 million, or 12% of the total population.

The population aged 80 and over stood at 657,000, or 2.4% of the total population—this is perhaps more critical for public policy development. The size of the elderly population and the very old population is the result of sustained growth rates over the past 40 years; this trend will continue well into the next century. In Chapter 5, the implications of the future growth of the elderly population are explored in detail.

The key feature of the growth of Canada's elderly population has been its gendered character. The preponderance of women at older ages has endured. While men's life expectancy has been improving relative to women's, the life-expectancy gap will likely persist for Canadians of all ages.

Public policy can only slowly change sex and dependency ratios and life expectancy, but one demographic variable that it can immediately affect is immigration. The effects of immigration on the elderly population are difficult to predict. However, in the years when family reunification was a priority, the proportion of immigrants who were elderly increased markedly, while in the years when economic/independent immigrants were a priority, a smaller proportion of elderly immigrants arrived.

Not only is the age composition of immigrants important in the short run, but where they locate also has ramifications for analysing the elderly population. As is shown in later chapters, the concentration of much of the new immigrant population in Toronto, Montréal and Vancouver affects the spatial distribution of the elderly population at the local level. However, in the long run, fertility and mortality, not immigration, are the primary factors influencing age and gender distributions.

What is observed at the national level plays itself out with much greater variation at other geographical levels. This theme is highlighted in Chapter 3, but suffice it to say that the elderly proportion of the population ranges from around 3.0% in the Northwest Territories to 15.0% in Saskatchewan. Looking at urban-rural differences, it is clear that the elderly population is greatest in Canada's largest cities, making demand for services, by elderly women in particular, a key issue in the coming years.

Even as the process of deinstitutionalization continues throughout Canada, this chapter demonstrates the importance of including the institutionalized elderly population in policy discussions. It would be a mistake to make generalizations—especially about the very old—without including the institutionalized elderly.

This chapter has set out the basic parameters of Canada's elderly population. The following chapters amplify many of the themes introduced here, to show a comprehensive picture of Canada's elderly population near the turn of the 21st century.

ENDNOTES

1. McDaniel (1987) argued that population aging has become a guiding paradigm for public policy because policy makers, the media and a large part of the public have grown to accept uncritically that a growing elderly population has serious implications for income, health and social policy. This has led to the perception of a population aging crisis. Northcott (1994) tests this argument and finds widespread support for it, explaining why there is now a "predisposition to accept policies that might otherwise be seen as unattractive."

2. The population total for 1991 excludes non-permanent residents to maintain consistency with reported totals for previous censuses.

3. $GR = (\frac{P_{t+n}}{P_t})^{1/n} - 1.0$

   The annualized growth rate between two time periods is:

   GR = the annualized growth rate;
   P_{t-n} = the population in the nth year of the period;
   P_t = the population in the initial year of the period;
   n = the number of years in the period.

4. Human capital theorists see social spending as increasing the economic potential of those for whom it is targeted, but it can also be extended to decision making. For example, decision making in a human capital theory of migration is dependent "on the income differential between places i and j, discounted for future income in i, less the costs of migrating from i to j" (Cadwallader, 1989, p. 499.)

5. Definitions of the types of immigrant are found in the Immigration Act, 1976 or the Immigration Regulations, 1978. Economic/independent immigrants are either those individuals who immigrate to Canada with no dependants (i.e., no dependent children, spouse, children classified as students or parents) or those who are classified as "entrepreneurs."

6. See p. 226.

7. For a complete discussion, see Chapter 4.

8. The Longitudinal Study of Aging (LSOA) began in 1984 with interviews of a representative sample of 7,527 individuals in the non-institutionalized population aged 70 and over in the United States. Subjects were reinterviewed in 1986, 1988 and 1990.

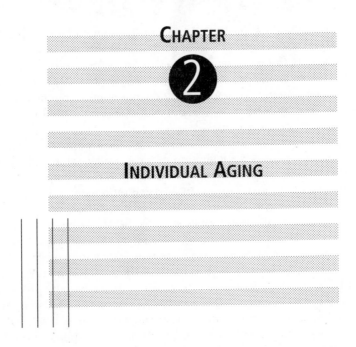

CHAPTER

2

INDIVIDUAL AGING

As people get older, their health and the range of social supports they need tend to change. The nature of this change and its implications for public policy depend not only on aging itself but also on each person's social, economic and demographic circumstances and community.

Central to any discussion of health and aging are individuals' marital status and living arrangements. Those who live with a spouse or partner have a different base of support in the event of poor health than those living alone, especially those who are far from other kin or close friends. Those living alone are more likely to turn to formal agencies for help, while those who live with others often share the tasks of daily living such as meal preparation, shopping and housework. Where people live is also important; in rural locations, access to informal and formal contacts for health services and social support is scarcer than in towns and cities.

A person's socio-economic attributes—income, wealth, ethnicity, age, education, employment status and so on—also affect health and social support. Historically, poor health and poverty have marched hand in hand, although the direction of causality—which causes which—is not always clear (McKeown 1988; Roberge, Berthelot and Wolfson 1993). Those with low incomes find it more difficult to provide adequate nutrition, shelter and preventive health care both for themselves and for their families. Poor health and nutrition at a young age lead to higher probabilities of poor health at an older age. As well, poor health can affect the likelihood of achieving educational goals and therefore employment prospects, thereby reducing income in later years.

Education influences a person's health experience, both indirectly through its relationship with economic success and directly through its effect on knowledge about health issues and the health care system. Those with more education tend to have more personal resources to deal with poor health and, more importantly, are more likely to better understand the health care system and use *its* resources more effectively. In an era of increasing financial constraints on the health care and social service systems, future progress depends as much on the ability to educate people to look after their own health as it does on the ability of the health care system to provide more extensive services.

The socio-demographic characteristics of any local population change constantly. People's propensity for migration or local residential mobility is strongly linked to their health status, although the relationship is complex (Litwak and Longino 1987). As individuals approach or reach retirement, they often contemplate moves to balmier climates such as those of British Columbia or the Niagara region, or to recreationally rich locales such as the Muskokas or Prince Edward Island. This is especially true of more affluent, healthy young-elderly couples (Northcott 1988). Often, they move to areas where they previously enjoyed holidays, places where the winters are less harsh or the summers more relaxing.

When the older elderly move, however, it is more likely to be precipitated by declining health, loss of independence and a need to be close to family and other sources of informal and formal support (Litwak and Longino 1987). Often such moves are return migrations by frail couples or a surviving spouse from the retirement location to a place where a stronger network of family and friends can provide support.

Moves by the elderly have effects for those who make them; they also affect the socio-demographic environments of both the areas they leave and the areas to which they move. When healthy, affluent couples move to British Columbia from areas such as Northern Ontario, they change not only the potential demand for health care in the two locations but also the character of the local population—the population they leave behind becomes progressively poorer in economic and health terms. When people move, they take their tax-paying capacity with them, thereby reducing their old community's ability to provide local services of good quality and quantity (Rosenberg and Moore 1990).

Each of these socio-demographic variables—marital status and living arrangements, poverty, education and mobility—will be examined in relation to aging. This discussion is a precursor to the measurement of health status and social support in Chapter 4, where the relationship between health status, aging and these socio-demographic variables will be explored in depth.

2.1 THE SOCIO-DEMOGRAPHIC CONTEXT OF AGING

2.1.1 Marital status and living arrangements

Canadian families have changed dramatically in the post-war years, particularly since the peak of the baby boom in the late fifties, and these changes are beginning to alter the contexts in which the elderly live out their later years. The most dramatic effects arose from the rapid increase in the disparity between male and female life expectancy after the Second World War. The proportion of women living beyond age 80 has increased much more rapidly than the proportion of men; as well, women are much more likely to be widowed at age 65 or older than are men (see Figure 2.1).

A second trend is now being overlaid on the first. As men's life expectancies also increase, the likelihood of a couple that has reached 65 remaining intact for many years after has increased among the young elderly; widowhood is occurring later (see Table 2.1). Women are still much more likely to survive their spouse or partner than vice versa, but the rapid growth in the number of widows is occurring at later ages than ever before. If men's survival rates continue to approach women's, as described in the previous chapter, then the ratio of men to women at higher ages would begin to increase. For the next 20 to 30 years, at least, the large proportion of widowed women will be a particular focus when considering the care of the older elderly. Often older women live alone and have limited access to friends or family for social support—help for daily activities such as shopping or housework. Every effort needs to be made to identify this population and its needs in the local community (Havens 1995).

Divorce and remarriage have emerged as significant events in Canadian social life since the 1950s (Ram 1990). Since then, younger adults have been more likely to divorce, but now the impact of the divorce explosion is being felt in the population 65 and over. In 1951, only 0.3% of men and 0.1% of women aged 65 to 74 were divorced; by 1991, these figures had risen to 5.0% and 6.1% respectively.[1] Undoubtedly these numbers will continue to grow simply as a function of the aging of those who were divorced at younger ages. For example, in 1991, 10.5% of women aged 55 to 59 were divorced and, with the current structure of older

FIGURE 2.1: PERCENTAGE WIDOWED, BY AGE AND SEX, CANADA, 1991

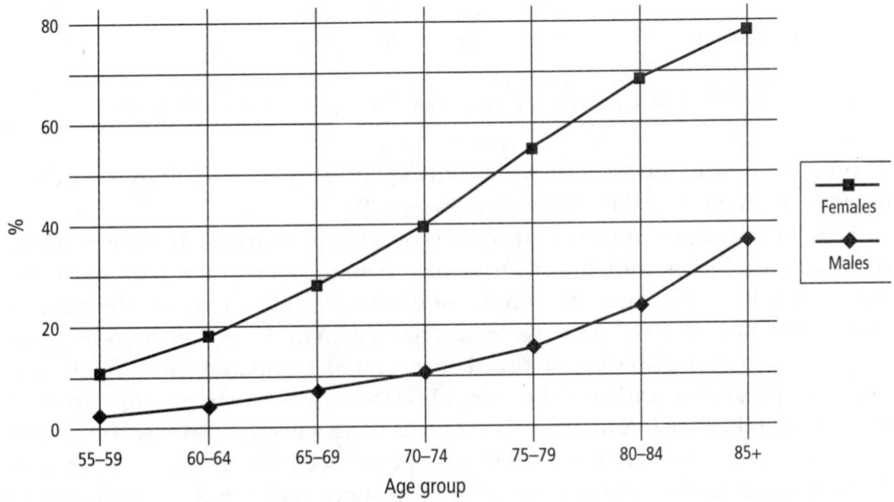

Source: Census of Canada, Public Use Micro-data File, 1991.

TABLE 2.1: MARITAL STATUS OF THE NON-INSTITUTIONAL PRE-ELDERLY AND ELDERLY, PERCENTAGES,[1] BY AGE AND SEX, 1991 AND 1981

				AGE GROUP			
	55–59	60–64	65–69	70–74	75–79	80–84	85+
MARITAL STATUS IN 1991				Females (%)			
Single	5.4	5.5	5.9	6.4	7.4	8.6	9.9
Married	73.9	68.2	60.2	48.5	35.7	22.3	11.7
Widowed	10.3	17.5	27.0	40.0	53.4	66.6	76.9
Divorced or separated	10.5	8.8	6.9	5.1	3.5	2.5	1.5
				Males (%)			
Single	6.0	6.3	6.3	5.4	5.2	5.7	6.7
Married	84.5	83.0	82.1	80.9	77.1	69.0	55.7
Widowed	2.0	3.7	6.2	9.1	14.1	21.8	34.3
Divorced or separated	7.6	7.0	5.4	4.5	3.6	3.5	3.2

				AGE GROUP			
	55–59	60–64	65–69	70–74	75–79	80–84	85+
MARITAL STATUS IN 1981				Females (%)			
Single	6.4	7.2	8.1	10.0	10.3	10.3	10.2
Married	73.8	66.1	55.3	42.5	29.0	18.2	9.2
Widowed	13.2	21.1	32.5	44.0	58.3	70.5	80.1
Divorced or separated	6.7	5.6	4.1	3.5	2.4	1.1	0.5
				Males (%)			
Single	8.1	7.8	7.7	8.4	8.7	10.0	8.8
Married	82.9	82.2	80.7	76.4	70.2	59.2	43.0
Widowed	2.7	4.2	6.4	11.0	17.4	28.1	46.2
Divorced or separated	6.3	5.8	5.2	4.2	3.7	2.7	2.0

1. Percentages may not add to 100 due to rounding.
Sources: Census of Canada, Public Use Sample Tape, 1981; Census of Canada, Public Use Micro-data File, 1991.

divorce and remarriage, in 2001 we would expect more than 9% of those aged 65 to 69 to be divorced, compared with 6.9% in 1991.

To some extent, the impact of divorce is offset by remarriage. However, remarriage rates are significantly lower for women than for men of the same age (Ram 1990), so that at older ages the number of divorced women exceeds the number of divorced men. In 1991, there were 82,100 women in the non-institutional population 65 and over who were divorced or separated, compared with 57,300 men. The main reason for watching these trends is that they change the support available to the individual in the home. Not only is there a loss of a spouse, but access to children and other family members may be reduced for one or both partners. Although individuals can find other systems of support (Rosenthal and Gladstone 1994), there is no question that the options available to the elderly divorced person tend to be reduced.

The changes in life expectancy, divorce and remarriage between 1981 and 1991 were dramatic (see Table 2.1). Among those 55 to 74, there was a notable decline in the proportion of both men and women who were single or widowed, and increases in the proportions of those married and divorced. For those 75 and over, the most dramatic change was among men; a smaller proportion was widowed in 1991 than in 1981, and a greater proportion was still married. The changes for women were much more modest. The most dramatic differences in 1991 were between men and women 85 and over. Among the men, 55.7% were married and 34.3% were widowed; among the women, 11.7% were married and 76.9% were widowed. There were more than twice as many women 85 and over as men, so it is no surprise that there were four times more widows than widowers in this age group. As observed above, the increasing survival rates of men will increase the ratio of men to women 85 and over, but the gap will be slow to close—older widows will greatly outnumber older widowers well into the next century.

These trends in marital status have a direct impact on older people's living arrangements. In turn, living arrangements dictate who is available to provide support when individuals have problems undertaking daily activities, particularly those of a more personal nature, such as getting in and out of bed, dressing or moving around the home. These support activities are much more likely to be provided by family than friends (Rosenthal and Gladstone 1994), although we should not assume that friends cannot take on this role. Men's increasing longevity means that older men and women were more likely in 1991 than in 1981 to be living with a spouse—either with or without children (see Table 2.2). As well, the proportion of individuals of most older ages living alone steadily increased between 1981 and 1991, although not dramatically. At the same time, both women and men at most ages 65 and over were less likely to be living with children or with others. This shows a continued movement away from traditional models of in-home, family-based elder care.

When institutional residents are included, the marital status statistics are interesting, particularly for the older elderly. Most notable are women 85 and over; among those living in the community (i.e., outside institutions) in 1991, 26% lived with their spouse. When women in institutions are included, this figure falls to 11.7%; 76.9% of all women 85 and over in 1991 were widowed. In other words, the great majority of those in institutions are widowed, with the implication that there may be no one to look after them even if they were able to live outside the institution.

It is difficult to project these trends very far into the future. The living arrangements of the very old depend on their economic circumstances, as well as the availability of affordable housing and provincial policies with respect to eligibility criteria, institutional funding and long-term care in general. The catch-up in male life expectancy and increases in remarriage rates (Ram 1990) will likely ameliorate some of the long-term effects of increasing divorce rates, particularly among the younger elderly. The critical issue for the future is whether affordable places in health-related institutions for the elderly who have no support from kin will be

TABLE 2.2: LIVING ARRANGEMENTS OF THE NON-INSTITUTIONAL PRE-ELDERLY AND ELDERLY, PERCENTAGES,[1] BY AGE AND SEX, 1991 AND 1981

	55–59	60–64	65–69	70–74	75–79	80–84	85+
LIVING ARRANGEMENTS IN 1991				Females (%)			
One-person household	13.5	18.7	26.2	36.5	45.6	54.1	51.1
Couple only	41.5	47.1	47.8	40.7	30.4	18.7	8.7
with children	27.3	16.4	9.8	7.1	6.8	7.1	8.8
with others	3.3	3.3	3.0	2.6	2.9	3.9	8.2
Multi-family household	3.2	3.4	2.5	2.0	1.6	1.5	1.3
Non-family household	3.3	4.2	4.9	5.3	6.4	7.7	11.4
Lone-parent family	7.9	7.0	5.8	5.7	6.4	7.0	10.6
				Males (%)			
One-person household	8.8	10.6	11.9	13.3	15.9	21.0	27.2
Couple only	39.6	50.7	59.4	64.5	63.6	57.6	42.9
with children	38.8	25.5	16.1	11.1	8.1	8.1	10.5
with others	3.4	3.7	3.7	3.1	3.1	3.4	4.6
Multi-family household	2.7	3.0	3.1	2.8	3.1	3.0	4.0
Non-family household	3.3	3.8	3.9	3.5	3.9	4.7	7.0
Lone-parent family	3.4	2.6	2.0	1.8	2.3	2.2	3.9

	55–59	60–64	65–69	70–74	75–79	80–84	85+
LIVING ARRANGEMENTS IN 1981				Females (%)			
One-person household	12.2	17.9	27.6	36.0	45.1	47.9	45.0
Couple only	38.0	46.1	45.1	36.9	25.5	16.4	8.3
with children	31.9	17.2	9.7	8.0	8.7	9.4	9.8
with others	3.3	3.7	3.3	3.0	3.2	4.9	8.8
Multi-family household	2.5	2.4	2.1	2.0	1.7	1.6	2.0
Non-family household	4.0	5.6	6.7	8.2	9.1	11.0	13.0
Lone-parent family	8.2	7.2	5.6	5.9	6.7	8.8	13.1
				Males (%)			
One-person household	8.1	9.0	11.0	13.1	15.4	21.2	22.0
Couple only	33.7	47.4	58.2	60.5	59.4	51.2	39.7
with children	45.4	30.9	17.9	12.5	10.5	10.9	11.2
with others	3.4	3.7	4.2	4.2	4.3	4.3	6.9
Multi-family household	2.2	2.6	2.9	3.0	2.6	3.2	4.1
Non-family household	3.6	3.4	3.6	4.6	5.3	5.8	9.2
Lone-parent family	3.7	3.1	2.2	2.1	2.4	3.4	6.8

1. Percentages may not add to 100 due to rounding.
Source: Census of Canada, Public Use Micro-data Files, 1981–1991.

available, or whether increasing numbers will remain in the community and depend on more extensive home-oriented services. For those who remain in the community, many will move to be closer to relatives or friends who can provide social support for various activities of daily living. However, even though such moves are quite common, less than 5% of the elderly population migrate to other communities for this purpose in a given five-year period (McGuinness 1996), and the effect of such moves on local demand for services is usually small.

2.1.2 Poverty

There are many common stereotypes about poverty among the elderly. But, in fact, of all age groups the elderly have seen the greatest decline in poverty rates over the last 20 years, reflecting significant policy successes in both benefits and taxation (Dooley 1994). During this period, there have been real increases in the value of Old Age Security and Guaranteed Income Supplements (OAS/GIS), the Canada and Quebec Pension Plans (CPP/QPP) and other government transfers. By 1990, the average income for older men and women was well above Statistics Canada's 1986 low-income cut-off (Dooley 1994).

The measurement of poverty is contentious (Sarlo 1992). The most commonly used measure is the low-income cut-off (Wolfson and Evans 1989). For a given year, it is based on an analysis of family expenditure patterns, and is determined by adding 20 percentage points to the average expenditure on food, shelter and clothing. Families that spend more than 58.5% of their income on these basic goods and services are defined as "low income." The low-income cut-off value is estimated from the relationship between expenditures on food, shelter and clothing and pre-tax income. It also takes into account family size, urban–rural differences and geographic region. These low-income cut-off values are adjusted as a function of the annual consumer price index (CPI).

Basing such measures on pre-tax income can lead to overestimates of the incidence of poverty among the elderly, argue Ruggieri, Howard and Bluck (1994). Using pre-tax income as a basis ignores special income tax exemptions available to the elderly, as well as employment-related expenses. Instead of pre-tax income, Ruggieri et al. (1994) propose a measure called net purchasing power, an after-tax measure that generates dramatically lower estimates of the incidence of low income—in 1991, 4.7% of the elderly were low-income by this measure, compared with 30.6% by the low-income cut-off measure.

This wide discrepancy does not suggest that either measure is without value. Although the *absolute* estimates are widely different, the *relative* poverty levels among different groups of elderly, however, tend to remain similar using either measure (Ruggieri et al. 1994). This is important, given that the measures available for a broad-based analysis of poverty and its links to health are limited to the low-income cut-off and similar pre-tax indicators. Low-income cut-off measurements are available for the 1986 and 1991 Health and Activity Limitation Surveys as well as for the Public Use Micro-data File in the same years. Although the low-income cut-off may have limitations as an absolute measure, it does serve as a useful indicator of relative likelihoods of being in the low-income category, and we will interpret it in that fashion.

Even the most elementary presentation showing the likelihood, by age and gender, of being considered low-income produces a fairly complex outcome. Since the low-income cut-off is a measure of family income, the proportion of men and women who live below it is influenced by the individuals' living arrangements (see Table 2.3). One of the reasons that women are consistently more likely to have low incomes at all ages—elderly or younger—is that they are also much more likely to live alone at all ages. Women living alone face—on average—lower lifetime earnings and associated public and private pension entitlements than do men. The proportions of women and men below the low-income cut-off crests at between the ages of 60 and 64 and then drops once individuals reach 65. It is at age 65 that most gain access to a range of seniors' benefits, including OAS/GIS and CPP/QPP (see Table 2.4); in fact, the proportion of those 70 to 74 years old who received these benefits in 1991 was even higher than the proportion of those 65 to 69. The proportion of those 70 to 74 who lived below the low-income cut-off tends to be lower than the proportion of those 65 to 69 (see Table 2.3).

TABLE 2.3: PERCENTAGE BELOW STATISTICS CANADA'S LOW-INCOME CUT-OFF, BY AGE, SEX AND LIVING ARRANGEMENTS, 1991

Age group	FEMALES (%)			Age group	MALES (%)		
	Living alone	With spouse	With others		Living alone	With spouse	With others
55–59	39.0	10.3	22.3	55–59	32.0	8.6	20.2
60–64	40.7	11.7	20.6	60–64	37.3	12.2	21.1
65–69	39.4	8.5	19.0	65–69	31.8	9.6	18.0
70–74	39.3	8.1	17.5	70–74	28.5	7.9	18.9
75–79	42.9	10.1	17.3	75–79	30.5	9.7	12.2
80–84	47.5	11.7	18.5	80–84	36.3	12.3	18.5
85+	53.0	9.0	17.2	85+	39.5	13.2	18.7

Source: Census of Canada, Public Use Micro-data File, 1991.

When the structure of individual income is examined separately for those above and below the low-income cut-off in 1991, some important differentials emerge (see Table 2.6). Among both women and men below the low-income cut-off, OAS and GIS were dominant income sources. Women had proportionately slightly higher incomes from these sources than men. As well, this proportion tended to increase sharply with age up until 75, indicating that women and older individuals are more likely to qualify for GIS.

Income for those above the low-income cut-off is structured quite differently. Average payments for OAS and GIS are less than for those below the low-income cut-off, but income from retirement pensions, CPP/QPP, investments and employment are significantly higher. Retirement and CPP/QPP incomes decline markedly

Age group	ABOVE LOW-INCOME CUT-OFF				BELOW LOW-INCOME CUT-OFF			
	OAS/GIS	CPP/QPP	Other government transfers	UI benefits	OAS/GIS	CPP/QPP	Other government transfers	UI benefits
				Females (%)				
55–59	0.0	10.1	6.4	9.6	0.0	15.0	28.7	5.7
60–64	17.6	34.9	11.9	5.7	24.7	34.1	30.8	3.2
65–69	83.9	62.1	50.0	2.3	79.3	52.5	49.9	1.2
70–74	97.5	62.8	55.0	0.8	94.2	52.8	55.9	0.4
75–79	97.6	59.5	57.5	0.5	96.9	48.5	56.6	0.3
80–84	98.0	54.6	61.3	0.5	97.5	46.5	57.4	0.5
85+	95.9	37.0	66.4	0.7	98.0	28.3	65.6	0.5
Total	**55.7**	**43.1**	**34.9**	**4.1**	**64.3**	**40.1**	**46.7**	**1.9**
				Males (%)				
55–59	0.0	5.9	8.1	13.7	0.0	12.3	31.9	10.3
60–64	2.6	32.8	11.1	10.5	4.2	37.5	34.5	5.9
65–69	72.9	81.4	61.4	4.7	56.8	59.2	61.4	2.9
70–74	97.8	87.4	58.4	0.7	91.5	57.6	57.0	0.3
75–79	98.3	83.5	58.5	0.5	94.5	55.6	52.9	0.5
80–84	98.2	79.9	59.9	0.6	96.4	58.5	52.1	0.0
85+	97.2	62.7	63.3	0.9	96.5	45.2	60.7	0.2
Total	**46.8**	**52.0**	**35.9**	**7.0**	**42.8**	**42.2**	**45.9**	**4.4**

Source: Census of Canada, Public Use Micro-data File, 1991.

with age, especially among men, indicating the importance of improvements in pension benefits over the last two decades. There are large gaps between women's and men's pension incomes; in fact, women's pension payments increase slightly for those in their seventies, as pensions often transfer from husbands to wives when the former die.

Although the last 20 years have seen significant improvement in older Canadians' economic circumstances (Dooley 1994), at the end of the 1980s both older men and older women saw an apparent deterioration.[2] As Table 2.4 shows, both men and women living with their spouse in 1991 were significantly less likely to have low incomes than were those living with others, while those living alone, particularly women, were much likelier to have low incomes than were those in other living arrangements. Between 1986 and 1991, the likelihood that those in most age categories 65 and over living with their spouse would have low incomes increased two to three times. The clear implication is that the downturn in the economy at the end of the 1980s ate into some of the gains the elderly made in the previous two decades.

Even given reservations about the use of the low-income cut-off measures for the elderly, some groups of the elderly are clearly much more economically vulnerable than others. This is particularly true of women living alone, who are often not eligible for CPP/QPP benefits if they spent little or no time in the labour force in their earlier years.

The overwhelming majority—about 90%—of those 65 and over had incomes of less than $15,000 in 1991; women were more likely than men to fall into this category. Among this group the likelihood was also high that more than 80% of income was derived from government transfers (see Table 2.5 and Figure 2.2). The likelihoods tended to be higher for those who live alone. For example, among women 75 and over who lived alone and had incomes between $5,000 and $10,000, 99.3% received more than 80% of their income from transfers; there were 45,000 such women in Canada in 1991. Among women who lived with others, 82.7%—104,867—received more than 80% of their income from transfers. Clearly, this is a group that lives at the margin, and is particularly vulnerable to public policy changes that affect either the range of benefits received or the costs of services.

TABLE 2.5: PERCENTAGE OF THE POPULATION THAT RECEIVES MORE THAN 80% OF TOTAL INCOME FROM GOVERNMENT TRANSFER PAYMENTS, BY AGE, SEX, INCOME, AND LIVING ARRANGEMENTS, 1991

| | FEMALES | | | | | MALES | | | |
| | 65–74 | | 75+ | | | 65–74 | | 75+ | |
	Not alone	Alone	Not alone	Alone		Not alone	Alone	Not alone	Alone
INCOME GROUP ($)					%				
0–4,999	86.2	65.5	94.6	54.2		65.1	63.9	83.2	66.7
5,000–9,999	74.3	94.6	82.7	99.3		87.5	91.2	92.4	99.7
10,000–14,999	43.8	69.0	58.3	64.2		68.1	74.2	55.2	65.0
15,000–19,999	10.7	14.1	12.1	14.8		18.5	18.1	11.6	15.7
20,000–24,999	5.1	9.6	6.4	9.3		6.5	9.6	5.3	10.2
25,000+	1.4	2.1	1.7	1.2		1.5	2.1	1.6	1.2
INCOME GROUP ($)					Population counts				
0–4,999	76,967	1,900	18,567	433		9,567	767	2,800	133
5,000–9,999	199,800	40,633	104,867	45,000		76,800	10,400	68,333	9,800
10,000–14,999	70,167	93,433	64,667	106,567		101,333	27,667	60,333	24,333
15,000–19,999	6,867	6,200	3,167	5,733		21,833	2,567	6,100	1,667
20,000–24,999	1,967	2,700	1,000	2,033		6,167	967	1,700	633
25,000+	1,067	1,233	500	567		3,867	600	1,167	200

Source: Census of Canada, Public Use Micro-data File, 1991.

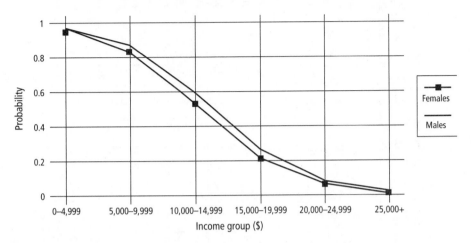

Source: Census of Canada, Public Use Micro-data File, 1991.

Changes in income and its sources are not the only indicators of economic well-being. Assets are also important; unfortunately, there are no direct sources of asset data in recent public micro-data files. Two types of assets are especially important: investments, which can generate income; and home ownership, which can reduce shelter costs. Those above the low-income cut-off received in 1991 an average income from investment 10 to 15 times as large as did those below the low-income cut-off (see Table 2.6). Those above the low-income cut-off are more likely to own than to rent. They also spend a smaller proportion of their income on shelter costs—whether they own or rent—than do those below the low-income cut-off (see Table 2.7). The role of shelter costs in the budgets of those 65 and over emphasizes the vulnerability of those who are poor; women are worse off in this regard than men.

The discussion of elderly people's conditions must focus not so much on some average or median set of characteristics but on those segments of the elderly that are most vulnerable because of their economic circumstances, their health and their access to supports, both informal and formal. Often individuals are vulnerable in more than one of these ways; they need particular attention from planners and policy makers. In 1991, very few individuals with incomes under $5,000 lived alone; that proportion rose rapidly with income, and women were much more likely than men to live alone. Across the country there were 350,000 individuals in 1991 who had incomes between $5,000 and $15,000, lived alone and received more than 80% of their income in transfers; 280,000 of them were women. This group contains the biggest concentration of economically vulnerable elderly.

TABLE 2.6: AVERAGE INCOMES OF THE ELDERLY, BY SOURCE OF INCOME, 1991

Sex	Income status	Age	Average income from wages and self-employment	Average income from OAS/GIS	Average income from investments	Average income from retirement pensions	Average income from CPP/QPP	Average total income
					$			
Females	Above low-income cut-off	65–69	2,086	4,061	4,025	2,094	2,319	15,909
		70–74	923	5,086	4,886	2,431	2,318	16,709
		75–79	706	5,358	5,722	2,413	2,065	17,457
		80–84	584	5,723	6,512	2,027	1,703	17,699
		85+	678	6,235	6,054	1,674	1,079	17,160
	Below low-income cut-off	65–69	161	6,007	397	253	1,284	9,008
		70–74	68	7,363	441	232	1,282	10,019
		75–79	47	7,608	547	244	1,179	10,266
		80–84	44	7,789	644	290	1,009	10,384
		85+	57	8,087	685	279	595	10,483
					$			
Males	Above low-income cut-off	65–69	6,376	3,654	4,532	6,848	4,295	29,199
		70–74	2,561	4,912	5,136	6,402	4,393	25,776
		75–79	1,587	5,035	6,095	5,428	3,702	23,599
		80–84	1,314	5,241	6,416	3,917	2,889	21,353
		85+	2,095	5,596	6,792	3,028	1,531	20,613
	Below low-income cut-off	65–69	366	4,515	398	456	1,835	9,391
		70–74	80	6,947	324	383	1,721	10,199
		75–79	95	7,080	337	361	1,586	10,071
		80–84	116	7,143	451	420	1,514	10,126
		85+	62	7,616	438	340	717	9,868

Source: Census of Canada, Public Use Micro-data File, 1991. Computation by authors.

TABLE 2.7: PERCENTAGE OF INCOME SPENT ON SHELTER, OWNERS AND RENTERS, 1991

	Income status	Age	Average percentage of income spent on shelter—owners	Average percentage of income spent on shelter—renters
			%	
Females	Above	65–69	32.0	41.0
	low-income	70–74	29.5	40.0
	cut-off	75–79	28.0	39.6
		80–84	28.1	36.4
		85+	31.0	36.5
	Below	65–69	38.3	45.9
	low-income	70–74	34.4	43.6
	cut-off	75–79	31.6	42.9
		80–84	30.8	41.3
		85+	30.4	40.5
			%	
Males	Above	65–69	19.1	31.8
	low-income	70–74	19.5	33.3
	cut-off	75–79	20.4	35.7
		80–84	22.2	36.7
		85+	24.3	35.7
	Below	65–69	37.5	46.5
	low-income	70–74	35.6	45.8
	cut-off	75–79	33.0	47.6
		80–84	31.0	46.8
		85+	29.9	44.3

Source: Census of Canada, Public Use Micro-data File, 1991. Computation by authors.

2.1.3 Employment status

Although 65 is the common age for retirement in Canada, many leave the labour force prior to this age. A significant minority, however, continue to work after 65, especially men (see Table 2.8). While the skill mix of those employed stays relatively constant with increasing age,[3] the nature of their employment changes significantly. The relative importance of self-employment and part-time work increases rapidly with age for men and women. Of the approximately 10% of men aged 75 to 79 who were still working in 1990, 53% were self-employed, and more than 40% worked part time. The corresponding figures for the 28% of 65- to 69-year-old men in the labour force were 31% and 25%. Occupation had little bearing on people's choice to work past age 65.

TABLE 2.8: LABOUR FORCE STATUS, PERCENTAGES, BY AGE AND SEX, 1990

Age group	NOT IN THE LABOUR FORCE	IN THE LABOUR FORCE			
		Mainly full time	Mainly part time	Self-employed	Self-employed as a percentage of the labour force
		Females			
		%			
55–59	45.9	38.3	15.8	4.9	9.1
60–64	67.3	21.5	11.2	3.6	11.0
65–69	87.3	7.0	5.7	2.3	17.9
70–74	94.2	2.8	3.0	1.6	27.5
75–79	96.5	1.6	1.8	1.3	36.2
80–84	97.6	1.5	0.9	1.1	44.1
85+	96.5	2.1	1.4	1.0	29.0
		Males			
		%			
55–59	18.8	75.6	5.6	13.1	16.2
60–64	39.3	53.4	7.3	11.6	19.0
65–69	71.6	20.9	7.5	8.8	30.9
70–74	84.9	9.1	5.9	6.2	41.3
75–79	90.6	5.4	4.0	4.9	52.5
80–84	93.8	3.6	2.6	3.5	55.7
85+	92.5	5.3	2.2	2.7	36.1

Source: Census of Canada, Public Use Micro-data File, 1991.

The elderly make a considerable contribution to both their own resources and to the general productivity of society. Although staying in the labour force significantly reduces an individual's likelihood of being classified as being of low income (see Table 2.11), the other impacts of continued employment on individual welfare deserve greater attention. Those who are still working are clearly fit enough to do so; but it is also relevant to ask whether those who continue to work are also more satisfied with their circumstances than those who do not.

2.1.4 Education

The educational attainment of the elderly largely reflects the educational experiences of those who grew up before or during the Second World War. Many elderly also came to Canada as immigrants after they had completed their school years. Consequently, a high proportion of those 85 and over (51% of women and 55% of men) had no high school education and less than 18% of women or men had any postsecondary experience (see Table 2.9). These percentages drop consistently and rapidly as we move down the age scale.

TABLE 2.9: EDUCATIONAL BACKGROUND OF THE PRE-ELDERLY AND ELDERLY, BY AGE AND SEX, PERCENTAGES,[1] 1991

EDUCATIONAL STATUS

Age group	Percentage with less than high school	Percentage with some high school	Percentage with some postsecondary	Percentage with degree	Average years of schooling
			Females		
			%		
55–59	26.5	42.9	30.5	5.7	10.5
60–64	31.8	42.1	26.1	4.9	10.1
65–69	35.3	42.4	22.4	3.2	9.7
70–74	37.3	42.0	20.8	3.4	9.5
75–79	40.6	39.3	20.0	3.3	9.3
80–84	45.6	35.3	19.0	2.5	8.8
85+	51.0	31.4	17.6	2.5	8.3
			Males		
			%		
55–59	26.7	38.8	34.5	11.0	10.8
60–64	32.1	37.8	30.1	9.7	10.3
65–69	35.5	37.1	27.4	8.7	10.0
70–74	37.1	38.6	24.2	7.5	9.7
75–79	41.7	35.8	22.4	7.1	9.4
80–84	48.7	31.4	19.9	6.4	8.7
85+	55.0	27.2	17.7	6.2	8.1

1. Percentages may not add to 100 due to rounding.

Source: Census of Canada, Public Use Micro-data File, 1991.

Not surprisingly, the average numbers of years of schooling increase significantly for younger age groups. The disparity between men's and women's average years of schooling was much smaller than the disparity between the percentages of men and women with a degree. This indicates that in the years before and during the Second World War women were much less likely to go on to postsecondary education than were women who were of school age in the last three decades.

There is a strong relationship between educational attainment and the likelihood of being classified as low income (see Table 2.10). Men and women who did not finish high school were more than twice as likely to fall below the low-income cut-off as those who had some postsecondary education. This was true at every age group, although the ratios tended to get smaller for the older elderly. The percentages were consistent for all age and gender sub-groups; those with some high school education fell between those who had none and those who continued their education after high school. In this context, the education variable acts as a surrogate measure for lifetime earnings and the accumulation of resources to cope with the retirement years.

TABLE 2.10: PERCENTAGE BELOW STATISTICS CANADA'S LOW-INCOME CUT-OFF, BY AGE, SEX AND EDUCATION, 1991

	FEMALES			MALES		
Age group	Percentage with less than high school	Percentage with some high school	Percentage with some postsecondary	Percentage with less than high school	Percentage with some high school	Percentage with some postsecondary
			%			
55–59	26.4	14.3	9.1	20.2	10.1	7.2
60–64	28.3	15.9	10.4	24.7	13.7	8.8
65–69	25.8	15.1	11.0	19.2	11.2	7.3
70–74	27.9	18.7	12.0	15.4	10.4	7.5
75–79	33.5	24.2	14.5	16.7	12.2	8.3
80–84	38.1	30.4	21.0	21.5	15.9	12.6
85+	36.4	33.9	23.6	24.3	17.7	16.5

Source: Census of Canada, Public Use Micro-data File, 1991.

Over the next two decades, the proportion of the elderly who have postsecondary schooling will continue to increase, simply because of the aging of cohorts with higher levels of education. In the last decade, more women have had postsecondary education in all spheres of learning, particularly in science, engineering and professional programs; there is every reason to believe that this trend will continue. Three types of effects should follow: greater educational attainment should be reflected in higher lifetime earnings and accumulated pension benefits, which will provide a financial cushion in old age for both men and women (Wolfson 1989); higher education levels should help make health prevention and promotion programs more effective; and better educated elderly people should be more able to navigate the intricacies of the health care system.

2.1.5 A model of low-income status

The previous discussion shows that the probability of being in the vulnerable group that lies below the low-income cut-off is a function of a range of socio-economic and demographic variables. Older women who live alone are a particularly vulnerable group. The likelihood of being in the low income group depends on age; those 85 and over are much less likely to receive CPP/QPP benefits (if they were too old to contribute to these programs when they were set up, they are not eligible to collect today), while the proportion of individuals who supplement their income with continued employment also falls sharply after 65. Those who are employed full time should realize greater income benefits than those who are employed part time.

The income generated after retirement reflects pension entitlements, which are driven by earnings during one's working life. These earnings are sensitive to levels of education; those with higher levels of educational attainment should be less likely to fall below the low-income cut-off in old age. We can model the likelihood of falling below the low-income cut-off using variables to measure these individual attributes in 1991, and assess whether there are still regional[4] variations in this likelihood once controls have been placed on the other variables.

The relationships are modeled using logistic regression (Kleinbaum 1994). The results of this analysis are presented in Table 2.11. The dependent variable (*low income*) is a binary variable—it takes the value of 1 if an individual falls below the Statistics Canada low-income cut-off and 0 otherwise. The coefficients in the regression equation have been converted to odds ratios, which measure the effect of the independent variable on the relative likelihood of being low-income, controlling for the other variables in the equation. Thus, someone who works full time is only about one-quarter as likely to be low income as someone who does not work at all. Someone who lives alone is more than four times as likely to be low income as someone who lives with others.

The odds ratios can be multiplied together to assess the impact of combinations of attributes. For example, we include one variable (*females alone*), which measures the interaction between the two variables *female* and *living alone* to assess the combined effects of being female and living alone relative to men who live with their spouse. We use the combination of the coefficients for the three variables, *female*, *alone* and *female-alone,* which is (.830 * 4.461 * 1.870) to show that someone with all three characteristics is almost seven (6.924) times as likely to be low income.

The relationships shown in Table 2.11 confirm several of the ideas developed above. The likelihood of being low income increases with age, but at a decreasing rate.[5] Living alone has the greatest impact on the probability of being below the low-income cut-off; women living alone are seven times more susceptible than men living with their spouse, as discussed above. Living in arrangements with someone other than a spouse is also associated with greater likelihoods of being below the low-income cut-off, but these likelihoods are generally lower—approximately twice those of individuals living with a spouse.

Education and employment have the expected effects. Each year of schooling reduces the likelihood of being in the low-income group, and having a university degree reduces the odds by an additional 30%. Full-time employment reduces the odds by 70%, while part-time employment cuts the odds by one-third relative to those not in the labour force.

There are regional differences over and above those captured by the variation in socio-demographic characteristics of individuals. With British Columbia and the territories forming the reference group, two of the other regions were associated with lower likelihoods, while Quebec's elderly had almost a 50% higher probability of falling below the low-income cut-off in 1991. It is important to note that including the regional effects does not change the magnitude of the other effects in any significant way; this increases our confidence in their interpretation.

A central point in this chapter's theme is that those who are at greater risk of being in the lowest income categories are also those who have particular profiles of health status and service needs (see Section 2.3 below). In particular, we focus

TABLE 2.11: LOGISTIC REGRESSION MODELS—CORRELATES OF LOW INCOME

DEPENDENT VARIABLE
LOW INCOME DEFINED AS: RESPONDENT LIVES BELOW STATISTICS CANADA'S LOW-INCOME CUT-OFF

Independent variables[1]	WITHOUT REGIONAL VARIABLES		WITH REGIONAL VARIABLES	
	Odds ratio	Significance level	Odds ratio	Significance level
Age	0.613	– – –[2]	0.604	– – –
Age squared	1.003	+ + +	1.003	+ + +
Female	0.830	– – –	0.827	– – –
Total years of schooling	0.898	– – –	0.907	– – –
University degree	0.736	– – –	0.682	– – –
Living arrangements (reference category = respondent lives with spouse)				
Lives alone	4.461	+ + +	4.547	+ + +
Lives with others	1.808	+ + +	1.783	+ + +
Employment status (reference category = respondent did not work in 1990)				
Full time	0.287	– – –	0.295	– – –
Part time	0.617	– – –	0.637	– – –
Females who live alone	1.870	+ + +	1.883	+ + +
Census metropolitan area	2.512	+ + +	2.690	+ + +
Regional indicators (reference category = respondent lives in British Columbia)				
Atlantic provinces			1.243	+ + +
Quebec			1.485	+ + +
Ontario			0.684	– – –
Prairie provinces			0.925	–

N = 88,157
1. See Table 2.20 for variable definitions.
2. + + +, – – –   Significant at .001
   + +, – –   Significant at .01
   +, –   Significant at .05
   The chi-square value for each model is significant for $p<.0001$

Source: Census of Canada, Public Use Micro-data File, 1991.

on the consistent problems of elderly women living alone, who are at especially high risk of having low incomes and are highly dependent on government transfers.

2.1.6 Availability of social support

As one grows older and more likely to be functionally limited, the availability of family and friends for social support becomes more important. Furthermore, as the need for help with the more personal aspects of daily life such as dressing and moving about in the home increases, access to family becomes relatively more important compared with access to friends (Stone 1993). In particular, the proximity of close family or friends one can turn to for help both increases one's ability to cope with everyday life and often reduces the pressures on formal agencies when the need for social support arises. While these relationships are common, we should not assume that the presence of close family always leads to support, nor that the need for support can always be transferred to the family. The quality of the relationships among family members (Stone 1993), the obligations for caregiving of other family members, particularly grandchildren (Menken 1985), and the individual's own mechanisms for coping (Rosenthal and Gladstone 1994) all contribute to determining whether the family will be the locus of support.

Data from the Survey of Ageing and Independence reveal the relationship between older people and the family members and friends to whom they feel close. What is striking is the frequency with which respondents said that there was either no one or only one person in each of these categories (see Table 2.12). Among those 75 and over, who tend to be more vulnerable because of their rapidly increasing likelihood of disabling conditions, 39.9% of women who live alone and 46.6% of men living alone identified one or no family members to whom they felt close. The numbers were even higher for close friends, with corresponding figures of 45.8% and 52.0%. While those who live with others most often have access to family in the same household, it is noteworthy that 13.9% of men and 8.2% of women 75 and over who lived with others claimed that there was no family member to whom they felt close (see Table 2.13).

The proximity of friends and family to whom one feels closest provides more insight into the availability of support for older people (see Table 2.13). As might be expected, family networks tend to be more geographically dispersed than networks of friends. Among those who lived alone in 1991, fully one-third of women 75 and over said that their closest family member lived in another town or city; only 5% said the same of their closest friend. The most dramatic responses, again, came from those who live alone. While the likelihood of having a close family member in the same neighbourhood increases with age, among both men and women 75 and over only 20% had a close family member in the same neighbourhood, and only 35% had their closest friend in the same neighbourhood. While this type of analysis is not definitive, it draws a clear picture about a significant proportion of older people; they live alone and have few resources in their social networks to turn to in the event that they need support. The implication is that the burden of support for many of these individuals will be carried by formal agencies and, given that a substantial proportion of these people are low income, the prime providers will be public-sector agencies.

2.2 MIGRATION AND MOBILITY

Canada is a mobile society. The elderly are less prone to move than younger people, but they do show a significant tendency to do so, whether it is moving across town or migrating to another province. Here we are concerned with relatively permanent moves, which cause changes in the population's distribution and

TABLE 2.12: DISTRIBUTION OF CLOSE FAMILY MEMBERS AND FRIENDS, BY AGE, SEX AND LIVING ARRANGEMENTS, PERCENTAGES,[1] 1991

	FEMALES			MALES		
	55–64	65–74	75+	55–64	65–74	75+
NUMBER OF CLOSE FAMILY MEMBERS			Not alone (%)			
0	5.0[2]	9.3	8.2	9.7	12.2	13.9
1	18.2	20.2	26.5	19.7	19.4	21.7
2–3	31.0	32.0	32.4	29.5	28.9	32.2
4+	45.8	38.5	32.9	41.0	39.5	32.2
			Alone (%)			
0	16.0	7.7	14.0	25.0	23.5	21.2
1	21.3	25.9	25.3	25.8	23.4	25.4
2–3	32.6	35.9	33.7	23.6	30.5	33.4
4+	30.1	30.5	27.0	25.6	22.7	19.9
NUMBER OF CLOSE FRIENDS			Not alone (%)			
0	21.9	27.1	36.1	26.9	31.2	37.6
1	12.6	14.9	12.7	9.0	8.7	9.6
2–3	35.9	32.0	30.1	30.7	23.3	20.1
4+	29.6	26.0	21.1	33.4	36.8	32.6
			Alone (%)			
0	21.0	20.3	29.5	33.6	28.7	36.4
1	17.1	16.7	16.3	9.3	13.2	15.6
2–3	34.5	31.6	24.8	27.6	31.2	21.6
4+	27.4	31.4	29.5	29.5	26.9	26.4

1. Percentages may not add to 100 due to rounding.
2. Percentage of female population aged 55 to 64 who report no close family members.
Source: Survey on Ageing and Independence, 1991.

characteristics. Many individuals, particularly the elderly, also make seasonal moves, which undoubtedly affect local service usage to some degree. However, there is insufficient data on such moves to support an effective analysis.[6]

Over the years, elderly migration[7] has had a different pattern from that of working-age people. The latter has clearly been sensitive to the shifts in rates of economic growth and possibilities for personal economic advantage; the pendulum has swung from Alberta during the oil boom years of the 1970s to Ontario during much of the 1980s and, more recently, to British Columbia. For the elderly, the pendulum has steadied at British Columbia, but there have been small net flows between other provinces (Northcott 1988; Bergob 1995) (Figure 2.3). The greatest net flows are made up of younger elderly; British Columbia is the prime destination, but there are also minor flows from Ontario to the Atlantic provinces.

These moves reflect the attraction of the milder winters of the West Coast and the return migration to the Atlantic provinces of former migrants to Ontario at the time of retirement (Newbold 1993).

Among the oldest age groups the salience of net flows declines; in fact the migration saldo[8] for interprovincial flows falls from 0.317 for the 55-to-64 age group to 0.140 for those 75 and older. This indicates that the redistribution effects of elderly migration are relatively much stronger at younger ages. The only variant for the older population compared with those under 65 is that a net flow is sustained from Quebec to Ontario, although in relative terms it is small.

TABLE 2.13: DISTRIBUTION OF THE PROXIMITY TO CLOSEST FAMILY MEMBER AND FRIEND, BY AGE, SEX AND LIVING ARRANGEMENTS, PERCENTAGES,[1] 1991

	FEMALES			MALES		
	55–64	65–74	75+	55–64	65–74	75+
PROXIMITY OF CLOSEST FAMILY MEMBER	Not alone (%)					
None	5.0	9.3	8.2	9.8	12.2	13.9
Same household	44.7[2]	42.7	50.4	56.9	50.8	46.9
Same neighbourhood	10.3	10.6	9.1	5.8	6.1	8.3
Same city or town	19.3	19.0	15.9	13.5	16.3	15.2
Different city or town	20.6	18.3	16.4	13.9	14.6	15.6
	Alone (%)					
None	16.0	7.7	14.0	25.0	23.5	21.3
Same household	0.8	0.7	0.8	2.0	1.0	2.1
Same neighbourhood	11.8	18.9	19.4	13.6	14.5	20.3
Same city or town	34.2	35.3	33.8	30.7	28.4	29.2
Different city or town	37.1	37.4	31.9	28.6	32.6	27.2
PROXIMITY OF CLOSEST FRIEND	Not alone (%)					
None	22.0	27.1	36.1	27.1	31.4	37.7
Same household	0.6	1.2	2.2	1.0	2.0	2.1
Same neighbourhood	25.2	27.7	26.5	23.1	25.6	25.7
Same city or town	36.1	28.4	26.5	32.3	30.1	27.0
Different city or town	16.0	15.6	8.6	16.5	11.0	7.5
	Alone (%)					
None	21.0	20.4	29.6	33.6	28.7	36.4
Same household	0.5	0.9	2.2	0.7	1.1	1.0
Same neighbourhood	25.3	36.5	34.3	21.7	27.5	35.8
Same city or town	35.6	30.0	28.3	32.0	29.0	21.1
Different city or town	17.7	12.2	5.7	11.9	13.6	5.6

1. Percentages may not add to 100 due to rounding.
2. Percentage of women aged 55 to 64 whose closest family member lives in the same household.
Source: Survey of Ageing and Independence, 1991.

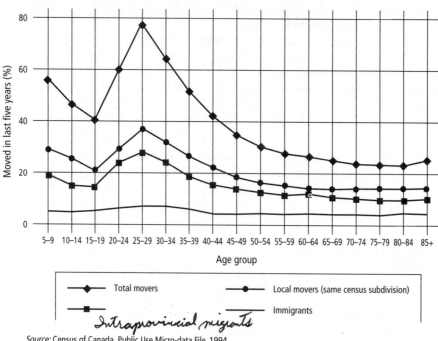

Source: Census of Canada, Public Use Micro-data File, 1994.

The long-run nature of these patterns, which are very similar to those provided in Northcott (1988) for the 1976-to-1981 period, has a significant impact on the cumulative mobility experience of the elderly population in different provinces (see Table 2.14). Moving from east to west, the 1991 proportion of the elderly population born in the province changes dramatically. In Newfoundland, the long history of out-migration and in-migration (mainly limited to those returning after an extended absence) produced an elderly population that was overwhelmingly home-grown and deeply intertwined in the local community. At the other extreme lies British Columbia, where only 20% of the elderly—and just 12% of those 85 and over—were born in the province. One-third of the elderly—and 60% of those 85 and over—were immigrants. The other provinces were somewhere along the spectrum between Newfoundland and British Columbia; the Maritime provinces and Quebec had high proportions of elderly who were born locally. Ontario and Alberta were similar; 40% to 50% of the elderly there were born locally. Manitoba and Saskatchewan occupied an intermediate position between Ontario and the Maritime provinces.

The major implication of these different provincial patterns is that in provinces with a low proportion of elderly born locally, many have their kin living far enough away that direct, regular support is difficult. Likelier sources of support in these areas are friendship networks and formal agencies. There could be a second,

TABLE 2.14: NET INTERPROVINCIAL MOBILITY STATUS SINCE BIRTH, PERCENTAGE,[1] BY AGE AND SEX, 1991

Province or territory of residence in 1991	FEMALES			MALES		
	Live in province of birth	Born in different province	Immigrants	Live in province of birth	Born in different province	Immigrants
	Percentage of population 55–64					
Newfoundland	97.5	2.4	0.2	96.9	2.7	0.5
Prince Edward Island	90.7	4.9	4.3	94.3	3.2	2.6
Nova Scotia	91.4	6.3	2.3	92.4	5.5	2.1
New Brunswick	94.7	4.3	1.0	93.8	4.5	1.7
Quebec	83.0	4.7	12.3	81.7	4.3	14.0
Ontario	49.6	13.5	36.9	47.5	13.9	38.6
Manitoba	64.4	17.4	18.2	66.3	15.5	18.2
Saskatchewan	80.7	10.5	8.8	81.2	9.9	8.9
Alberta	43.4	30.7	25.9	41.1	31.2	27.7
British Columbia	22.7	42.3	35.0	23.2	41.6	35.2
Yukon/Northwest Territories	84.4	11.1	4.4	79.7	8.7	11.6
	Percentage of population 65–74					
Newfoundland	96.0	3.6	0.4	98.1	1.5	0.4
Prince Edward Island	91.8	6.4	1.8	91.9	4.4	3.7
Nova Scotia	90.5	7.5	2.0	92.0	6.0	2.0
New Brunswick	92.7	6.4	1.0	93.9	4.7	1.4
Quebec	82.3	5.7	12.0	81.3	5.2	13.5
Ontario	50.7	15.0	34.3	49.6	14.1	36.3
Manitoba	62.2	16.4	21.4	68.7	12.9	18.3
Saskatchewan	78.5	10.2	11.2	83.7	7.5	8.9
Alberta	42.9	28.4	28.7	44.8	27.7	27.5
British Columbia	20.4	45.9	33.7	21.9	44.0	34.1
Yukon/Northwest Territories	85.7	10.7	3.6	86.2	3.5	10.4
	Percentage of population 75–84					
Newfoundland	98.2	1.8	0.0	99.0	1.0	0.0
Prince Edward Island	94.8	3.5	1.7	96.1	2.6	1.3
Nova Scotia	95.0	4.2	0.8	90.6	7.9	1.5
New Brunswick	93.6	5.8	0.6	93.9	5.1	1.0
Quebec	81.8	6.3	11.9	79.3	5.7	15.0
Ontario	52.7	13.9	33.4	50.0	12.9	37.1
Manitoba	64.3	12.3	23.4	61.3	15.0	23.7
Saskatchewan	68.0	13.1	18.8	67.9	10.2	21.9
Alberta	40.1	26.5	33.4	40.3	27.1	32.6
British Columbia	19.4	45.1	35.5	21.1	42.3	36.7
Yukon/Northwest Territories	80.0	20.0	0.0	87.5	6.3	6.3
	Percentage of population 85+					
Newfoundland	98.2	1.9	0.0	96.6	3.5	0.0
Prince Edward Island	79.3	20.7	0.0	94.7	5.3	0.0
Nova Scotia	94.1	4.7	1.2	94.4	1.4	4.2
New Brunswick	85.6	11.7	2.7	83.6	14.6	1.8
Quebec	73.5	6.3	20.2	76.6	4.8	18.6
Ontario	45.8	10.1	44.1	44.3	7.8	48.0
Manitoba	43.8	13.8	42.4	39.0	8.1	52.9
Saskatchewan	31.5	22.5	46.1	26.5	22.3	51.2
Alberta	15.0	23.6	61.4	14.7	20.3	65.0
British Columbia	13.0	26.3	60.7	11.9	29.4	58.7
Yukon/Northwest Territories	100.0	0.0	0.0	0.0	100.0	0.0

1. Percentages may not add to 100 due to rounding.
Source: Census of Canada, Public Use Micro-data File, 1991.

more subtle effect; people who have moved around are likely to have less parochial views of public services. Expectations formed from experiences in other places may well be transferred to the new local environment, and create pressures for changes in social service delivery.

Turning to a shorter-term perspective on mobility, the role of local moves and migration on the recent lives of older people should be examined. While the elderly are less likely to move or migrate than younger people (Rogers 1988) (Figure 2.3), their propensity to move is far from trivial. Even among those aged 80 and over, more than one-quarter of all renters and 15% of owners moved between 1986 and 1991 (see Table 2.15). Older people are less affected by the important life events associated with household formation and labour force activities that cause younger people to move or migrate.

However, there are other influences and events that are more important for older people (Wiseman 1980; Litwak and Longino 1987). Retirement—its anticipation and its aftermath—plays a major role, particularly in encouraging moves for the purpose of enjoying physical amenities such as milder climate, more scenic

TABLE 2.15: MOBILITY STATUS[1] AND TENURE STATUS OF THE ELDERLY, PERCENTAGES, BY AGE, SEX AND TENURE STATUS, 1991

Age group	FEMALES				MALES			
	Stayers[2]	Local movers[3]	Migrants in Canada[4]	Immigrants[5]	Stayers	Local movers	Migrants in Canada	Immigrants
				Owners (%)				
55–59	79.5	9.1	10.1	1.4	79.9	9.0	10.0	1.1
60–64	80.7	7.7	10.2	1.4	81.0	7.3	10.5	1.2
65–69	82.4	7.1	9.2	1.3	82.8	6.5	9.7	1.0
70–74	85.1	6.3	7.5	1.2	85.1	5.9	7.9	1.1
75–79	85.3	6.6	7.1	1.1	86.1	6.0	7.2	0.8
80–84	85.2	7.2	6.2	1.3	87.7	6.1	5.4	0.8
85+	82.1	7.7	8.5	1.8	84.6	7.6	6.4	1.4
				Renters (%)				
55–59	48.6	31.6	15.1	4.6	47.0	31.1	17.5	4.4
60–64	52.9	29.1	14.4	3.6	51.9	29.3	15.6	3.1
65–69	55.9	27.3	14.3	2.5	52.1	28.5	16.1	3.3
70–74	61.9	24.1	12.5	1.5	59.3	24.0	14.0	2.6
75–79	66.2	21.8	11.1	0.9	61.0	25.6	12.2	1.2
80–84	70.0	19.3	10.1	0.5	66.5	19.2	12.8	1.5
85+	73.4	17.4	8.3	0.8	63.8	22.1	13.0	1.1

1. "Mobility status" refers to the respondent's mobility history for the period 1986 to 1991.
2. Stayers are those who remained in the same dwelling in 1986 and 1991.
3. Local movers are those who moved to a different dwelling in the same census subdivision between 1986 and 1991.
4. Migrants in Canada are those who moved to a different census subdivision between 1986 and 1991.
5. Immigrants are those who immigrated to Canada between 1986 and 1991.
Source: Census of Canada, Public Use Micro-data File, 1991.

landscape or better recreation opportunities. These are often the motives behind relocation to British Columbia, Prince Edward Island and the Niagara and Muskoka regions of Ontario. As such moves accumulate in the destination areas, the infrastructure to support an active elderly lifestyle also expands, attracting others. Such movers are economically better off than those who do not migrate, and they are more likely to be healthy, intact couples than those who stay behind.

In later years, changes in health status and the ability to continue to live independently create a different set of pressures and induce new forms of movement. Older elderly often need to move to smaller housing if it becomes difficult to maintain a large house and grounds, and to an area offering appropriate social support. If it becomes difficult to look after an aging spouse or if one spouse dies or is institutionalized, older elderly often move closer to long-time friends and family who may be able to give the necessary support (Litwak and Longino 1987).

There is no sudden transformation of the structure of mobility with age; rather there is a steady shift in the distribution of the motivations for moving (see Table 2.16).[9] The most significant change is in the increase in moves to be closer to sources of social support: from 11.9% of movers aged 65 to 69 to 28.2% of those 75 and over. Housing-related reasons, which often reflect changing needs and abilities to cope with care of the home, remain important throughout the age distribution. Even amenity-related reasons still applied to 8.8% of those 75 and over. Many of these health-related moves may have been return migrations to the places in which individuals lived prior to retirement.

The propensity to move, for whatever reason, does decline gradually as people age (see Table 2.15). However, as with younger populations, the most dramatic differences are between owners and renters. Greater attachment to place and much higher moving costs make owners—of all ages—markedly less likely to move. Furthermore, since over 70% of elderly owners are mortgage-free, staying in the home is often the cheapest alternative (Moore and Rosenberg 1993).

TABLE 2.16: REASONS CITED FOR PRE-ELDERLY AND ELDERLY MOBILITY, BY AGE, PERCENTAGES AND NUMBERS, 1991

Reasons for moving	AGE GROUP 55–59	60–64	65–69	70–74	75+
			%		
Support	8.7	11.9	18.6	19.7	28.2
Amenities	9.8	5.8	7.0	15.6	8.8
Housing	33.5	24.9	28.9	25.8	27.1
Retirement	7.0	16.3	17.6	10.8	5.9
Separation/divorce	7.2	6.6	5.9	6.9	8.7
Financial	10.4	8.9	10.7	7.6	6.9
Employment	7.0	10.0	1.2	0.3	1.0
Other	16.4	15.6	10.0	13.3	13.5
Number	304,681	299,502	281,898	188,537	220,275

Source: Survey on Ageing and Independence, 1991.

Among older home-owners of both genders, only 15% to 20% moved between 1986 and 1991. The percentage of stayers was small, but rose steadily from ages 55 to 59 to ages 80 to 84. Those in the oldest age group were dramatically likelier to move in with other family members. It is also at the oldest age that the propensity to move to an institution is greatest, but the migration data from the census only records moves for individuals living in households.

The pattern is different for renters (see Table 2.15); a higher proportion of them were recent movers (30% to 50% between 1986 and 1991). Age has a much stronger effect than it does with owners. While 51.4% of 55- to 59-year-old women renters moved in the reference period, only 26.4% of those 85 and over (who are not in institutions) moved. Clearly, a significant number of people move from the community into institutions, but there is no satisfactory way of estimating their numbers at present.[10] Among the adults in the community who moved between 1986 and 1991, renters were twice as likely to have been local movers than migrants. Rental markets are much more flexible than owned markets, and housing moves are easier and cheaper to make. Among the population as a whole, moves from one rental unit to another are much more likely to be made within the same local area than at a distance.

Other relationships between socio-demographic variables and mobility are played out in the housing arena. Elderly people still living with their spouse or partner are the most likely to be living in stable, owner-occupied settings, and they are least likely to move (see Table 2.17). In contrast, single, divorced or widowed people, while their demographic status is probably stable, are more likely to be renters. This strongly influences their likelihood of moving, and when single people move they are also more likely to be a local mover than a migrant.

Widows and those who are divorced or separated are more likely to be movers, since both groups are more likely to have lower incomes and to be renters. Those who have recently left a marriage are likely to have responded to their new circumstances by moving—those who are divorced or separated are more likely to move than are widows. Given the higher divorce rates at younger ages and the modest remarriage rates (Ram 1990), the size of the divorced elderly population is likely to continue to grow over the next 20 years; it will contribute to greater elderly mobility. At the same time, however, the increased longevity of men will mean larger proportions of couples will remain intact during their later years. This will offset the divorce effects, since intact couples are the least mobile group.

We must not fall into the trap of assuming that higher levels of residential mobility are necessarily socially undesirable. A modest level of mobility is necessary as individuals adjust to changing personal circumstances. Stress is produced by three types of situations: moves that are imposed on individuals by circumstances beyond their control (e.g., by eviction or inability to pay the rent); situations that may or may not be precipitated by other events such as sickness or loss of spouse; and inability to move for lack of opportunity or financial resources. Stress arising from forced moves and blocked moves is more likely to happen to those with limited incomes (Moore and Clark 1987). In particular, there is a propensity for older people to become "trapped" in owner-occupied dwellings in

TABLE 2.17: DISTRIBUTION OF MOBILITY STATUS[1] OF THE PRE-ELDERLY AND ELDERLY, BY AGE, SEX AND MARITAL STATUS, PERCENTAGES, 1991

Age group	FEMALES				MALES			
	Stayers[3]	Local movers[4]	Migrants in Canada[5]	Immigrants[6]	Stayers	Local movers	Migrants in Canada	Immigrants
Married (%)								
55–59	76.8[2]	10.5	10.8	1.9	76.0	11.4	10.8	1.8
60–64	77.8	9.5	11.0	1.7	77.3	9.8	11.2	1.7
65–69	79.4	9.4	9.8	1.4	78.2	9.4	10.8	1.5
70–74	81.8	8.7	8.8	0.8	80.6	8.7	9.1	1.6
75–79	81.6	9.4	8.5	0.5	81.4	9.8	7.9	0.9
80–84	81.6	9.3	8.2	0.9	83.4	8.7	7.0	1.0
85+	81.5	11.2	6.6	0.7	80.4	11.3	7.3	1.0
Single (%)								
55–59	69.5	19.4	9.4	1.7	71.5	18.5	9.4	0.6
60–64	71.4	17.5	8.8	2.3	74.9	15.7	9.0	0.4
65–69	73.4	15.5	10.1	1.0	73.8	16.1	9.8	0.3
70–74	79.5	13.4	6.8	0.4	80.0	12.5	7.1	0.4
75–79	82.1	12.1	5.5	0.3	79.5	13.0	7.2	0.3
80–84	84.0	10.0	5.7	0.2	85.6	8.7	5.1	0.5
85+	78.4	15.0	5.2	1.4	72.6	12.8	12.8	1.7
Widowed (%)								
55–59	66.6	18.6	11.1	3.7	72.0	15.1	8.9	4.0
60–64	68.9	17.1	11.1	2.9	69.7	15.9	12.2	2.1
65–69	70.3	15.9	11.3	2.4	73.5	14.2	9.7	2.6
70–74	73.9	14.8	9.2	2.1	75.9	13.2	9.6	1.3
75–79	75.5	14.2	8.9	1.4	76.5	13.3	9.7	0.6
80–84	77.5	13.7	7.7	1.0	75.2	13.0	10.6	1.2
85+	78.2	11.7	8.9	1.2	76.2	13.7	8.4	1.7
Divorced or separated (%)								
55–59	53.7	30.3	14.6	1.3	53.1	26.0	19.9	1.1
60–64	57.8	26.5	14.3	1.4	57.5	25.1	16.5	0.9
65–69	59.9	24.4	14.2	1.6	59.3	24.0	15.9	0.8
70–74	65.7	19.2	13.5	1.6	66.4	21.0	12.4	0.2
75–79	70.4	16.9	11.9	0.8	61.4	20.1	16.9	1.6
80–84	64.0	17.3	17.3	1.3	76.7	17.1	4.7	1.6
85+	70.9	12.7	12.7	3.6	66.1	12.9	21.0	0.0

1. "Mobility status" refers to mobility experience for the period 1986 to 1991.
2. Percentages may not add to 100 due to rounding.
3. Stayers are those who remained in the same dwelling in 1986 and 1991.
4. Local movers are those who moved to a different dwelling in the same census subdivision between 1986 and 1991.
5. Migrants in Canada are those who moved to a different census subdivision between 1986 and 1991.
6. Immigrants are those who immigrated to Canada between 1986 and 1991.

Source: Census of Canada, Public Use Micro-data File, 1991.

remote locations that they can neither afford to sell nor maintain properly. This situation could become more widespread as the burgeoning suburban population in metropolitan areas ages (Golant 1992). As this population loses its ability to get around independently, the lack of public transportation makes access to health and social services more difficult; if this population cannot relocate to more central locations, then per capita costs of delivering services will increase.

A central issue in the literature on aging has been elderly people moving to be closer to social support. As indicated above, this often occurs in later life, when they encounter problems coping with the activities of daily living. The frequency of support-related moves increases markedly with age (see Table 2.16). These moves also have consequences for the relationship between the older person and close family and friends at the destination (see Table 2.18). While those who move for support reasons often move to be near a close family member, they often leave friends behind. Those who make support-related moves are much more likely to have their closest friend in another town or city; the implication is that the support-related move is often a trade-off between family and friends. In fact, support-related movers tend to express less satisfaction with their lives after the move than others (McGuinness 1996), which may be as much a function of the reduction in their social interaction as it is of the decline in their functional abilities.

TABLE 2.18: PROXIMITY TO CLOSEST FAMILY MEMBER OR FRIEND FOR THOSE 75 AND OVER WHO MOVED BETWEEN 1986 AND 1991, BY TYPE OF MOVE

	Non-movers	Other movers	Support movers
PROXIMITY OF CLOSEST FAMILY MEMBER			
		Unmarried respondents (%)	
Same household	21.4	22.7	35.4
Within neighborhood	18.6	17.1	16.6
Within same city or town	30.5	30.4	29.9
In different city or town	29.5	29.8	18.1
PROXIMITY OF CLOSEST FRIEND			
		All respondents (%)	
Same household	3.8	0.4	6.4
Within neighborhood	45.3	44.7	26.3
Within same city or town	42.1	41.3	40.6
In different city or town	8.8	13.6	26.7

Source: Survey on Ageing and Independence, 1991.

2.2.1 A model of migration

The socio-demographic influences on migration interact with each other; we need to place these influences in a multivariate structure to assess their relative importance. Since the theoretical literature on migration emphasizes that different processes assume different degrees of importance at different ages (Wiseman 1990), we decided to conduct three separate analyses using logistic regression (see Tables 2.19 and 2.20). The first focuses on individuals aged 55 to 64, most of whom had not yet retired and most of whom saw attachment to the labour force as crucial. The second analysis is of individuals aged 65 to 74; for them amenity-oriented moves took on added significance, and migrations tended to be strongly associated with intact couples. The third analysis is of individuals 75 and over, for whom support-related moves assumed greater importance (Litwak and Longino 1987).

In the pre-retirement group (aged 55 to 64), women were much less likely to be migrants than men; since one-half of a couple that moves is usually female, this result expresses the tendency for those women who live alone or in lone-parent situations to be less likely to migrate. Participation in the labour force was the strongest deterrent to migration. However, those at the upper end of the income and education scales were much more likely to migrate (the mobility coefficient for low income is negative and that for postsecondary education is strongly positive). It is also the only model for which severe functional limitation emerges as a deterrent to migration (see Chapter 4 for detail on the definition of *severe*).

Among 65- to 74-year-olds, women were still less likely to be recent migrants, while living alone emerged as a significant negative correlate of migration. The odds ratios for the income variables show that those with higher incomes were significantly more likely to have been migrants than those with low or moderate incomes. As well, postsecondary education is an even stronger differentiator between migrants and non-migrants in this age range than in the first. Attachment to the labour force is a marginally positive correlate, suggesting that migrants were more likely to continue working when they reached their destination than were those who do not move. Rural residents were much less likely to have migrated.

Among the 75-and-over group, women's likelihood of migration was dramatically lower again. However, living alone was a greater factor in this group than in younger groups, reflecting the greater importance of widowhood as a cause of migration. The income effects are more dramatic—the lower likelihood of low-income individuals moving and the higher likelihood for high-income individuals are accentuated. Those in the labour force, though a very small proportion of the population (see Table 2.8), had much higher propensities to be recent migrants. Rural residents in this age range had even lower migration rates than those in the first two age ranges, while the high value for mild and moderate disability indicates that, at this age, declining health status had a noticeable effect on the likelihood of moving.

The regional effects consistently stress that British Columbia is a favoured destination for migration (Bergob 1995). The importance of the regional coefficients

TABLE 2.19: LOGISTIC REGRESSION MODELS—CORRELATES OF MIGRATION

Dependent variable

MIGRATION DEFINED AS: RESPONDENT LIVED IN A DIFFERENT CENSUS SUBDIVISION FIVE YEARS AGO

	Population 55–64		Population 65–74		Population 75+	
			Without regional variables			
Independent variables[1]	Odds ratio	Significance level	Odds ratio	Significance level	Odds ratio	Significance level
Female	0.738	– –[2]	0.831	– – –	0.572	– – –
Lives alone	1.029	NS	0.663	– – –	1.173	+
Census family income (in $'0,000)	0.855	NS	0.418	– – –	0.195	– – –
Census family income, squared	0.989	NS	1.100	+ + +	1.271	+ + +
Low income	0.761	– –	0.864	NS	0.500	– – –
Postsecondary education	1.649	+ + +	3.003	+ + +	0.897	NS
Professional job classification	1.074	NS				
In labour force	0.556	– – –	1.128	NS	2.405	+ + +
Size-of-place indicators (reference category = respondent lives in an "other urban" area)						
Census metropolitan area	0.938	NS	0.935	NS	1.016	NS
Rural area	0.889	NS	0.616	– – –	0.546	NS
Disability status (reference category = respondent is not disabled)						
Mild or moderate disability	0.914	NS	1.106	NS	1.520	+ + +
Severe disability	0.800	–	0.956	NS	1.161	NS
Number of observations	19,587		19,898		14,250	

1. See Table 2.20 for variable definitions.
2. + + +, – – –   Significant at .001
   + +, – –   Significant at .01
   +, –   Significant at .05
   The chi-square value for each model is significant for $p<.0001$

TABLE 2.19: LOGISTIC REGRESSION MODELS—CORRELATES OF MIGRATION (CONTINUED)

Dependent variable

MIGRATION DEFINED AS: RESPONDENT LIVED IN A DIFFERENT CENSUS SUBDIVISION FIVE YEARS AGO

Independent variables[1]	Population 55–64		Population 65–74		Population 75+	
	Odds ratio	Significance level	Odds ratio	Significance level	Odds ratio	Significance level
			With regional variables			
Female	0.744	– – –[2]	0.837	– – –	0.569	– – –
Lives alone	1.022	NS	0.641	– – –	1.227	+ +
Census family income	0.858	NS	0.406	– – –	0.195	– – –
Census family income, squared	0.988	NS	1.105	+ + +	1.271	+ + +
Low income	0.759	– –	0.876	NS	0.486	– – –
Postsecondary education	1.58	+ + +	2.925	+ + +	0.877	NS
Professional job classification	1.077	NS				
In labour force	0.569	– – –	1.169	+	2.509	+ + +
Size-of-place indicators (reference category = respondent lives in an "other urban" area)						
Census metropolitan area	0.908	NS	0.912	NS	0.978	NS
Rural area	0.928	NS	0.683	– – –	0.55	– – –
Disability status (reference category = respondent is not disabled)						
Mild or moderate disability	0.933	NS	1.105	NS	1.559	+ + +
Severe disability	0.822	NS	0.954	NS	1.193	NS
Regional indicators (reference category = respondent lives in British Columbia)						
Atlantic provinces	0.369	– – –	0.31	– – –	0.798	NS
Quebec	0.557	– – –	0.422	– – –	0.862	NS
Ontario	0.579	– – –	0.557	– – –	0.69	– – –
Prairie provinces	0.467	– – –	0.405	– – –	0.554	– – –
Number of observations	19,587		19,898		14,250	

1. See Table 2.20 for variable definitions.
2. + + +,– – – Significant at .001
+ +, – – Significant at .01
+, – Significant at .05
The chi-square value for each model is significant for $p < .0001$

Source: Health and Activity Limitation Survey, 1986.

VARIABLES DERIVED FROM THE 1991 PUBLIC USE MICRO-DATA FILE

DEPENDENT VARIABLES

1. Low income	1 = Respondent lives below the low-income cut-off; 0 otherwise

INDEPENDENT VARIABLES

Socio-demographic indicators:

1. Age	Single years of age from 65 to 85
2. Age, squared	Respondent's age squared
3. Female	1 = Respondent is female; 0 otherwise
4. Total years of schooling	Total years of schooling at the elementary, secondary, university, and other postsecondary levels
5. University degree	1 = Respondent has received bachelor or first professional degree; 0 otherwise

Living arrangements: reference category = respondent lives with spouse

6. Lives alone	1 = Respondent lives alone; 0 otherwise
7. Lives with others	1 = Respondent lives with someone other than his or her spouse; 0 otherwise

Employment status: reference category = respondent did not work in 1990

8. Full-time	1 = Respondent worked mainly full-time weeks in 1990
9. Part-time	1 = Respondent worked mainly part-time weeks in 1990
10. Females who live alone	1 = Female respondent who lives alone; 0 otherwise

Size-of-place indicator:

11. Census metropolitan area	1 = Respondent lives in a census metropolitan area; 0 otherwise

Regional indicators: reference category = respondent lives in British Columbia

12. Atlantic provinces	1 = Respondent lives in Newfoundland, Prince Edward Island, Nova Scotia or New Brunswick; 0 otherwise
13. Quebec	1 = Respondent lives in Quebec; 0 otherwise
14. Ontario	1 = Respondent lives in Ontario; 0 otherwise
15. Prairie provinces	1 = Respondent lives in Manitoba, Saskatchewan, or Alberta

VARIABLES DERIVED FROM THE 1986 HEALTH AND ACTIVITY LIMITATION SURVEY

DEPENDENT VARIABLES

1. Migration	1 = Respondent lived in a different census subdivision five years ago

INDEPENDENT VARIABLES

Socio-demographic indicators:

1. Female	1 = Respondent is female; 0 otherwise
2. Lives alone	1 = Respondent lives alone; 0 otherwise
3. Census family income	Census family income in $'0,000 (values range from 0 to 5 (indicating a census family income of $50,000)

4. Census family income, squared	Census family income squared (ranges from 0 to 25)
5. Low income	1 = Respondent lives below the low-income cut-off; 0 otherwise
6. Post secondary education	1 = Respondent has received bachelor or first professional degree; 0 otherwise
7. Professional job classification	1 = Respondent is classified as upper-level manager, middle-level manager or other manager, or professional in the employment equity occupation groupings; 0 otherwise
8. In labour force	1 = Respondent last worked in 1986 (and is now in the labour force) 0 = Respondent last worked before 1986 or never worked in lifetime

Size-of-place indicators: reference category = respondent lives in an "other urban" area

9. Census metropolitan area	1 = Respondent lives in a census metropolitan area; 0 otherwise
10. Rural area	1 = Respondent lives in a rural area; 0 otherwise

Disability status: reference category = respondent is classified as not disabled

11. Mild or moderate disability	1 = Respondent is classified as mildly or moderately disabled; 0 otherwise
12. Severe disability	1 = Respondent is classified as severely disabled; 0 otherwise

Regional indicators: reference category = respondent lives in British Columbia

13. Atlantic provinces	1 = Respondent lives in Newfoundland, Prince Edward Island, Nova Scotia or New Brunswick; 0 otherwise
14. Quebec	1 = Respondent lives in Quebec; 0 otherwise
15. Ontario	1 = Respondent lives in Ontario; 0 otherwise
16. Prairie provinces	1 = Respondent lives in Manitoba, Saskatchewan, or Alberta

The chi-square value for each model is significant for $p<.0001$
Sources: Census of Canada, 1991 Public Use Micro-data File; Health and Activity Limitation Survey, 1986.

is that they have virtually no effect on the underlying structure of the influences of the socio-demographic variables on the likelihood of migrating. This makes us more confident about the interpretation of the basic relationships.

2.3 CONCLUSION

Not only is Canada's population experiencing rapid aging, but the structure of that aging population has important implications for planning health and social services in the next 20 years. This structure is changing, but slowly, such that its general characteristics should hold for at least the next two decades.

The most remarkable attributes of the elderly are the predominance of women in the population 75 and over and the large gap in the proportions of men and women in that age group who are widowed and live alone. Fully 30% of the total non-institutional population 75 and over are women living alone. Forty percent of these (or 12% of all older elderly) live below the Statistics Canada low-income cut-off.[11] Members of this group need others nearby who will help them, when needed, conduct their activities of daily living.

While most of the elderly are strongly independent and able to cope in the community, a significant number have limited social networks on which to call in times of need. In a mobile society, children often move away to pursue higher education and careers; parents are left behind and, even when strong family ties persist, family members may be so far apart that everyday support is difficult or impossible. We have seen that, among men and women 75 and over who live alone, only 20% reported they have a close family member in the same neighbourhood, and only 35% had their closest friend in the same neighbourhood. The majority without family or friends nearby form a core of demand for social support from public agencies.

Migration and local moves play an important role in the lives of the elderly. Elderly people's propensity to move is lower than that of working-age people, but it is certainly not insignificant. As recent writers have emphasized, mobility serves different functions at different ages; support becomes a relatively more important reason to move for those 75 and over. For those responding to decreasing functional abilities, moves are usually in one of two directions. The first is to be closer to those who can provide support for the activities of daily living—more often family than friends. The second is within the local housing market to more manageable accommodations given diminished functional abilities.

Both support and housing-related moves can be made in anticipation of future needs as well as of current needs. However, money is a central issue for those making either type of move; how many elderly cannot afford such moves is impossible to ascertain with the types of data available from national sources. It is difficult, for example, for an elderly person to move from slower-growing urban areas where housing prices are modest to the higher-priced housing markets of larger, growing centres. If the latter are where children live, parents would often have difficulty moving close by without downgrading their housing or having to take advantage of considerable financial support from family.

While individual mobility is important for the elderly, how it changes communities is less clear. In any given year, significant numbers of both elderly and non-elderly move in and out of almost every community. Whether they change the characteristics of the elderly population or the relative size of the elderly population depends on the aggregate characteristics of in- and out-migration. It is to this issue that we turn in the next chapter.

ENDNOTES

1. The source of the 1951 percentages are Ram (1990), and the 1991 percentages are calculated from Table 2.1.

2. The structure of seniors' benefits favours couples in determining low-income cut-offs, since the benefits for both partners have grown at a faster rate than have combined expenditures.

3. In 1990, 11.1% of women 60 to 64 and 10.7% of men 60 to 64 were professionals; the corresponding figures for women and men 75 to 79 were 9.4% and 12.2%, respectively.

4. For the purposes of this discussion, "region" refers to the five regions of Canada—the Atlantic provinces, Quebec, Ontario, the Prairie provinces, and British Columbia and the territories.

5. The positive coefficient for age and negative coefficient for age squared defines a curve which increases at a decreasing rate.

6. There has been some interesting research on "snowbirds" that has portrayed their socio-economic characteristics (e.g., Tucker et al. 1992). However, how one defines seasonal moves (for example, the duration) and therefore how one measures the magnitude of this phenomenon remain complex issues that go beyond the scope of this analysis.

7. Local moves are defined as a change of permanent residence within a specified administrative area—in Canada, a census subdivision, typically a rural township or urban municipality—while migrations are moves between census subdivisions.

8. The migration saldo is the ratio of net migration to total in- and out-migration for a given flow or set of flows. It is a measure of the redistributional impact of migration.

9. The data in Table 2.16 refer to all moves. This downplays the role of "amenity orientation," which applies primarily to migrations, which in total constitute less than one-third of all moves.

10. The lower bounds for proportions moving to institutions by age, however, can be estimated (see Chapter 1).

11. These proportions will decline as men's longevity approaches women's, but they will be offset by the growing numbers of divorced people reaching old age.

CHAPTER

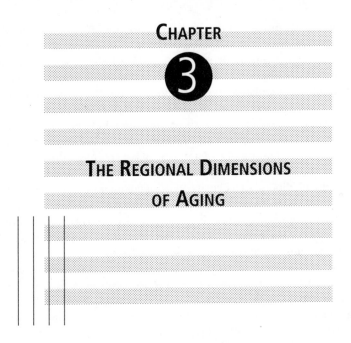

THE REGIONAL DIMENSIONS
OF AGING

Chapter 2 discussed the mobility patterns of the younger elderly and older elderly. The younger elderly often seek out places that offer recreational opportunities in a climate with moderate winters and moderate living costs, especially housing and local taxes (Fournier, Rasmussen and Serow 1988). But as their health deteriorates, elderly people need more support from both informal and formal services. If such support, particularly from family and friends, is not available locally, then it is likelier that they will move. The return migration of older people to places where they were brought up or spent much of their lives, and where family supports are available, deserves special attention (Newbold 1993).

Several excellent profiles have been written of the elderly population's geographical distribution and mobility at the national and provincial levels (e.g., Northcott 1988; Statistics Canada 1990b). However, little has been published in Canada that examines the changing geographical distribution of the elderly population at the sub-provincial level,[1] and what this means for the demand for health care and social services.[2]

Although the elderly have received less than their share of attention—largely because they are considered a low-mobility group (Rogers 1988)—it is recognized that flows of both the elderly and non-elderly, whether in good or poor health, of high or low income, retired or still in the labour force, can have a significant impact on both source and destination communities (McCarthy 1983; Bekkering 1990).

Changes in individual circumstances associated with elderly migration and aging in place also have consequences at the aggregate level for local and provincial governments as the demand for health services changes. To better estimate future demand for health services at the provincial and local levels, we need to better understand the processes that underlie the aging of local populations.

To create a clear picture of the spatial distribution of Canada's elderly and the roles that aging in place and migration play at the local level, this chapter focuses on variations among census divisions. Section 3.1 discusses the influences on local population distributions. Section 3.2 examines geographical variations in the percentages of the population aged 65 and over and the population 80 and over, as well as the sex ratios of the population 65 and over and the old component of the dependency ratio. Changes in these measures between 1986 and 1991 are analysed. In Section 3.3, shares and rates of change are examined. Section 3.4 assesses the relative importance of aging in place and migration. Based on a categorization of the relative importance of aging in place and elderly migration, in Section 3.5 the likelihood of a census division falling into a category is linked to its socio-economic characteristics. In other words, we examine differences in the geographical distribution of the elderly and the characteristics of the communities in which they live. The general relations between the aging variables and community profiles are illustrated using regression analyses.

There are practical and analytical reasons to choose census divisions as the geographical unit of analysis. Census divisions are equivalent to counties, cantons, regional municipalities or districts in many provinces. Provincial rates and even those calculated by urban size obscure the tremendous variation in the absolute and relative size of the elderly population at the local level. Since much of the planning and delivery of health and social services is carried out at the local level, it is critical to understand how the size of the elderly population is changing at this scale. For analytical purposes, census divisions are the smallest spatial units at which five-year age cohorts and socio-economic data are available for developing the measures used in this chapter. If we were to use the smaller census subdivisions, the small numbers in each five-year age category would make the estimates of the migration numbers unreliable.

3.1 CHANGE IN POPULATION AGING AT THE LOCAL LEVEL

In Canada, the primary influence on population aging has been the long-run decline in fertility and mortality rates (McDaniel 1986). With progressively fewer children being born and proportionately more people surviving to the age of 80, it is not surprising that the proportion of the population 65 and over has risen continuously for the last 50 years (see Chapter 1). This increase at the national level has only been mitigated slightly by immigration; because immigrants are on average younger than the resident population, immigration has a tendency to reduce the rate of population aging.

In any set of subnational regions, such as provinces or census divisions, the degree of population aging varies considerably, and the relative importance of different components of change also tends to vary. Because people are much likelier to migrate shorter distances (Shaw 1985), it follows that the smaller the area, the greater the potential role played by migration in changing populations. Interprovincial migration changes provincial population distributions; but migration between census divisions changes population distributions even more. People of all ages are more likely to move from one census division to an adjacent census division than from one province to another. So migration tends to have a greater impact on population aging at the census division scale.

Since population change is brought about by births, deaths and migration (see Appendix 3.1), variation in aging is attributable to long-run differences in fertility, mortality and migration rates. Change is cumulative so that, for any five-year intercensal period, the rate of population aging is dependent primarily on two demographic influences: the demographic structure of the area at the beginning of the period, and the impact of the demographic structure of migration into and out of the area during the period.

An area's demographic structure at the beginning of an intercensal period determines the magnitude of aging in place—the increase in the proportion of the population 65 and over that is attributable to births and deaths in the initial population. In a given five-year period, the dominant predictors of the increase in the proportion 65 and over are:

- the ratio of the population aged 60 to 64 to that aged 65 to 69. This ratio represents the potential for those approaching 65 to increase that segment of the population. If the 60-to-64 age group is significantly larger than the one above it, the number in this group who survive to 65 will more than offset the accumulated number of deaths in the elderly population;

- the proportion of those 65 and over who are 80 and over. This variable defines the shape of the elderly age pyramid; the smaller the ratio, the younger the elderly population and the greater the potential for rapid increase.

A simple regression for census division data for the period 1986 to 1991 shows that 73% of the variation in aging in place among the population 65 and over (the variable a_{65} in Appendix 3.1) is attributable to these two variables.

The second major factor determining the rate of population aging is the impact of the demographic structure of migration into and out of the area during the intercensal period. If the net migration rate into the area for those 65 and over is greater than that for those under 65,[3] then migration will increase the rate of population aging in the area.

In the short run, these two factors are more important than local variations in fertility and mortality rates. In the longer run, however, sustained differences in local fertility and mortality would produce different rates of aging. Higher mortality rates or fertility rates would tend to slow the population-aging process. It is also worth noting that over longer periods of time it is necessary to take into account the fertility, mortality and subsequent migration experience of the migrants themselves (Rogers 1975; Rees and Wilson 1977), which can change the rate of population aging. However, in a five-year period, the effect of the differential experiences of migrants is small.

Population aging is a cumulative process. The demographic characteristics of an area at the beginning of an intercensal period may have more to do with the previous decades' complex history of fertility, mortality and migration than with any recent events or current characteristics. This is well illustrated by the low proportion of males in those age cohorts that experienced the First World War; these men were concentrated in the 70-to-79 age group in 1971. They were not only less numerous than women of the same age group, but also much less numerous than subsequent male age groups. Similar long-run demographic impact is also associated with the small cohorts born in the Great Depression years and the large cohorts of the post-war baby boom (see Chapter 1; Peron and Strohmenger 1985).

In large part, mortality and fertility effects are macro-scale influences: they permeate every part of the country. The decline in fertility has occurred in all segments of society, although fertility remains higher in rural than in urban areas. The primary reason for differences in mortality is the variation in local populations' socio-economic conditions; those in lower socio-economic classes have consistently higher mortality rates (Wilkins, Adams and Brancker 1989). The net effect of these mortality differentials on geographical distribution is small.

There are also systematic demographic processes, present for many decades, that produce geographical variations in the distribution of the elderly. The history of migration in Canada—as in other countries—is of young adults moving from areas with limited economic opportunities to areas where they are better. In general, these moves have been from rural and small-town Canada to bigger towns and cities. Younger people migrate at consistently higher rates than older people, whose established social networks and greater job security are associated with much lower propensities to migrate (Northcott 1988). A prime consequence of this process has been that many parts of rural Canada, particularly in the Prairie and Atlantic provinces, have seen significant aging as the older people remain while the younger ones depart.

However, there are other reasons for migration besides the search for better economic opportunities. A newer trend, discussed in Chapter 2, is more and more affluent elderly migrating to high-amenity areas, particularly those with moderate winters. Again, however, selective migration by one group leads to concentration of others who are less mobile; the less affluent elderly will become concentrated in more disadvantaged origin areas. That concentration can be compounded by older elderly migrants returning to their areas of origin to be close to family and to other services.

The pervasive differences between male and female mortality, particularly at older ages, also have implications for the geographical distribution of the elderly population. Since women are more likely to survive at every age than men, the ratio of men to women declines with age, and the number of women without partners increases (see Chapter 1). It is particularly difficult for single elderly individuals to cope with rural life, especially if living in a remote area hampers access to social supports and services. Often single elderly people overcome this difficulty by moving from rural areas to nearby urban centres. Therefore, we would expect greater concentrations of elderly single women in urban areas, with corresponding implications for the types of services that must be provided. Women living alone are greater users of formal agencies for support (see Chapter 4), and continued growth of this population will increase pressure on service providers.

TABLE 3.1: VARIABLES USED IN REGRESSION ANALYSES

	VARIABLES USED IN ANALYSES OF 1991 STRUCTURE	VARIABLES USED IN ANALYSES OF CHANGE 1986 to 1991
Urban variables	Percentage of census division population defined as urban metropolitan area (=1 if census metropolitan area; 0 otherwise)	Percentage of census division population defined as urban metropolitan area (=1 if census metropolitan area; 0 otherwise)
Socio-economic variables	Percentage of census division population who immigrated between 1986 and 1991	Percentage of census division population who immigrated between 1986 and 1991
	Percentage of households falling below low-income cut-off in 1991	Percentage of 15+ population unemployed in 1986
	Percentage 15+ population unemployed in 1991	Percentage change in average income 1986 to 1991
	Average income in 1991	Percentage change in unemployment rate 1986 to1991
	Population growth 1986 to 1991	Average income in 1986
	Percentage over 15 with university degree in 1991	Percentage over 15 with university degree in 1986
	Percentage over 15 with less than Grade 9	
	Percentage 15 to 24 not in labour force	
Health services environment	Health services employees per thousand population	Health employees per thousand population
	Physicians per thousand population	Physicians per thousand population
Climate	Mean July temperature	Mean July temperature
	Mean January temperature	Mean January temperature
	Number of hours of sunshine in year	Number of hours of sunshine in year
Regional dummy variables	Atlantic (=1 if census division is in Atlantic provinces; 0 otherwise)	Atlantic
	Quebec	Quebec
	Ontario	Ontario
	Prairies	Prairies
	(reference category is British Columbia and territories)	
1986 demographic characteristics		Percentage of population who were women aged 20–35 in 1986
		Ratio of (population aged 60–64/65–69 in 1986)
		Percentage of population 65+ in 1986
		Percentage of the elderly population who were 80+ in 1986

Our current understanding of population aging suggests that the country-wide aging caused by shifts in fertility and mortality is geographically differentiated by a complex web of other social, economic and demographic variables. The dominant message, however, is that we would expect to find a strong association at the local level between population aging and economic disadvantage. Although the majority of any elderly population is likely to be active and healthy, communities with fewer local resources can expect to see disproportionate increases in demand for services for the elderly compared with affluent communities.

The structure of and change in population aging described above suggest that the demographic indicators of aging have multivariate links with certain social, economic and demographic variables. In the later sections of this chapter, we will verify the existence of these links between aging and community profiles with a series of two types of regression analyses using the independent variables set out in Table 3.1. The first analysis relates demographic characteristics in 1991 to socio-economic characteristics in 1991; the second relates measures of change between 1986 and 1991 to characteristics in 1986 and changes in socio-economic measures between 1986 and 1991. Because of the complexity of the relations underlying aging, these regression analyses are meant to be descriptive rather than explanatory, characterizing the types of communities associated with particular aging scenarios.

As part of these analyses, we include regional dummy variables to represent the broad demographic differences among the five main regions (the Atlantic provinces, Quebec, Ontario, the Prairie provinces, and British Columbia and the territories). In many cases there are additional regional differentials over and above those attributable to the independent variables included in the analyses. The analyses use British Columbia as the reference region, so the coefficients for the other four regions reported in Tables 3.2 to 3.5 represent the differences between British Columbia and each region after controlling for differences in the other socio-economic variables.

3.2   THE SPATIAL DISTRIBUTION OF CANADA'S ELDERLY POPULATION

In 1991, 11.7% of Canadians were 65 and over, and 2.4% were 80 and over. However, at the census division level these percentages varied considerably. The elderly made up more than 11.7% of the population in 56% of the census divisions across Canada in 1991 (see Figure 3.1). What is striking is the contrast between a *young* northern Canada and an *old* southern Canada. To a large extent, this contrast reflects the differences in the proportion of Native people living in northern Canada compared with southern Canada, and the differences in fertility and mortality patterns of Native people compared with non-Native people.[4] It also reflects the tendency of older people to leave areas with harsher climates for areas with moderate conditions, particularly western destinations, while younger people are attracted northward by adventure and high wages.

In Southern Canada, there was also considerable spatial variation in the elderly population. In Atlantic Canada, parts of Cape Breton, much of Nova Scotia and the

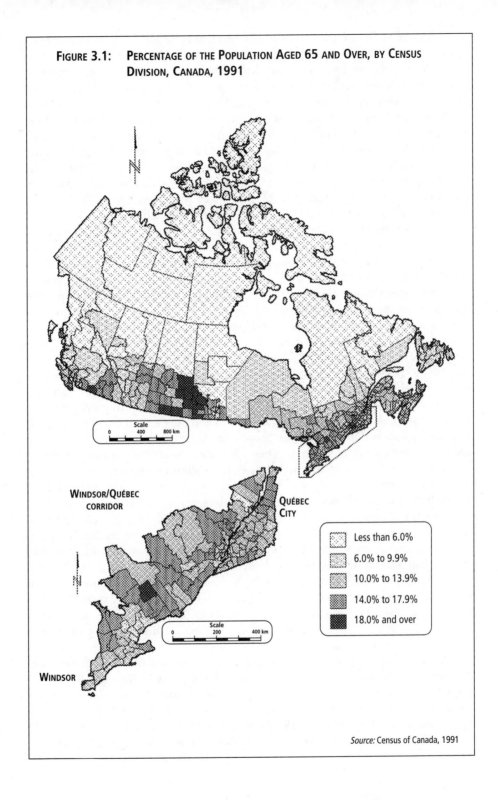

FIGURE 3.1:   PERCENTAGE OF THE POPULATION AGED 65 AND OVER, BY CENSUS
               DIVISION, CANADA, 1991

Scale
0   400   800 km

WINDSOR/QUÉBEC
CORRIDOR

QUÉBEC
CITY

Less than 6.0%
6.0% to 9.9%
10.0% to 13.9%
14.0% to 17.9%
18.0% and over

Scale
0   200   400 km

WINDSOR

Source: Census of Canada, 1991

THE REGIONAL DIMENSIONS OF AGING

census divisions around the Bay of Fundy had relatively large elderly populations (greater than 14.0%). In Quebec, it was mainly in the non-metropolitan census divisions along the St. Lawrence and Ottawa rivers where higher concentrations of the elderly lived. In Ontario, there were three distinct clusters of census divisions with high proportions of elderly: rural Eastern Ontario; a wedge of census divisions stretching from Lake Ontario to the north shore of Georgian Bay; and the rural census divisions along Lake Huron and the southern shore of Georgian Bay. On the Prairies, there was a growing number of rural census divisions along the southern borders of Manitoba and Saskatchewan, where more than 18.0% of the population was elderly. In British Columbia, the census divisions of the south-central interior and the southern part of Vancouver Island, which are well-known retirement destinations, had relatively large elderly populations.

The spatial distribution of the population aged 80 and over (see Figure 3.2) was very similar to the spatial distribution of the population aged 65 and over (see Figure 3.1); the ecological correlation[5] between the proportion 65 and over (f_{65+}) and the proportion 80 and over (f_{80+}) for census divisions is 0.95. In many census divisions across Canada, the population aged 80 and over in 1991 made up more than 3.0% of the total population and, as was indicated for the population of Canada as a whole, was often the fastest-growing segment of the community.

Our general ideas about the concentrations of elderly are confirmed by regression analysis relating f_{65+} and f_{80+} to the socio-economic conditions in census divisions in 1991 (see Table 3.2). In both cohorts, Quebec's population was generally younger and Ontario's older than British Columbia's, once the other variables were controlled. Strong negative associations were found between f_{65+} and f_{80+} and average income, recent population growth and the percentage of the population aged 15 to 24 not in the labour force—the latter often a sign of higher post-secondary education enrolment. The association with the degree of urban population in a census division was also negative, although the relation was not as high. Strong positive associations were found with mean January temperature, highlighting the importance of moderate winters, and with the proportion of the population with less than Grade 9 education. The aging measures were also positively associated with the concentration of health services workers. It is tempting to assign a causal link to the latter association, but the relationship was probably more a function of the fact that concentrations of both older people and health service workers were lower in larger, high-growth urban areas. High values for the number of health service workers per thousand population were found in many medium-sized communities with teaching hospitals (such as London, Ontario, Kingston, Ontario and Sherbrooke, Quebec), although these communities did not grow particularly rapidly in the 1980s.

The ratio of the proportion 80 and over to the proportion 65 and over measures the overall age of the elderly population—the higher the ratio, the older the elderly population. It had a particular geographical distribution: the Atlantic provinces, Ontario and the Prairies had older elderly populations than did Quebec or British Columbia. Many of the other relationships with aging are reinforced, as one might expect, by these two variables that are so highly correlated. Communities with

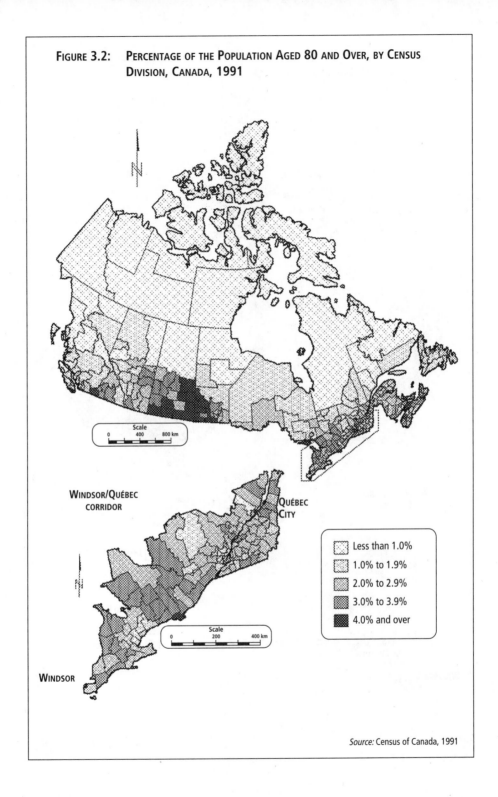

FIGURE 3.2:   PERCENTAGE OF THE POPULATION AGED 80 AND OVER, BY CENSUS
DIVISION, CANADA, 1991

WINDSOR/QUÉBEC
CORRIDOR

QUÉBEC
CITY

WINDSOR

Scale
0   400   800 km

Scale
0   200   400 km

Less than 1.0%

1.0% to 1.9%

2.0% to 2.9%

3.0% to 3.9%

4.0% and over

Source: Census of Canada, 1991

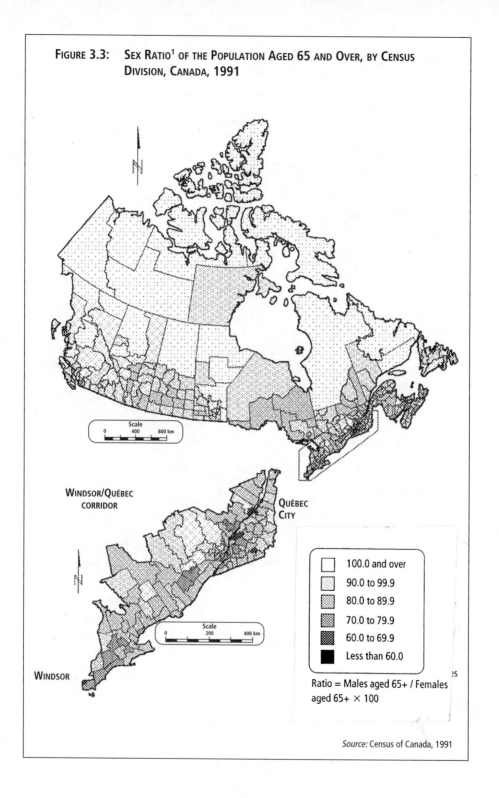

FIGURE 3.3:   SEX RATIO[1] OF THE POPULATION AGED 65 AND OVER, BY CENSUS
DIVISION, CANADA, 1991

WINDSOR/QUÉBEC
CORRIDOR

QUÉBEC
CITY

WINDSOR

Scale
0   400   800 km

Scale
0   200   400 km

	100.0 and over
	90.0 to 99.9
	80.0 to 89.9
	70.0 to 79.9
	60.0 to 69.9
	Less than 60.0

Ratio = Males aged 65+ / Females
aged 65+ × 100

Source: Census of Canada, 1991

high ratios were more likely to have below-average incomes and to have had low growth rates in the previous five years. They were also those communities with moderate winters and above-average amounts of sunshine. There was a negative association with the proportion of urban dwellers in the area, as well as with areas of high unemployment and concentrations of families with low incomes (see Table 3.2).

When the percentage of the population that is elderly is decomposed by gender, the spatial patterns are similar to those in Figure 3.1. On a division-by-division basis, the percentage of the female population that is elderly, however, tended to be higher than the percentage of the male population that is elderly, reflecting men's lower life expectancy.

The implied imbalance between the elderly male and female populations can be presented more accurately by the calculation of sex ratios for each census division. Sex ratios are calculated in the following manner:

$$SR = \frac{P_{m,65+}}{P_{f,65+}} * 100$$

where

SR = the sex ratio
$P_{m,65+}$ = the total male population aged 65 and over in Canada
$P_{f,65+}$ = the total female population aged 65 and over in Canada

Values above 100 indicate that there are more elderly men than women in a census division, values of 100 indicate a balance between elderly men and women, and values below 100 indicate there are more elderly women than men.

In almost all of the census divisions in southern Canada in 1991, sex ratios for the elderly population were below 100 (see Figure 3.3). These ratios are even lower—more predominately female—when the ratios are calculated for the population aged 80 and over (see Figure 3.4). In many of Canada's census divisions, the sex ratio approached or passed 2 women to 1 man over the age of 80 (SR = 50). The sex ratio for the elderly was strongly associated with urban areas; the more urbanized areas had significantly fewer males per 100 females.

Comparing the spatial distribution of the elderly population to that of the working-age population by means of the ODR reveals those communities where the need for health and social services is likely to be greatest among the elderly population.[6]

$$ODR = \frac{P_{65+}}{P_{15-64}} * 100$$

where

ODR = the old component of the dependency ratio
P_{65+} = the population aged 65 and over in Canada
P_{15-64} = the remainder of the adult population in Canada

Many of the census divisions with high ODRs (see Figure 3.5) were also the census divisions previously known to have relatively large elderly populations, relatively large populations aged 80 and over, and sex ratios highly biased towards

TABLE 3.2: MODELS OF DEMOGRAPHIC CHARACTERISTICS IN 1991 FOR CENSUS DIVISIONS

DEPENDENT VARIABLES

Independent variables	Percentage 65 and over 1991		Percentage 80 and over 1991		Proportion of elderly 80 and over in 1991		Sex ratio 65 and over 1991	
	Model 1	Model 2	Model 3	Model 4	Model 5	Model 6	Model 7	Model 8
Intercept	24.0374***	26.2728***	5.0670***	6.1741***	17.4316***	22.3861***	1.0585***	0.9300***
% urban	-0.0189*	-0.0253**	-0.0041**	-0.0064**	-0.0082	-0.0190*	0.0024***	0.0021***
Metropolitan area	-0.3100	0.2990	-0.0968	0.0704	-0.3001	0.2183	0.0297	0.0321
% immigrants 1986–1991	0.0676	0.3327*	0.0489	0.1281**	0.2503*	0.4777**	-0.0000	-0.0128*
% low-income families	-0.0132	-0.1181*	-0.0219	-0.0511**	-0.1343*	-0.1931***	0.0011	0.0062*
% unemployed	-0.3001***	-0.2448***	-0.0770***	-0.0553***	-0.0809	-0.0042	-0.0122***	-0.0100***
Average income	-0.3894***	-0.3827***	-0.0904***	-0.1002***	-0.0777*	-0.1641***	-0.0067***	-0.0040***
Population growth 1986–1991	-0.2934**	-0.3418***	-0.1141***	-0.1421***	-0.3245***	-0.5079***	-0.0007	-0.0034
% with degree	0.1216	0.0503	0.0478*	0.0455*	0.1209	0.2206*	0.0124*	0.0194***
% with less than Grade 9	0.1311***	0.0615*	0.0475***	0.0200*	0.2020*	0.0890*	0.0020	0.0049***
% 15–24 not in labour force	-0.0986***	-0.1050***	-0.0286***	-0.0286***	-0.0846***	-0.0746	-0.0003	-0.0005
Health employees per thousand	0.1221***	0.1403***	0.0451***	0.0524***	0.1745***	0.2152***	0.0054***	0.0064***
Physicians per thousand	0.0442	-0.1644	-0.1109	-0.2461**	-0.3799	-1.2537***	0.0025	-0.0087
Mean July temperature	0.0831	0.1344	0.0260	0.0174	0.1263	0.0078	0.0040	0.0157***
Mean January temperature	0.2564***	0.2581***	0.0615***	0.0622***	0.1429***	0.1303*	0.0057***	0.0065***
Number of hours of sunshine	0.3143***	0.2520*	0.0645**	0.0707**	0.0700	0.2305*	0.0028	-0.0086*
Atlantic	-0.0947		0.1958		2.4101***		0.1724***	
Quebec	-1.6959**		-0.4969**		-0.6431		0.1436***	
Ontario	1.8834***		0.4240**		1.4218**		0.1449***	
Prairies	-0.4578		0.1213		2.7265***		0.0253	
Degrees of freedom	270	274	270	274	270	274	270	274
R-square	0.7685	0.7182	0.7852	0.7308	0.3947	0.2387	0.7547	0.6862

*** $p < 0.001$
** $p < 0.01$
* $p < 0.05$

Source: Census of Canada, 1986, 1991.

elderly women. The implication is that these are census divisions facing the challenge of high need, especially among their very old female populations, with fewer resources for health and social services.

Although the emphasis in this chapter is on population aging, which measures the *relative* concentration of the elderly population, it is important to remember that the *absolute* distribution of the elderly is central to many service decisions. A simple measure is the *share* of elderly population within each census division as a percentage of the total elderly population in Canada, which can be expressed as follows (Rogers 1989):

$$S_{65+,i} = \frac{P_{65+,i}}{P_{65+,tot}} *100$$

where

$S_{65+,i}$ = the share of the elderly population in the ith census division
$P_{65+,i}$ = the population aged 65 and over in the ith census division
$P_{65+,\,tot}$ = the total population aged 65 and over in Canada

Using the share measure, it is clear that the distribution of Canada's elderly population reflected the distribution of the total population; the largest *populations* were located in Ontario's census divisions, and most of the census divisions with shares over 2.0% in 1991 were metropolitan census divisions (see Figure 3.6). This contrasts sharply with Figure 3.1, which shows that many small-town and rural census divisions had relatively large *proportions* of elderly. Although the elderly proportion of the population varied substantially from place to place, the underlying population of Canada was so highly concentrated in big cities (Simmons 1991) that the absolute distribution of the elderly mirrored to a large degree the distribution of the total population.

It is important to remember the differences between the absolute and relative sizes of the elderly population when assessing the impact of aging on both the public and private sectors. When issues of equity come to the fore, the higher relative concentrations of elderly in rural and economically disadvantaged areas are significant; if the question is one of allocation of resources in response to the magnitude of demand for services, the concentrations of elderly in urban areas take precedence.

3.2.1 The elderly population of Canada's largest metropolitan areas

Much of Canada's elderly population lives in its largest cities, but within these cities the distribution of the elderly population is far from uniform. In this section we focus on the three largest census metropolitan areas in 1991: Toronto, Montréal and Vancouver. The elderly population represented 10.3% of Toronto's population, 11.4% of Montréal's and 12.8% of Vancouver's. Toronto was therefore slightly younger and Vancouver slightly older than the national average of 11.7%. The three cities together made up 30.0% of the Canadian elderly population.

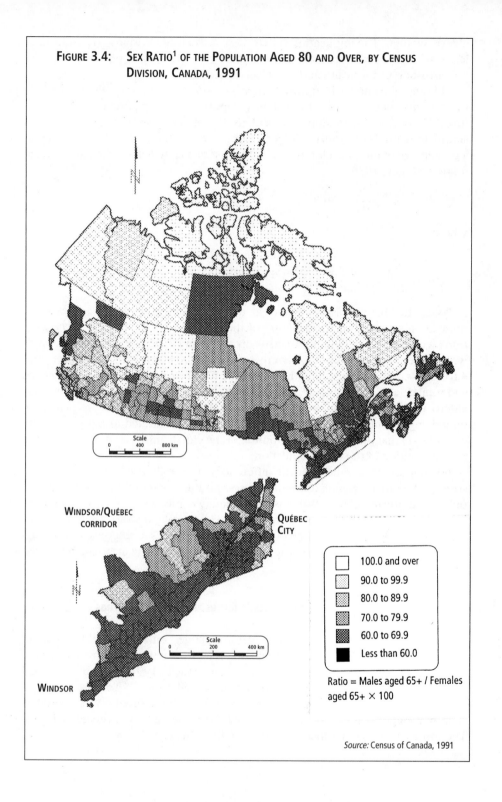

FIGURE 3.4: SEX RATIO[1] OF THE POPULATION AGED 80 AND OVER, BY CENSUS
DIVISION, CANADA, 1991

Scale
0   400   800 km

WINDSOR/QUÉBEC
CORRIDOR

QUÉBEC
CITY

Scale
0   200   400 km

WINDSOR

☐	100.0 and over
	90.0 to 99.9
	80.0 to 89.9
	70.0 to 79.9
	60.0 to 69.9
■	Less than 60.0

Ratio = Males aged 65+ / Females
aged 65+ × 100

Source: Census of Canada, 1991

Scale
0   400   800 km

WINDSOR/QUÉBEC
CORRIDOR

QUÉBEC
CITY

N

Scale
0   200   400 km

WINDSOR

Less than 7.0

7.0 to 12.9

13.0 to 18.9

19.0 to 24.9

25.0 and over

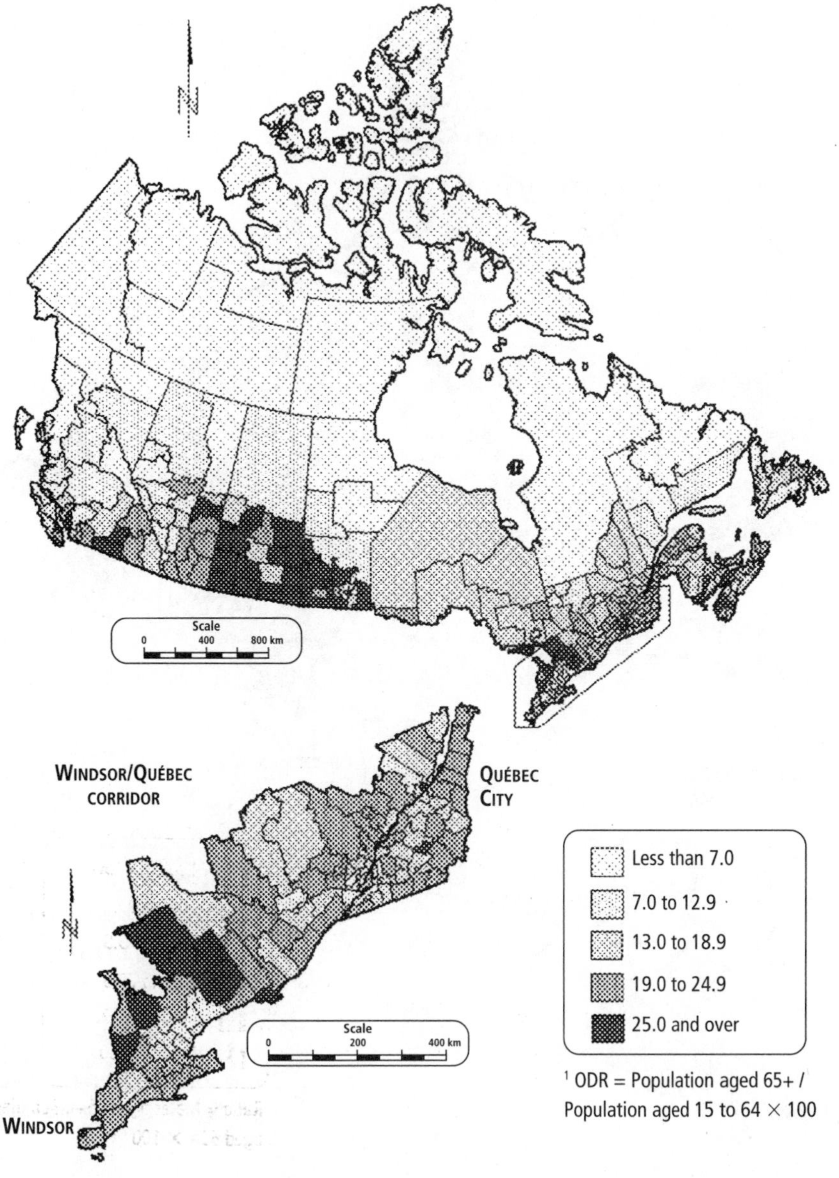

[1] ODR = Population aged 65+ /
Population aged 15 to 64 × 100

Source: Census of Canada, 1991

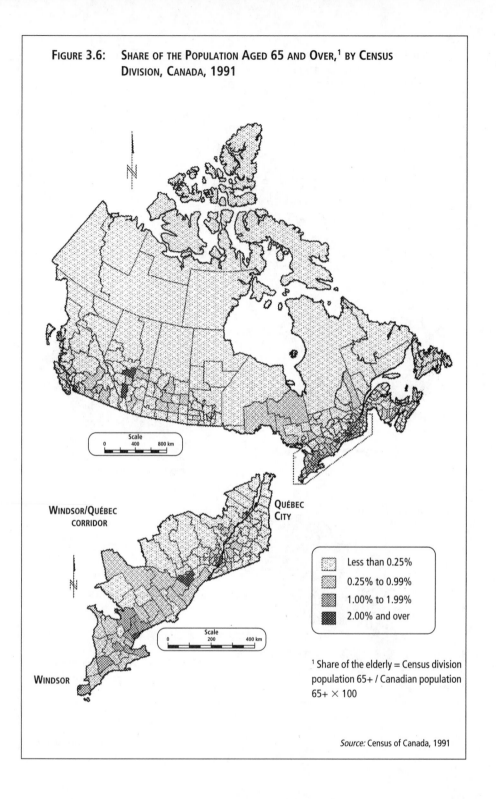

FIGURE 3.6: SHARE OF THE POPULATION AGED 65 AND OVER,[1] BY CENSUS DIVISION, CANADA, 1991

WINDSOR/QUÉBEC CORRIDOR

QUÉBEC CITY

WINDSOR

Scale
0   400   800 km

Scale
0   200   400 km

	Less than 0.25%
	0.25% to 0.99%
	1.00% to 1.99%
	2.00% and over

[1] Share of the elderly = Census division population 65+ / Canadian population 65+ × 100

Source: Census of Canada, 1991

In all three cities, the spatial distribution of the elderly population resembles a bull's-eye with two rings surrounding it. The bull's-eye contains the census tracts of the central business district and immediately adjacent neighbourhoods, where there were relatively few people 65 and over. This region is surrounded by a ring of census tracts taking in the older suburbs, where the elderly proportion of the population was—and is—growing rapidly. These are the census tracts of Etobicoke, North York and East York in Metropolitan Toronto (see Figure 3.7). In Montréal, they are the census tracts found mainly south and west of the central business district, but still on the island of Montréal (see Figure 3.8). In Vancouver, they are the census tracts in North Vancouver and West Vancouver along Burrard Inlet (see Figure 3.9). The newer suburbs of the three census metropolitan areas make up the outer ring, where the elderly population 65 and over is relatively small.

In all three census metropolitan areas, the sex ratios favoured elderly women over elderly men almost uniformly, except in some of the tracts in the outer suburbs, where the incidence of women living alone was small. (The large houses of the outer suburbs are often not suitable for individuals living alone; this encourages the elderly living alone to leave if they can afford to do so.) Overall, suburban populations tended to be much younger, the elderly population there was likely to be under 80, and most suburban elderly live with a spouse or partner (see Figures 3.10 to 3.12).

The most notable aspect of aging in the three metropolitan areas was the rapid increase in aging of the inner suburbs. These areas now have some of the highest elderly growth rates in the country and, given the large absolute numbers of elderly involved, will be the source of huge new demand for specialized goods and services in the coming years. However, suburbs' lower population densities pose a problem for those delivering services to the burgeoning elderly population.

3.3 CHANGES IN GEOGRAPHIC DISTRIBUTION OF THE ELDERLY POPULATION

Our concern here is not only with the current distribution of the elderly population but also with the way in which it is changing. Change itself can be measured in many ways, reflecting both absolute and relative growth.

Canada's elderly population grew at an annualized rate of 3.2% a year between 1986 and 1991.[7] The growth rates for individual census divisions, however, ranged from a small number of negative rates to a high of 9.5% a year. High growth rates for the elderly were clearly an urban phenomenon, although they tended to be lower in metropolitan areas than in smaller cities and towns (see Figure 3.13 and Table 3.3). In particular, the areas adjacent to metropolitan regions, especially Toronto, saw very high growth rates during this period. Particularly prone to higher rates were those communities with low proportions of elderly in 1986. Suburban Toronto is particularly ripe for growth; many who moved into new suburbs in the 1950s are now reaching retirement age. Unlike the measures of population aging, the growth rates themselves have a strong positive association with

FIGURE 3.7: PERCENTAGE OF THE POPULATION AGED 65 AND OVER, BY CENSUS TRACT, TORONTO CENSUS METROPOLITAN AREA, 1991

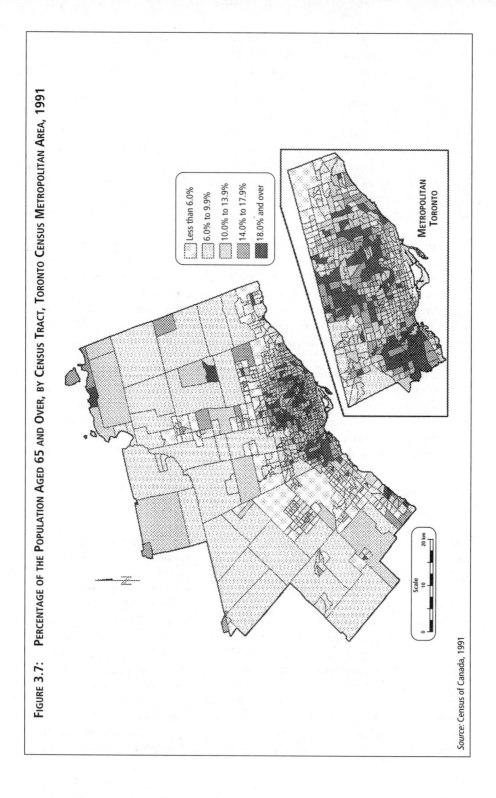

Less than 6.0%
6.0% to 9.9%
10.0% to 13.9%
14.0% to 17.9%
18.0% and over

METROPOLITAN TORONTO

Scale
0   10   20 km

Source: Census of Canada, 1991

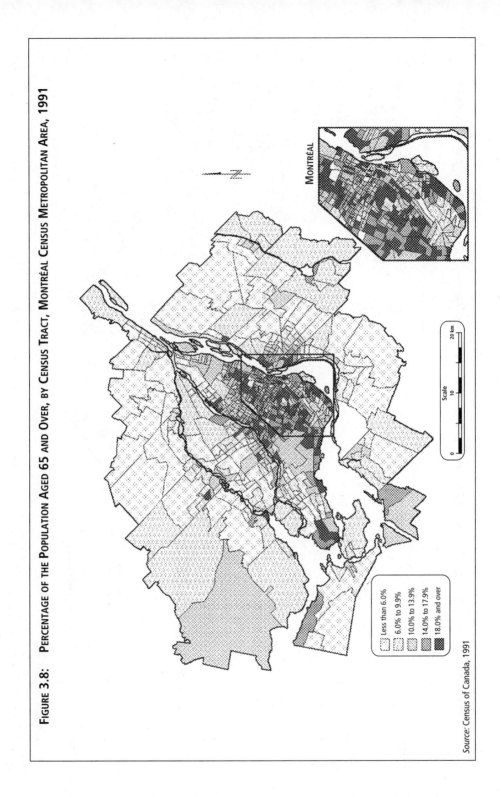

FIGURE 3.8: PERCENTAGE OF THE POPULATION AGED 65 AND OVER, BY CENSUS TRACT, MONTRÉAL CENSUS METROPOLITAN AREA, 1991

MONTRÉAL

Scale
0   10   20 km

Less than 6.0%
6.0% to 9.9%
10.0% to 13.9%
14.0% to 17.9%
18.0% and over

Source: Census of Canada, 1991

THE REGIONAL DIMENSIONS OF AGING

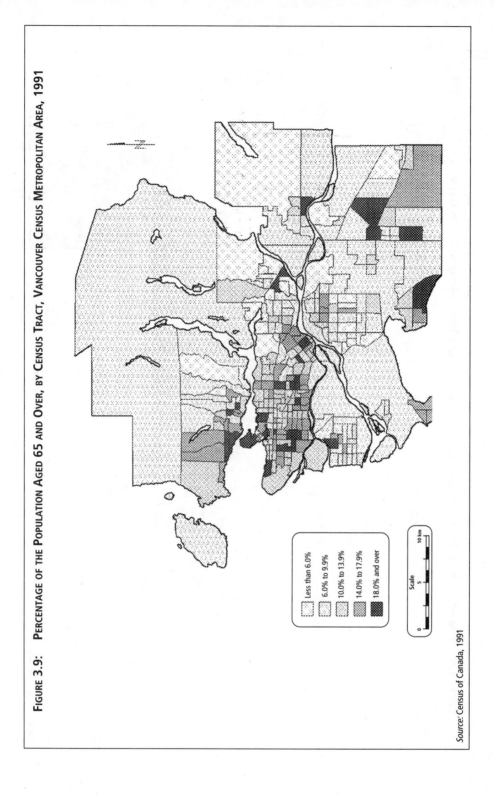

FIGURE 3.9:   PERCENTAGE OF THE POPULATION AGED 65 AND OVER, BY CENSUS TRACT, VANCOUVER CENSUS METROPOLITAN AREA, 1991

Less than 6.0%
6.0% to 9.9%
10.0% to 13.9%
14.0% to 17.9%
18.0% and over

Scale
0   5   10 km

Source: Census of Canada, 1991

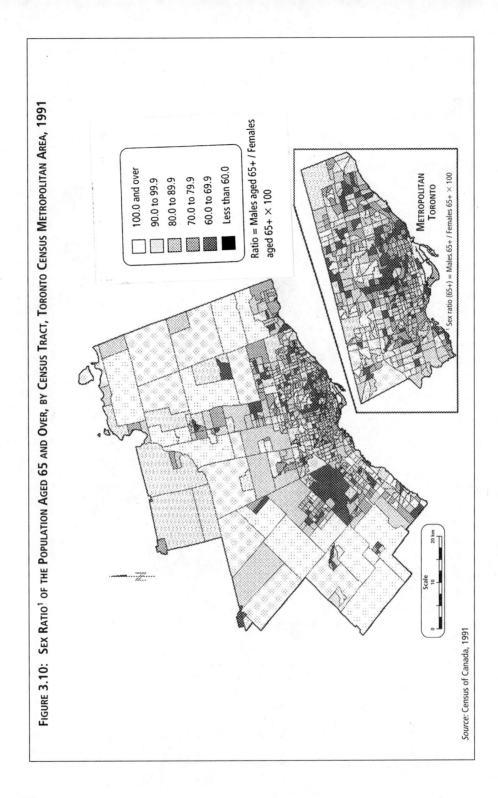

FIGURE 3.10:   SEX RATIO[1] OF THE POPULATION AGED 65 AND OVER, BY CENSUS TRACT, TORONTO CENSUS METROPOLITAN AREA, 1991

100.0 and over
90.0 to 99.9
80.0 to 89.9
70.0 to 79.9
60.0 to 69.9
Less than 60.0

Ratio = Males aged 65+ / Females aged 65+ × 100

METROPOLITAN TORONTO

Sex ratio (65+) = Males 65+ / Females 65+ × 100

Scale
0   10   20 km

Source: Census of Canada, 1991

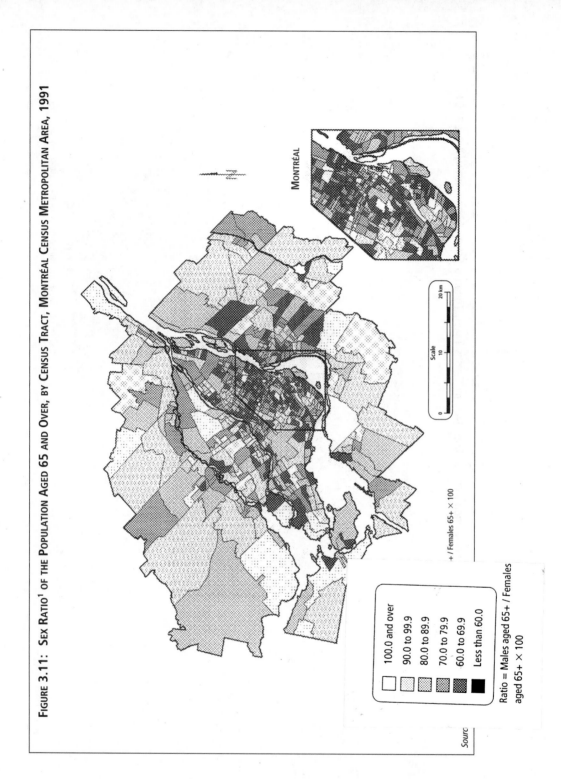

FIGURE 3.11: SEX RATIO[1] OF THE POPULATION AGED 65 AND OVER, BY CENSUS TRACT, MONTRÉAL CENSUS METROPOLITAN AREA, 1991

MONTRÉAL

Scale

0   10   20 km

100.0 and over

90.0 to 99.9

80.0 to 89.9

70.0 to 79.9

60.0 to 69.9

Less than 60.0

+ / Females 65+ × 100

Ratio = Males aged 65+ / Females
aged 65+ × 100

Source

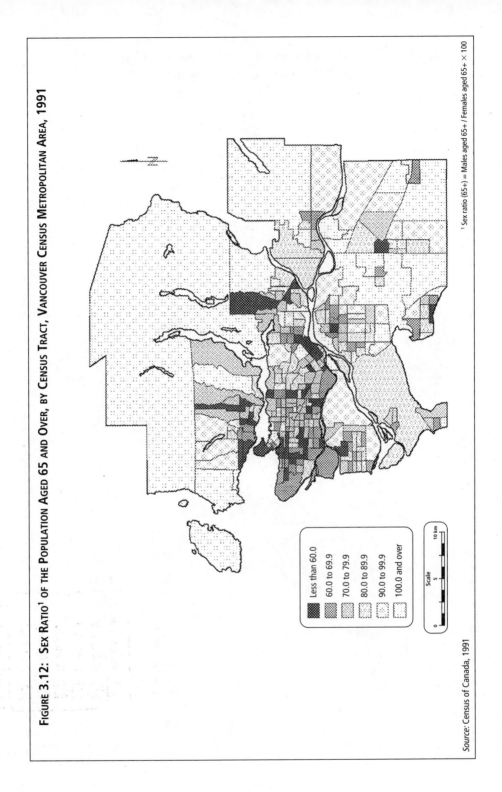

Figure 3.12: Sex Ratio[1] of the Population Aged 65 and Over, by Census Tract, Vancouver Census Metropolitan Area, 1991

Less than 60.0
60.0 to 69.9
70.0 to 79.9
80.0 to 89.9
90.0 to 99.9
100.0 and over

Scale

0   5   10 km

[1] Sex ratio (65+) = Males aged 65+ / Females aged 65+ × 100

Source: Census of Canada, 1991

FIGURE 3.13: ANNUAL RATE OF GROWTH[1] OF THE POPULATION AGED 65 AND OVER, BY CENSUS DIVISION, CANADA, 1986 TO 1991

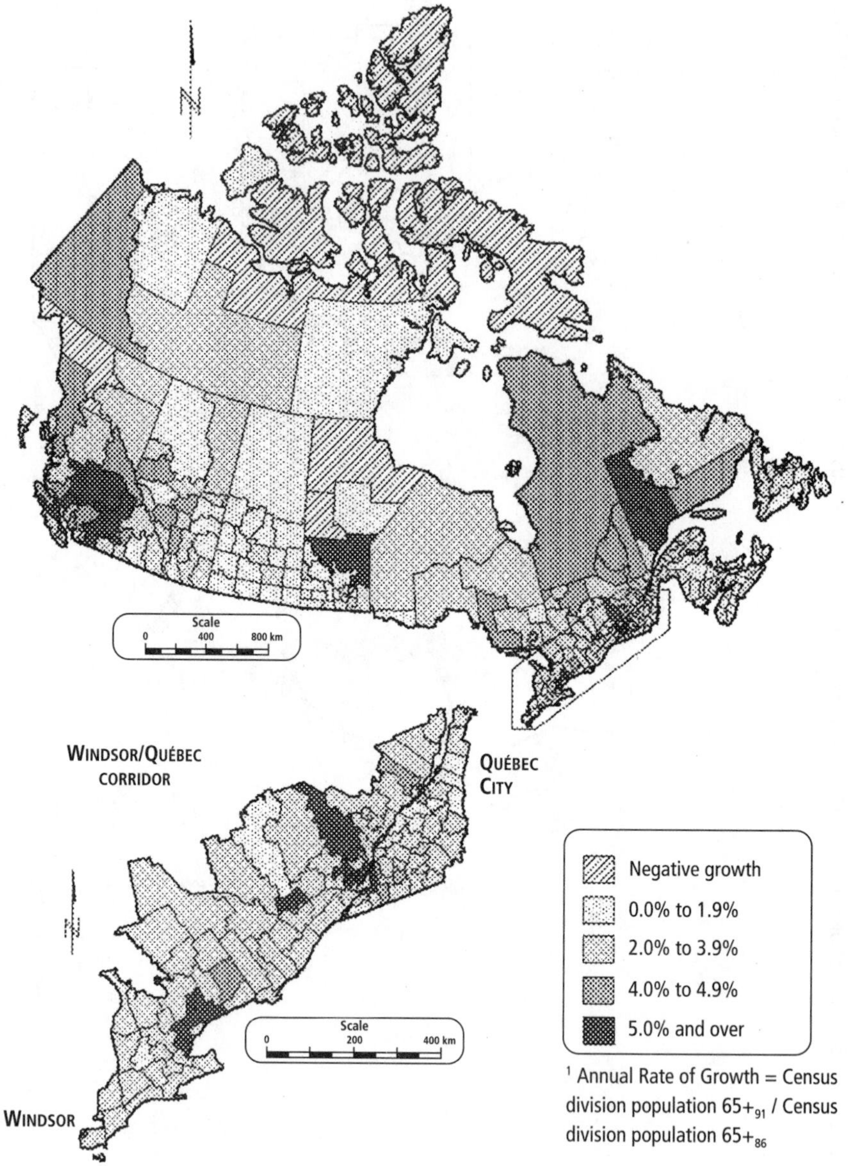

Scale
0   400   800 km

WINDSOR/QUÉBEC
CORRIDOR

QUÉBEC
CITY

Scale
0   200   400 km

WINDSOR

Legend:
- Negative growth
- 0.0% to 1.9%
- 2.0% to 3.9%
- 4.0% to 4.9%
- 5.0% and over

[1] Annual Rate of Growth = Census division population 65+$_{91}$ / Census division population 65+$_{86}$

Source: Census of Canada, 1986 and 1991

TABLE 3.3: MODELS OF GROWTH IN ELDERLY POPULATION FOR CENSUS DIVISIONS, 1986 TO 1991

DEPENDENT VARIABLES

Independent variables	C(65)		Growth rate >65 1986–1991		C(80)	
	Model 1	Model 2	Model 3	Model 4	Model 5	Model 6
Intercept	0.8859***	0.8480***	−0.0246*	−0.0350*	1.6054***	1.9331***
% urban	0.0011***	0.0008***	0.0002***	0.0002***	0.0009	0.0000
Metropolitan area	−0.0247*	−0.0255*	−0.0049*	−0.0051*	−0.0224	−0.0228
% immigrants 1986–1991	0.0018	0.0039	0.0003	0.0007	−0.0051	0.0147
% unemployed	0.0069***	0.0043***	0.0013***	0.0008**	0.0158***	0.0105**
% change in income 1986–1991	0.0004	−0.0006	0.0001	−0.0001	−0.0040*	−0.0038*
% change in unemployment 1986–1991	−0.0005*	−0.0005**	−0.0001*	−0.0001**	−0.0011	−0.0009*
Average income	0.0034**	−0.0008	0.0006**	−0.0001	−0.0069*	−0.0080*
Population growth 1986–1991	−0.0221***	−0.0229***	0.0060***	0.0058***	0.0095	−0.0105
% with degree	−0.0063*	−0.0030	−0.0012*	−0.0006	−0.0015	−0.0006
Health employees per thousand	−0.0006	0.0012*	−0.0001	0.0002*	−0.0015	0.0044**
Physicians per thousand	0.0084	0.0062	0.0018	0.0014	0.0331	0.0040
Mean July temperature	0.0027	−0.0006	0.0007	0.0001	0.0141*	0.0110*
Mean January temperature	0.0026**	0.0050***	0.0005***	0.0010***	−0.0026	0.0013
Number of hours of sunshine	−0.0000	0.0001***	−0.0000	0.0000***	−0.0003***	−0.0001*
Atlantic	0.0020	0.0478***	0.0015	0.0099***	−0.0349	0.0497
Quebec	0.0689***	0.0750***	0.0134***	0.0145***	0.0087	0.0293
Ontario	0.0368*	0.0584***	0.0073*	0.0112***	0.0460	0.0975***
Prairies	0.0612***	0.0681***	0.0127***	0.0140***	0.1730***	0.2011***
% women aged 20–35		−0.0118*		−0.0020*		−0.0060
Ratio 60–64/65–69		0.2801***		0.0524***		0.1453
% 65 and over 1986		0.0001		0.0001		0.0048
Proportion of elderly 80 and over		−0.0061***		−0.0011***		−0.0382***
Degrees of freedom	272	268	272	268	272	268
R-square	0.5616	0.7191	0.6774	0.7899	0.2735	0.5220

*** $p < 0.001$
** $p < 0.01$
* $p < 0.05$

Source: Census of Canada, 1986, 1991.

communities with higher average incomes and growing local economies. From a regional perspective, rates of growth were higher in Quebec than elsewhere; the areas that started out with relatively smaller elderly populations experienced the higher growth rates.

Most of the negative growth rates occurred in small northern communities, where out-migration of older people was the main contributing factor (see Section 3.4). In general, the Prairie and Atlantic provinces had consistently low growth rates, while British Columbia and Quebec saw significant growth in non-metropolitan areas. As we will see later, the differences in rates of growth are attributable to different mixes of aging in place and migration in different parts of the country.

In Canada as a whole, the proportion 65 and over (C_{65+}) grew by 9.5% between 1986 and 1991, from 10.7% to 11.7%. The proportion 80 and over (C_{80+}) grew 14.5%, from 2.1 to 2.4%.[8] High values of C_{65+} are concentrated in Newfoundland, Quebec, Northern Ontario, Saskatchewan, Alberta and the British Columbia Interior (see Figure 3.14). C_{65+} is a complex measure, in that it is positively associated with larger centres but has a strong negative association with high-growth areas (see Table 3.3). High-growth areas, particularly the Vancouver and Victoria regions and those in Ontario, attracted more than enough younger migrants to offset elderly growth.

Similar procedures can be used to calculate values for C_{80+}, the growth in the proportion 80 and over. Although there is some correlation (.42) between the distributions of C_{65+} and C_{80+}, there are also notable differences (see Figure 3.15 and Table 3.3). The distribution of C_{80+} tends to be less a function of economic circumstances—although values do tend to be higher for low-income, high-unemployment areas. Instead, the distribution is strongly driven by the previous aging of the population. Those areas that had a high proportion of the elderly 80 and over in 1986 tended to have faster-growing older populations than did other areas. For example, the Prairies had a much higher 80-and-over growth rate than did the other regions.

The above discussion shows some of the complexity of the geography of Canada's aging population. There were indications of the early stages of the "greying" of Canada's inner suburbs, and more evidence of the importance of the British Columbia Interior as a destination for Canada's elderly. In contrast, in regions like Atlantic Canada the growth of the elderly population was apparently in step with the growth of the non-elderly population. To understand these complex patterns, we must understand the roles that aging in place and elderly migration play in relation to the growth and migration of the non-aging population.

3.4 AGING IN PLACE, NET MIGRATION AND POPULATION AGING

The previous sections provide clues to the complexity of the process of population aging. In any given area or community, population aging or the increase in the proportion of the population 65 and over arises from two components: aging in place and net migration.

FIGURE 3.14: CHANGE IN THE PROPORTION OF THE POPULATION AGED 65 AND OVER (C_{65+}),[1] BY CENSUS DIVISION, CANADA, 1986 TO 1991

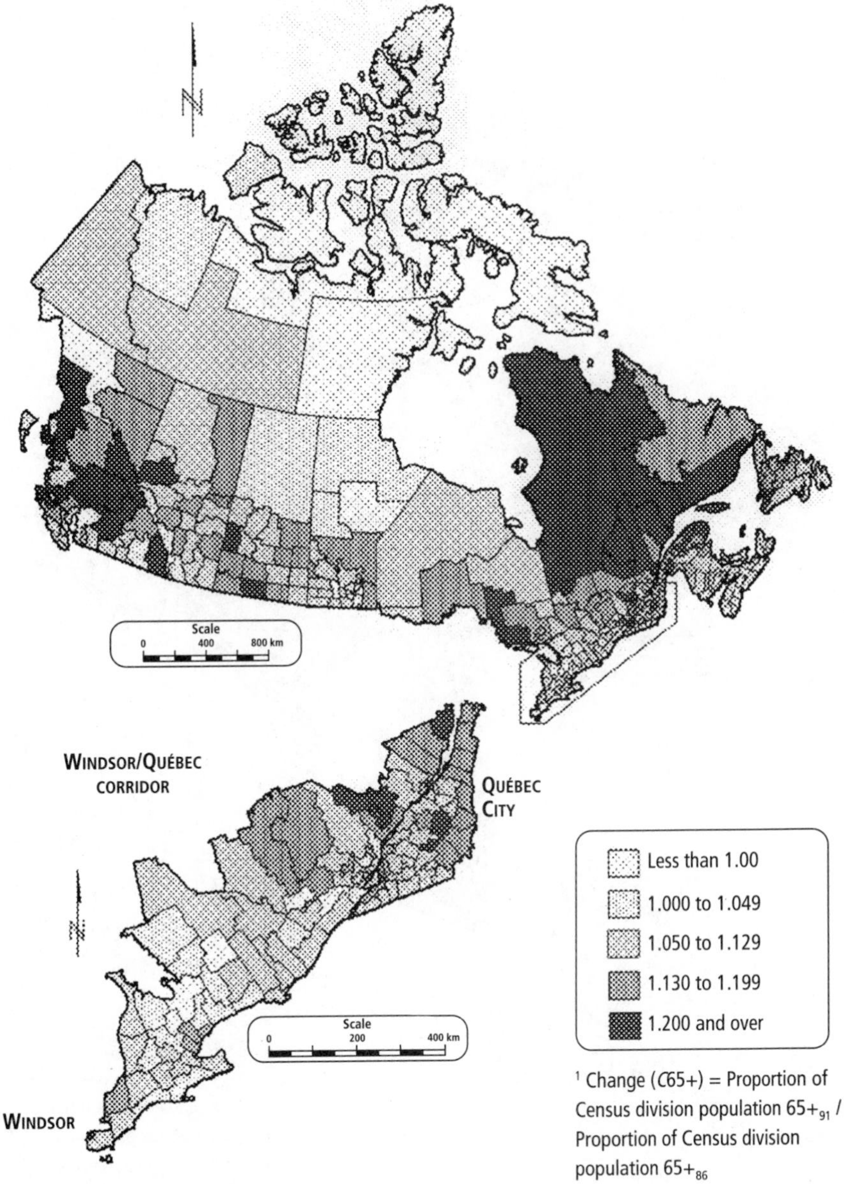

Scale
0   400   800 km

WINDSOR/QUÉBEC CORRIDOR

QUÉBEC CITY

WINDSOR

Scale
0   200   400 km

Less than 1.00
1.000 to 1.049
1.050 to 1.129
1.130 to 1.199
1.200 and over

[1] Change ($C65+$) = Proportion of Census division population $65+_{91}$ / Proportion of Census division population $65+_{86}$

Source: Census of Canada, 1986 and 1991

FIGURE 3.15: CHANGE IN THE PROPORTION OF THE POPULATION AGED 80 AND OVER (C_{80+}),[1] BY CENSUS DIVISION, CANADA, 1986 TO 1991

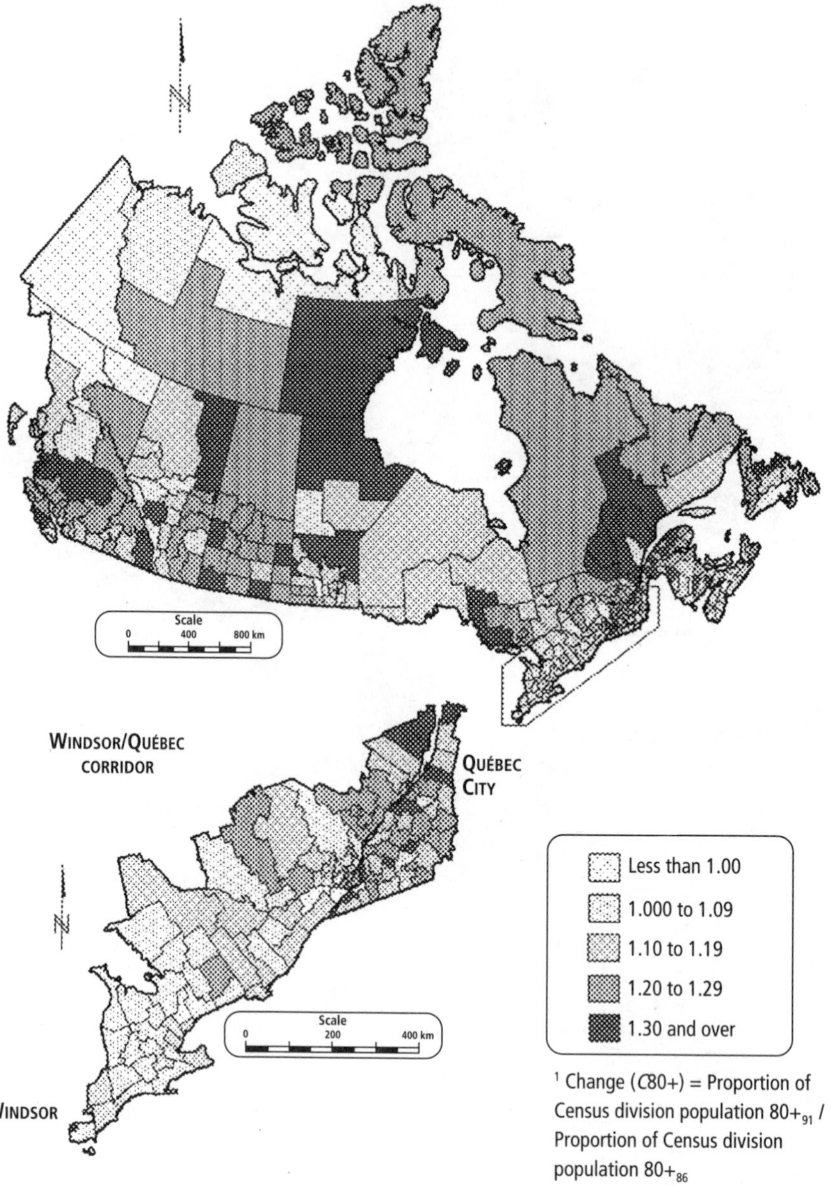

Scale
0   400   800 km

WINDSOR/QUÉBEC CORRIDOR

QUÉBEC CITY

Scale
0   200   400 km

WINDSOR

Less than 1.00

1.000 to 1.09

1.10 to 1.19

1.20 to 1.29

1.30 and over

[1] Change ($C80+$) = Proportion of Census division population $80+_{91}$ / Proportion of Census division population $80+_{86}$

Source: Census of Canada, 1986 and 1991

Aging in place is the net effect of births and deaths on the age structure of a local population; more precisely, it is the net effect of aging on the populations under 65 and 65 and over, considered separately.[9] If $a_{<65}$ and a_{65+} are the rates at which the two components of the population are growing as a function of births and deaths, then, if a_{65+} is greater than $a_{<65}$, aging in place will increase population aging.

Net migration is the net effect of migration into and out of the area for those under 65 and 65 and over. If $n_{<65}$ and n_{65+} are the net migration rates for the two segments of the population then, if n_{65+} is greater than $n_{<65}$, net migration will increase population aging.

The degree to which local populations age—if they age at all—therefore depends on the interaction between these two elements and their constituent rates. The rates themselves are outcomes of births, deaths and in- and out-migration. In exploring the nature of these changes, we consider the geographical distribution of the four constituent rates ($a_{<65}$, a_{65+}, $n_{<65}$, and n_{65+}) and the relative contributions of aging in place (α) and net migration (η) to population aging where:[7]

$$C_{65+} = 1 + \alpha + \eta$$

Each of the parameters cited above ($a_{<65}$, a_{65+}, $n_{<65}$, and n_{65+}) can be estimated directly from census data for census divisions in 1986 and 1991 (see Appendix 3.2).

The rates of increase in the populations under 65 and 65 and over due to aging in place ($a_{<65}$, a_{65+}) had similar general distributions (see Figures 3.16 and 3.17). Although the rates were consistently higher for the 65-and-over population, the rates tended to be relatively higher for both distributions in the northern parts of Quebec, the northern Prairies and northern British Columbia. As well, Newfoundland posted moderately high values. The two rates contrasted strongly in southern British Columbia, where the population under 65 grew at a rate far below average, as well as in Central Ontario and the census divisions around Montréal.

In all of Nova Scotia outside Halifax, the elderly population grew much faster due to aging in place relative to the younger population. Below-average values for $a_{<65}$ were found in areas where women of child-bearing age were a smaller fraction of the local population (see Table 3.4). Values were also lower in metropolitan areas, where fertility rates tended to be lower than in rural areas. As well, $a_{<65}$ tended to be higher in areas with higher unemployment. Higher valves of a_{65+}, on the other hand, were strongly associated with urban areas, and with areas that had higher average incomes and rates of income growth. This is because the driving force behind the growth of the elderly from aging in place is the shape of the age structure at the beginning of the period. Areas with high ratios of people 60 to 64 to people 65 to 69 and low proportions of elderly 80 and over—many metropolitan regions fit this description—are often associated with high values of a_{65+}.

Turning to the net migration rates $n_{<65}$ and n_{65+}, the two spatial distributions also had some commonalities (see Figures 3.18 and 3.19). The net migration pattern for those under 65 was predominantly one of out-migration from most census divisions; virtually all of the Prairies, northern Quebec and the Atlantic provinces

FIGURE 3.16: RATES OF INCREASE IN THE POPULATION AGED LESS THAN 65 DUE TO AGING IN PLACE, BY CENSUS DIVISION, CANADA, 1986 TO 1991

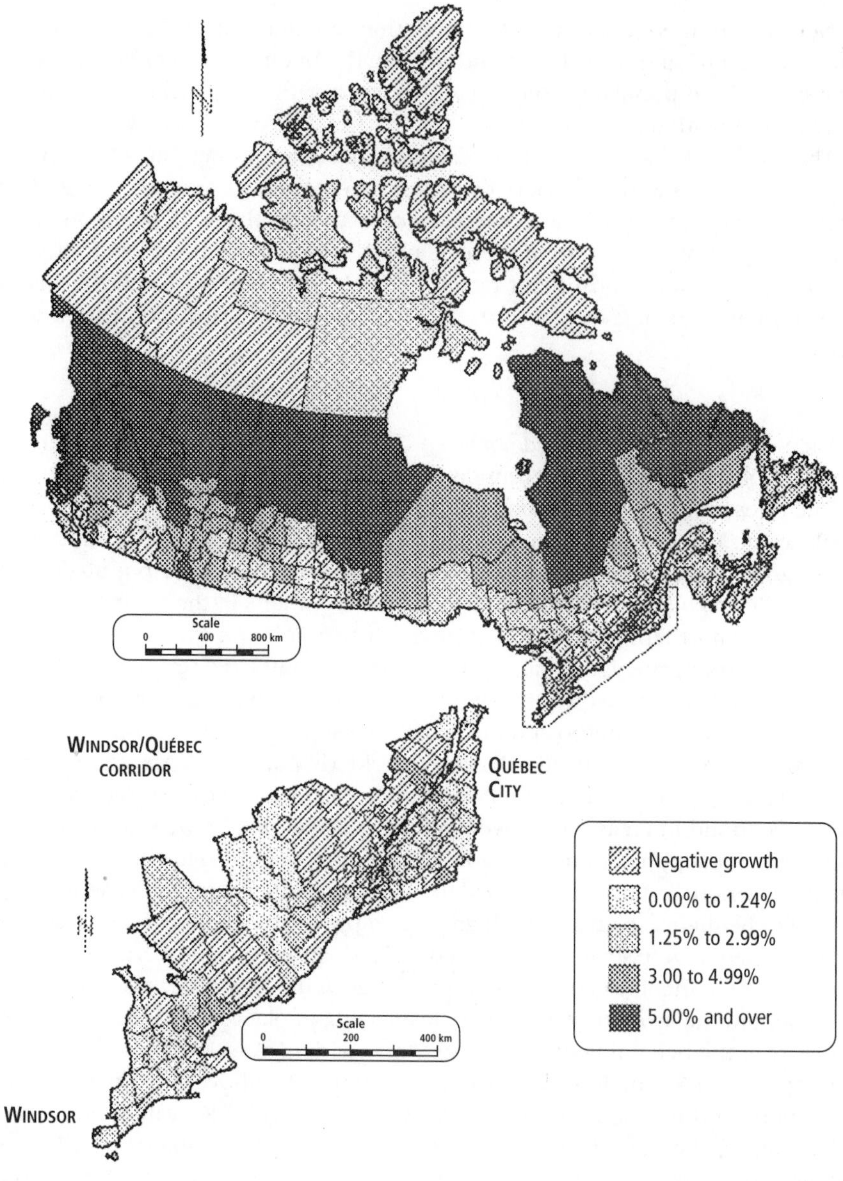

Scale
0   400   800 km

WINDSOR/QUÉBEC
CORRIDOR

QUÉBEC
CITY

Negative growth
0.00% to 1.24%
1.25% to 2.99%
3.00 to 4.99%
5.00% and over

Scale
0   200   400 km

WINDSOR

Source: Census of Canada, 1986 and 1991

FIGURE 3.17: RATES OF INCREASE IN THE POPULATION AGED 65 AND OVER DUE TO AGING IN PLACE, BY CENSUS DIVISION, CANADA, 1986 TO 1991

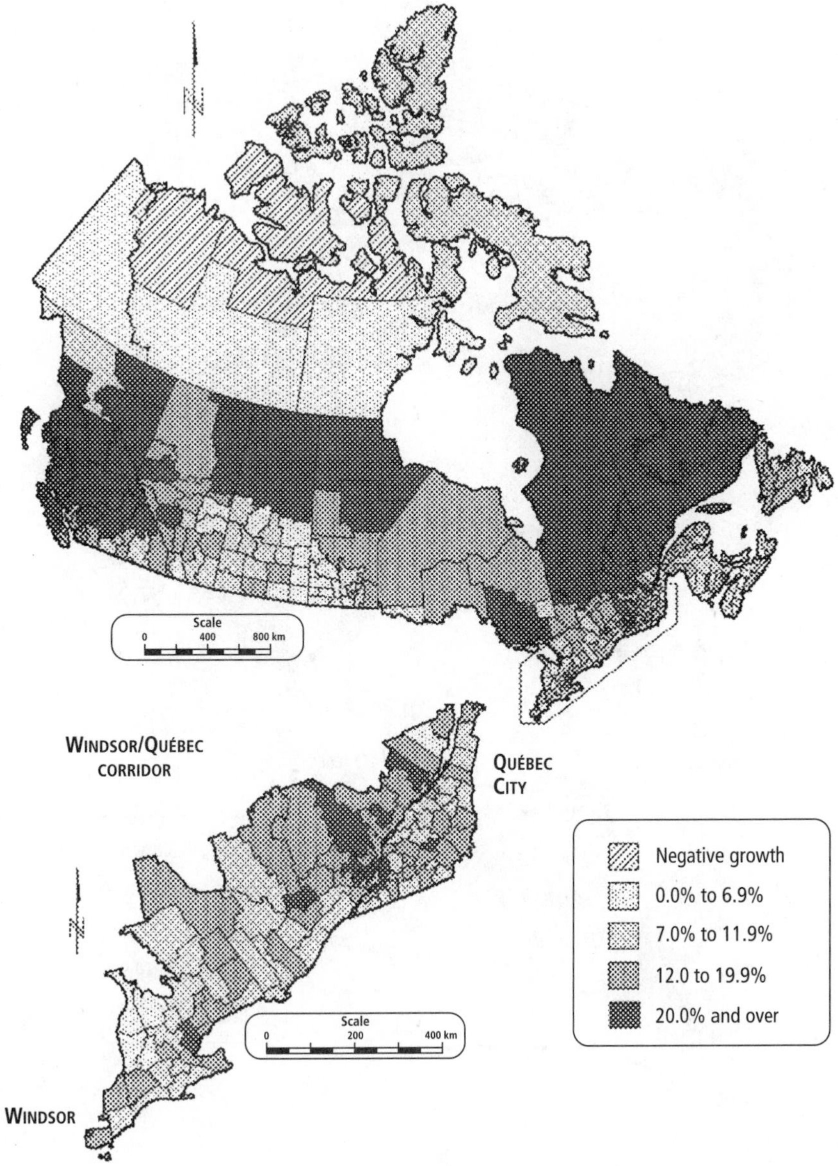

Scale
0   400   800 km

WINDSOR/QUÉBEC
CORRIDOR

QUÉBEC
CITY

Scale
0   200   400 km

WINDSOR

Negative growth
0.0% to 6.9%
7.0% to 11.9%
12.0 to 19.9%
20.0% and over

Source: Census of Canada, 1986 and 1991

THE REGIONAL DIMENSIONS OF AGING

FIGURE 3.18: NET MIGRATION RATES FOR THE POPULATION AGED LESS THAN 65, BY CENSUS DIVISION, CANADA, 1986 TO 1991

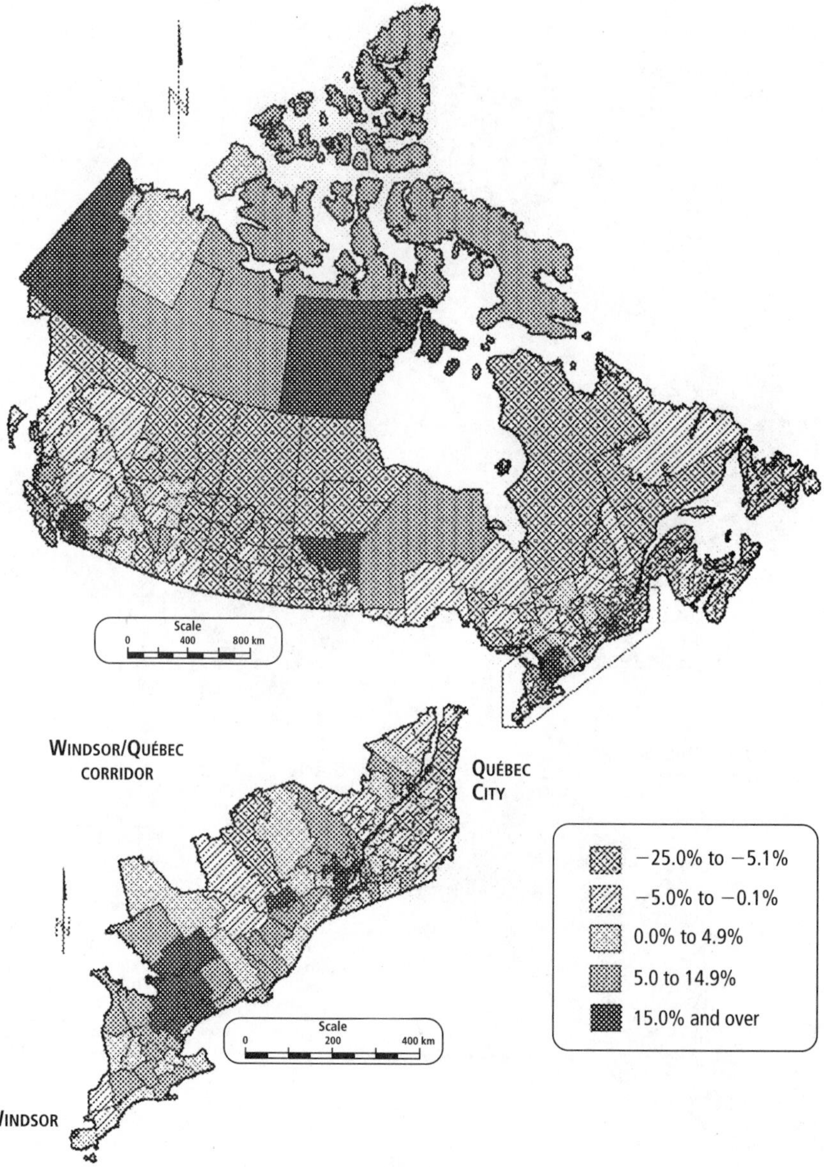

Scale
0   400   800 km

WINDSOR/QUÉBEC
CORRIDOR

QUÉBEC
CITY

	−25.0% to −5.1%
	−5.0% to −0.1%
	0.0% to 4.9%
	5.0 to 14.9%
	15.0% and over

Scale
0   200   400 km

WINDSOR

Source: Census of Canada, 1986 and 1991

FIGURE 3.19: NET MIGRATION RATES FOR THE POPULATION AGED 65 AND OVER, BY CENSUS DIVISION, CANADA, 1986 TO 1991

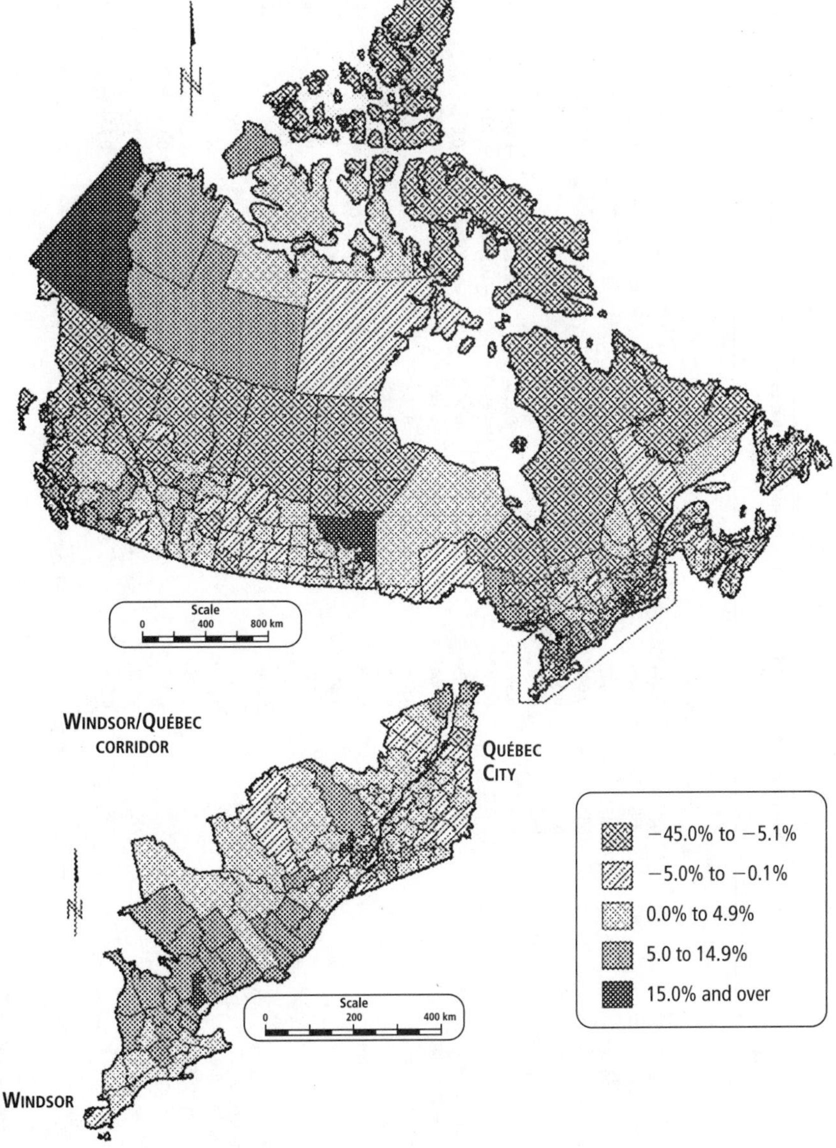

Source: Census of Canada, 1986 and 1991

TABLE 3.4: MODELS OF MIGRATION AND AGING IN PLACE FOR CENSUS DIVISIONS

DEPENDENT VARIABLES

Independent variables	Net migration under 65 M(<65)		Net migration 65 and over M(65+)		Aging-in-place under 65 A(<65)		Aging in place 65 and over A(65+)	
	Model 1	Model 2	Model 3	Model 4	Model 5	Model 6	Model 7	Model 8
Intercept	-40.354***	-38.293**	-30.577***	-22.109	-2.699	20.500***	-8.383	-3.922
% urban	-0.020	-0.044*	0.016	0.035	0.005	-0.001	0.105***	0.032*
Metropolitan area	-1.978	-2.126	-4.302*	-4.007**	-0.453	-0.150	-0.024	-0.222
% immigrants 1986–1991	-0.967*	-0.463	0.066	0.314	0.001	0.115	-0.429	-0.042
% unemployed	-0.583***	-0.648***	-0.045	0.196	0.220***	-0.019	0.523***	-0.151
% change in income 1986–1991	0.672***	0.674***	0.303***	0.327***	0.004	0.007	0.161*	0.019
% change in unemployment 1986–1991	0.073*	0.077*	0.042	0.040	-0.010	-0.018***	-0.063*	-0.064***
Average income	0.437**	0.530***	-0.296*	0.070	0.223***	-0.092*	1.025***	0.088
% with degree	1.280***	0.975***	0.906*	0.691*	-0.080	-0.109	-0.817*	-0.469*
Health employees per thousand	-0.095	0.039	0.216*	0.165*	-0.075*	-0.025	-0.397***	-0.038
Physicians per thousand	-0.862	-2.068*	-1.308	-1.430	-0.037	0.292	1.653	1.052
Mean July temperature	0.612*	0.645*	0.293	0.387	0.017	0.054	0.457*	0.037
Mean January temperature	0.067	0.080	0.311**	0.165	0.018	0.103***	0.026	0.479***
Number of hours of sunshine	0.002	0.003	0.010*	0.007*	-0.002*	-0.001	-0.010*	0.003
Atlantic	-8.114***	-7.409***	-0.522	-1.343	1.500*	1.060**	-3.034*	3.054*
Quebec	-3.994	-4.148*	1.336	2.184	1.230*	0.509	4.446*	3.930***
Ontario	-8.145***	-7.149***	-0.312	-0.729	1.587**	2.280***	0.130	3.992**
Prairies	-10.318***	-9.064***	-2.216	-1.818	4.760***	4.326***	5.657***	6.624***
% women aged 20–35		1.520*		0.074		-0.256**		-0.697*
Ratio 60–64/65–69		-7.811*		-14.518**		-4.561***		36.732***
% 65 and over 1986		0.466		0.225		-0.829***		-0.425*
Proportion of elderly 80 and over		-1.037***		-0.189		0.143***		-1.016***
Degrees of freedom	272	268	272	268	272	268	272	268
R-square	0.575	0.625	0.330	0.368	0.448	0.704	0.523	0.801

*** $p < 0.001$
** $p < 0.01$
* $p < 0.05$

Source: Census of Canada, 1986, 1991.

outside the metropolitan areas saw net losses of those under 65. The metropolitan fringes and southern British Columbia saw net gains during this period and, in general, $n_{<65}$ was strongly associated with higher incomes and positive economic growth.

Net migration for the elderly, n_{65+}, also tended to be negative for much of the Prairies and northern Quebec, although often the net losses were lower than for the younger population. Gains were seen in central Ontario, the fringes of Montréal and in southern British Columbia. While showing a general preference for growing areas, these migrants tended to avoid metropolitan areas, and tended more strongly to migrate according to climatic variables, indicating the attraction of moderate winters (see Table 3.4).

When we combine these various rates, we start to see a clearer picture of the components of aging. We first calculate the relative contributions of aging in place (α) and net migration (η) to the increase in population aging between 1986 and 1991. For the country as a whole the value of α was 0.106 (or a 10.6% increase in the proportion 65 and over), and η was −0.013 (a 1.3% decrease), which indicates both the magnitude of aging in place and the small negative effect on aging produced by net migration. The values for individual census divisions were fairly varied, although in most cases the aging-in-place component dominated net migration. The aging-in-place component was a strongly urban phenomenon, and was higher in places with higher-than-average incomes. The climatic variables took on major significance only when the regional dummy variables were removed, as the latter values were consistently higher in Quebec and lower in the Atlantic provinces (Table 3.5).

The net migration effects (η) were quite different. Although both $n_{<65}$ and n_{65+} had positive associations with growing areas and higher-income areas, the net difference between these rates produced the opposite relation—strong associations between higher values of η and low-growth, lower-income areas (see Table 3.5). This is because the net in-migration of younger individuals to high-growth areas consistently dominated the in-flow of older people, and thus lowered rates of population aging. At the same time the net effect of migration on aging was consistently higher in the four other regions relative to British Columbia and the territories, indicating the importance to the latter region of the migration of younger working-age people.

3.5 A CLASSIFICATION OF AGING SCENARIOS

The roles of α and η interact in different ways across the country to produce aging effects, as do the components of η. We can use the joint distribution of these values to produce a classification of aging scenarios.[10] In this classification we distinguish according to the effect on population aging between areas where aging in place is dominant but migration is still influential and areas where migration is dominant. Based on the values of α and η and the values of $n_{<65}$ and n_{65+}, the following nine scenarios were identified. In Scenarios 3 to 6, aging in place is the

TABLE 3.5: MODELS OF NET EFFECTS OF AGING IN PLACE AND MIGRATION ON POPULATION AGING

Independent variables	Net effects of aging in place (α)		Net effects of migration (η)	
	Model 1	Model 2	Model 3	Model 4
Intercept	−6.131	−22.590**	10.872	14.166
% urban	0.091***	0.031*	0.023	0.061**
Metropolitan area	0.264	−0.190	−1.764	−1.419
% immigrants 1986–1991	−0.371	−0.145	0.933*	0.669*
% unemployed	0.281*	−0.127	0.558***	0.828***
% change income 1986–1991	0.139*	0.011	−0.363***	−0.343***
% change in unemployment 1986–1991	−0.049*	−0.043**	−0.027	−0.032
Average income	0.752***	0.169*	−0.648***	−0.408**
% with degree	−0.656*	−0.309*	−0.450	−0.354
Health employees per thousand	−0.284***	−0.007	0.286***	0.120*
Physicians per thousand	1.416	0.615	−0.262	0.693
Mean July temperature	0.389*	−0.019	−0.376*	−0.326
Mean January temperature	−0.009	0.328***	0.228**	0.089
Number of hours of sunshine	−0.008**	0.003*	0.007**	0.004
Atlantic	-3.753*	2.040*	6.684***	5.340***
Quebec	3.032*	3.127***	4.926***	5.771***
Ontario	-1.417	1.423	7.633***	6.322***
Prairies	0.792	1.984*	7.636***	6.852***
% women aged 20–35		−0.398		−1.248**
Ratio 60–64 / 65–69		37.273***		−4.822
% 65 and over 1986		0.316*		−0.177
Proportion of elderly 80 and over		−1.002***		0.774***
Degrees of freedom	272	268	272	268
R-square	0.517	0.824	0.540	0.605

*** $p < 0.001$
** $p < 0.01$
* $p < 0.05$
Source: Census of Canada, 1986, 1991.

dominant phenomenon, and in Scenarios 7 to 9 migration is the dominant phenomenon.

1. *Stable:* The total effect of aging in place and migration produces changes of less than 3.5% in the proportion of the population who were 65 and over between 1986 and 1991, and neither individual effect was larger than 3.5%.

2. *Deconcentration*: The combined effects of aging in place and migration produced a decline in population aging ($\alpha + \eta < 0$).

3. *Aging in place—migration stable or reduces aging*: The net effects of migration were either insignificant or they acted to reduce the rate of population aging ($\alpha > 3.5$; $\eta <= 0$).

4. *Aging in place—migration produces congregation*:[11] Congregation is defined (McCarthy 1983) as the situation when there was net in-migration among both the elderly and non-elderly, but the in-migration rate for the elderly was higher ($\alpha > \eta$; $\eta > 0$; $n_{<65}, n_{65+} > 0$,[12] $n_{<65} < n_{65+}$).

5. *Aging in place—migration produces recomposition*: Recomposition is defined as the situation when the elderly were net in-migrants and the non-elderly were net out-migrants ($\alpha > \eta$; $\eta > 0$; $n_{<65}, < 0, n_{65+} > 0$), $n_{<65} < n_{65+}$).

6. *Aging in place—migration produces accumulation*: Accumulation is defined as the situation when both elderly and non-elderly experienced net out-migration but the out-migration rates were higher for the non-elderly ($\alpha > \eta$; $\eta > 0$; $n_{<65}, < 0, n_{65+} < 0$), $n_{<65} < n_{65+}$).

7. *Migration produces congregation*: Migration was more important than aging in place, and the elderly were gaining at a faster rate than were the non-elderly ($\alpha > \eta$; $\eta > 0$; $n_{<65}, n_{65+} > 0, n_{<65} < n_{65+}$).

8. *Migration produces recomposition*: ($\alpha > \eta$; $\eta > 0$; $n_{<65}, < 0, n_{65+} > 0$), $n_{<65} < n_{65+}$).

9. *Migration produces accumulation*: ($\alpha > \eta$; $\eta > 0$; $n_{<65}, < 0, n_{65+} < 0$), $n_{<65} < n_{65+}$).

The aging scenarios are dominated by aging-in-place processes (see Table 3.6). Significant aging in place was seen in 42.8% of census divisions in which this aging was mitigated by migration, while 28.2% saw both aging in place and increased aging due to migration: 8.9% of census divisions were either stable or experienced a decline in aging, and 20.1% of areas were subject to migration-dominated aging. Among the migration scenarios, recomposition was the most frequent; accumulation was much less important than in earlier intercensal periods (Bekkering 1990). Congregation was the least important, and more often occurred in areas where aging in place was dominant.

The scenarios were far from uniformly distributed geographically (see Figures 3.20 and 3.21; Table 3.6 provides both the percentage distributions by region and an index of concentration).[13] The migration-dominated aging areas were much more likely to be found in the Atlantic provinces and the Prairies than elsewhere. Congregation was the exception, but this was associated with net in-migration of the non-elderly, and it occurred only in parts of British Columbia and Ontario and the environs of Montréal. Stable areas, with little change caused either by aging in place or migration, were found primarily in the Atlantic region, while declining aging and migration-moderated aging were most likely to be found in British Columbia and Ontario.

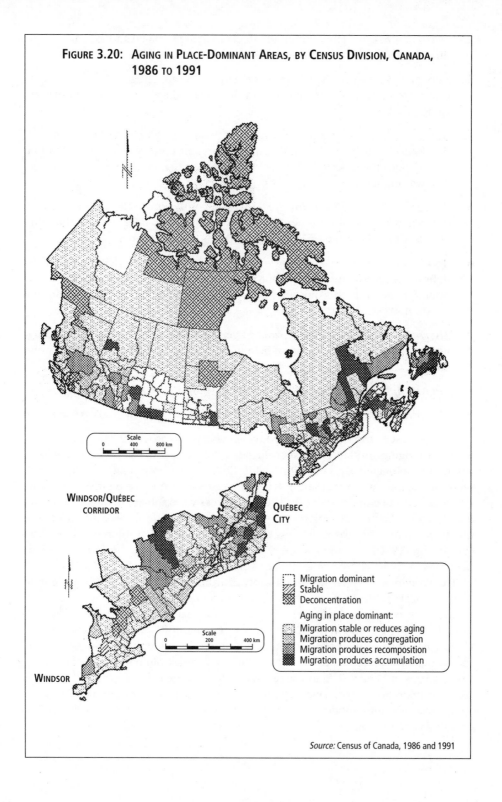

FIGURE 3.20: AGING IN PLACE-DOMINANT AREAS, BY CENSUS DIVISION, CANADA, 1986 TO 1991

Scale
0   400   800 km

WINDSOR/QUÉBEC
CORRIDOR

QUÉBEC
CITY

Scale
0   200   400 km

WINDSOR

Migration dominant
Stable
Deconcentration

Aging in place dominant:
Migration stable or reduces aging
Migration produces congregation
Migration produces recomposition
Migration produces accumulation

Source: Census of Canada, 1986 and 1991

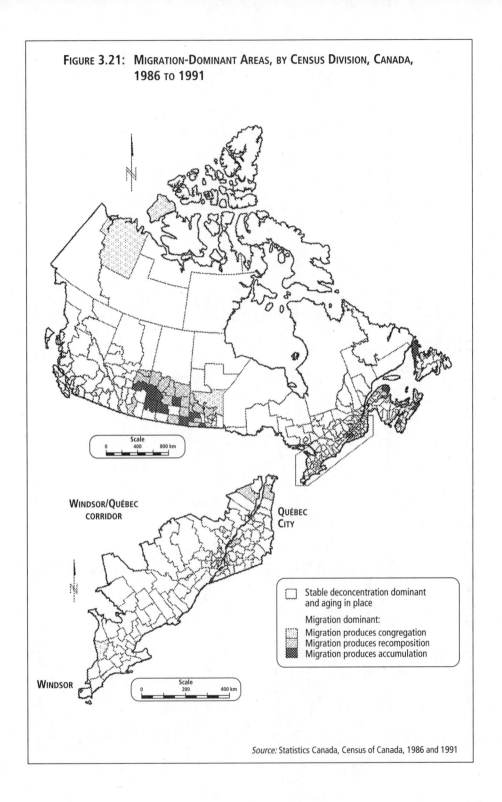

FIGURE 3.21: MIGRATION-DOMINANT AREAS, BY CENSUS DIVISION, CANADA, 1986 TO 1991

Scale
0   400   800 km

WINDSOR/QUÉBEC
CORRIDOR

QUÉBEC
CITY

Stable deconcentration dominant
and aging in place

Migration dominant:
Migration produces congregation
Migration produces recomposition
Migration produces accumulation

WINDSOR

Scale
0   200   400 km

Source: Statistics Canada, Census of Canada, 1986 and 1991

THE REGIONAL DIMENSIONS OF AGING

TABLE 3.6: DISTRIBUTION OF AGING SCENARIOS, BY REGION AND PROVINCE, 1991

AGING SCENARIOS

				AGING IN PLACE DOMINATES			MIGRATION DOMINATES		
	Stable (1)	Decline in aging (2)	Migration reducing aging (3)	Congregation (4)	Recomposition (5)	Accumulation (6)	Congregation (7)	Recomposition (8)	Accumulation (9)
Regions									
Atlantic	15.2[1]	0.0	15.2	2.2	13.0	19.6	0.0	26.1	8.7
Quebec	0.0	1.0	46.5	11.1	18.2	13.1	0.0	7.1	3.0
Ontario	4.1	8.2	69.4	10.2	6.1	0.0	2.0	0.0	0.0
Prairies	1.7	6.7	25.0	5.0	5.0	8.3	1.7	30.0	16.7
British Columbia and territories	0.0	19.4	61.1	8.3	5.6	0.0	5.6	0.0	0.0
Total	3.4	5.5	42.8	7.9	11.0	9.3	1.4	12.8	5.9
Index of concentration for scenarios[2]									
Atlantic	4.4	0.0	0.4	0.3	1.2	2.1	0.0	2.0	1.5
Quebec	0.0	0.2	1.1	1.4	1.6	1.4	0.0	0.6	0.5
Ontario	1.2	1.5	1.6	1.3	0.6	0.0	1.5	0.0	0.0
Prairies	0.5	1.2	0.6	0.6	0.5	0.9	1.2	2.4	2.8
British Columbia and territories	0.0	3.5	1.4	1.1	0.5	0.0	4.0	0.0	0.0
Numbers of census divisions by province and territory									
Newfoundland	0	0	2	0	2	3	0	2	1
Prince Edward Island	1	0	0	0	0	0	0	1	1
Nova Scotia	6	0	1	0	1	1	0	7	2
New Brunswick	0	0	4	1	3	5	0	2	0
Quebec	0	1	46	11	18	13	0	7	3
Ontario	2	4	34	5	3	0	1	2	3
Manitoba	0	4	7	0	0	1	1	0	3
Saskatchewan	0	0	2	0	3	2	0	8	6
Alberta	1	0	6	3	3	2	0	3	1
British Columbia	0	4	20	3	2	0	1	0	0
Yukon and Northwest Territories	0	3	2	0	0	0	1	0	0
Total	10	16	124	23	32	27	4	37	17

1. Percentage of census divisions in Atlantic provinces with "stable" aging scenarios.
2. Percentage of scenario in region/percentage of scenario in nation.
Source: Census of Canada, 1991.

The "average" or "typical" profiles of areas associated with the different scenarios provide more insights into the structure of population aging (see Table 3.7). Demographically, the stable areas and the census divisions dominated by recomposition and accumulation were the oldest when measured both by the proportion of the population 65 and over and by the relative importance of the very old. The younger populations were to be found in those census divisions where aging was declining or migration was moderating the aging process. Both those characteristics were also associated with higher average incomes and high annual growth rates. Census divisions associated with congregation were clearly differentiated from those associated with recomposition and accumulation because of these economic variables; they were also much more likely to be urban. The average growth rates were strongly positive in areas with congregation, and they were negative in areas classified in the four recomposition and accumulation categories.

The areas of declining aging were sharply differentiated from those with migration-moderated aging. The former were for the most part non-urban areas; many were northern. The latter were for the most part growing areas in Ontario, Quebec and British Columbia.

When health service variables are examined, their most important relationship is with population growth rates—the higher the growth rate, the lower the ratios of health service employees and beds per thousand population. This reinforces the view that smaller settlements continue to benefit from earlier investments on behalf of a relatively larger population base in smaller urban and rural communities. After controlling for the detailed age distributions of the population 65 and over, there were no great differences in the rates of disability among the elderly, apart from the higher rates in the few stable areas.

3.6 CONCLUSION

Aging in place is now the dominant process at virtually every geographical scale in Canada, although it interacts with migration in different ways in various parts of the country (Morrison 1992). The greatest rates of aging, as might be expected, were found in areas where aging in place was augmented by migration. However, even in areas where aging in place was moderated by migration, the average increase in the proportion 65 and over was 10% between 1986 and 1991.

Since the structure of the migration effects is strongly associated with the economic performance of local communities, any significant shifts in the economic attractiveness of communities are likely to produce marked changes in the rate of local aging. This was particularly the case in Ontario, where 70% of census divisions fell into Class 3, in which migration reduces the effect of aging in place; if major shifts in flows of immigrants and younger migrants were to favour the West, the rate of aging in Ontario could increase substantially.

Thirty-nine percent of census divisions in Canada were directly affected by recomposition and accumulation, and experienced the highest rates of aging. These communities were less urban, poorer, already older and experiencing

TABLE 3.7: PROFILES OF AGING SCENARIOS

| | | | | AGING SCENARIOS | | | | | |
| | | | | AGING IN PLACE DOMINATES | | | MIGRATION DOMINATES | | |
Variables	Stable (1)	Decline in aging (2)	Migration reducing aging (3)	Congregation (4)	Recomposition (5)	Accumulation (6)	Congregation (7)	Recomposition (8)	Accumulation (9)
Percentage over 65 in 1991	14.2[1]	8.8	10.6	12.7	11.8	12.7	10.1	15.1	15.8
Percentage elderly over 80	0.232	0.181	0.191	0.202	0.199	0.197	0.210	0.237	0.230
Sex ratio for elderly	1.33	1.06	1.25	1.39	1.24	1.23	1.06	1.23	1.18
Percentage of area urban	35.3	24.5	58.0	67.5	47.5	41.3	40.2	35.5	29.7
Average income in 1991	37,753	44,448	43,703	41,002	37,582	35,456	40,630	35,030	34,598
Annual growth rate 1986–1991	0.009	0.033	0.016	0.014	-0.000	-0.007	0.033	-0.006	-0.013
Mean January temperature	-6.4	-15.2	-10.6	-9.6	-11.4	-11.7	-13.7	-12.4	-13.1
Health services workers per thousand	27.9	19.2	24.7	30.2	24.9	24.4	19.7	26.9	24.9
Hospital beds per thousand	6.2	2.7	4.9	7.0	5.9	6.1	4.5	7.3	7.0
Disability rate of elderly per thousand	26.3	21.9	20.6	19.7	18.3	18.6	24.6	20.2	18.6
$C_{(65)}$	1.03	0.94	1.10	1.13	1.18	1.16	1.08	1.12	1.13

1. Unweighted average over census divisions in the "stable" scenario.
Source: Census of Canada, 1991.

population declines. They were also communities where resources for services to the elderly were likely to be more limited and, given the population's structure and the local economy, the ability to raise money through local taxes was also limited (Rosenberg and Moore 1990). Although many of these areas may be well served now, maintaining service levels in future that will be commensurate with the demands of a growing elderly population will require some form of transfer payment system. This issue has interprovincial and intraprovincial dimensions; the Prairie and Atlantic provinces feature much more prominently in these migration-dominated scenarios than do the other provinces. The importance of recomposition in both regions suggests that the phenomenon of return migration of the elderly is significant, and requires more critical attention than it has received to date. If the return migration is made up of older elderly, with their greater needs for health and social services, the problems of providing these services will be particularly acute.

APPENDIX 3.1:

POPULATION AGING: CONCEPTS AND MEASURES

Population aging is defined as the change in the proportion of the population of an area that is 65 and over. The following notation is used.

$P_{65+}(0)$, $P_{65+}(1)$ are the number of people 65 and over at times 0 and 1, respectively.

$P_{<65}(0)$, $P_{<65}(1)$ are the number under 65 at times 0 and 1, respectively.

$P_{tot}(0)$, $P_{tot}(1)$ are the total population at times 0 and 1, respectively.

$f_{65+}(0)$, $f_{65+}(1)$ are the proportions of the population 65 and over, where

$$f_{65+}(0) = P_{65+}(0) / P_{tot}(0) \tag{1}$$

Measures of Population Aging

$$C_{65+} = f_{65+}(1) / f_{65+}(0) \tag{2}$$

is the ratio of the proportions of the population 65 and over at times 0 and 1, respectively.

$$g_{65+} = P_{65+}(1) / P_{65+}(0) - 1 \tag{3}$$

is the proportionate increase in the population 65 and over between times 0 and 1.

If the time interval from 0 to 1 is five years, then

$$g^*_{65+} = (P_{65+}(1) / P_{65+}(0))^{1/5} - 1 \tag{4}$$

is the annualized growth rate of the population 65 and over.

Similar measures can be defined for the total population, P_{tot}, and the population under 65, $P_{<65}$.

Components of population aging

Any area population changes as a function of births and deaths, in-migration and out-migration. Thus,

$$P_{tot}(1) = P_{tot}(0) + B - D + I - O \tag{5}$$

where B = births in the interval 0, 1;[1]

D = deaths;

I = in-migrants to the areas in the interval 0, 1; and

O = out-migrants from the area in the interval 0, 1.

Using the concepts of "births" to an age group from the immediately younger age group and "deaths" from an age group to the next older age group, the equation in (5) can be used to define changes in those younger than 65 and 65 and older.

Thus,

$$P_{65+}(1) = P_{65+}(0) + B_{65} - D_{65+} + I_{65+} - O_{65+} \tag{6}$$

where B_{65} is the number of individuals who turn 65 during the interval 0, 1;

$$P_{<65}(1) = P_{<65}(0) + B - D_{<65} + I_{<65} - O_{<65} \tag{7}$$

where $D_{<65}$ is the number who die plus the number who turn 65 during the interval 0, 1; B is the number of births in the interval 0,1.

In equation (6), we can regard the value $(B_{65} - D_{65+})$ as contributing to the aging in place of the population 65 and over (A_{65}), and ($I_{65+} - O_{65+}$) as defining net migration of the population 65 and over (N_{65+}).

Thus,

$$P_{65+}(1) = P_{65+}(0) + A_{65+} + N_{65+} \tag{8}$$

$$= P_{65+}(0)(1 + a_{65+} + n_{65+}) \tag{9}$$

where a_{65+}, n_{65+} are the proportionate changes in the population 65 and over due to aging in place and net migration, respectively.

Similarly,

$$P_{<65}(1) = P_{<65}(0)(1 + a_{<65} + n_{<65}) \tag{10}$$

Combining the above information, it can be shown that:

$$C_{65} = \frac{1 + a_{65+} + n_{65+}}{f_{65+}(0)(1 + a_{65+} + n_{65+}) + (1 - f_{65+}(0))(1 + a_{<65} + n_{<65})} \tag{11}$$

It follows directly that C_{65} increases if $(a_{65+} + n_{65+}) > (a_{<65} + n_{<65})$. However, since $a_{65+} > a_{<65}$ in the majority of communities and a_{65+} is greater than n_{65+} virtually everywhere, it follows that the overall net migration defined by n_{65+} and $n_{<65}$ serves to reinforce or moderate the dominant aging-in-place effects.

In general, C_{65+} increases as a_{65+} and n_{65+} increase and decreases as $a_{<65}$ and $n_{<65}$ increase.

---

1. A complete accounting would also consider births and deaths to in-migrants and out-migrants (Rees and Wilson 1977), but only small errors are introduced by ignoring such multiple events.

In Chapters 1 and 3, attention is given to the separate components a_{65+}, $a_{<65}$, $n_{<65}$, n_{65+} as they respond to different conditions in local communities.

Decomposing C_{65+}

It is useful to decompose the ratio of the proportions 65 and over at intervals 0 and 1 into the components of change attributable to aging in place and to net migration.

Thus,

$$C_{65} = 1 + \alpha + \eta \tag{12}$$

where α is the proportionate change due to aging in place; and η is the proportionate change due to net migration.

If,

S_{65+} (1) is the population that survives in the area from 0 to 1 and is 65 and over at 1; and
$S_{<65}$ (1) is the population that survives from 0 to 1, including those born to residents of the area between 0 and 1 and is under 65 at 1
then

$$C_{65+}(S) = \frac{S_{65+}(1)}{S_{tot}(1)} \bigg/ \frac{P_{65+}(0)}{P_{tot}(1)} = 1 + \alpha \tag{13}$$

then

$$\alpha = C_{65+}(S) - 1 \tag{14}$$

and

$$\eta = C_{65+} - C_{65+}(S) \tag{15}$$

Because a_{65+} and $a_{<65}$ are defined by the populations at risk who are 65 and over or under 65 and are the contribution of aging in place to aging of the total population, the relation between the parameters is not straightforward.

$$\alpha = \frac{1 + a_{65+}}{f_{65+}(0)(1 + a_{65+}) + (1 - f_{65+}(0))(1 + a_{<65})} - 1 \tag{16}$$

However, it follows directly from (16) that

$$\alpha \lesseqqgtr 0 \text{ as } a_{65+} \lesseqqgtr a_{<65}$$

Similarly,

$$\eta \lesseqqgtr 0 \text{ as } \eta_{65+} \lesseqqgtr \eta_{<65}$$

APPENDIX 3.2:

A BRIEF TECHNICAL NOTE ON BOUNDARY CHANGES BETWEEN 1986 AND 1991

To compare the elderly population between 1986 and 1991 at the census division level, boundary changes made in the intervening years, mostly in Quebec, had to be taken into account. The solution was to examine the census subdivisions that made up the census divisions in 1986 and allocate them to the 1991 census division to which they corresponded completely, or divide the population between census divisions on an equal basis where a census subdivision crossed more than one census division boundary. In this way, only 99 census subdivisions from 1986 were divided between two or more 1991 census subdivisions. While there is no way of knowing whether the boundary changes had any effect on the data, it was likely minimal in most cases.

ENDNOTES

1. More attention has been paid in the United States to the regional dimensions of aging; there, the tax implications for local communities are more transparent. Frey (1986, 1992, 1995) has written extensively on elderly redistribution in the United States, while Morrison (1992) recently argued that the process of aging in place should be a major focus of both demographic inquiry and public policy in the coming years. Migration (or lack of it), however, has lain at the core of the literature on population redistribution.

2. See Moore and Rosenberg 1988; Moore et al. 1989; and Rosenberg and Moore 1990.

3. This is defined in an algebraic sense; thus if both net migration rates are negative and the out-migration rate is larger for those under 65 than those 65 and over, then the net migration rate for the elderly is algebraically greater than that for the population under 65.

4. Although both fertility and mortality rates of Canadian Native people have declined over the past two decades, in relative terms Native people living in remote settlements in Northern Canada continue to have higher fertility and mortality rates than non-Native people in Southern Canada.

5. Ecological correlations are those between area-based measures rather than between measures of individuals.

6. See Chapter 1 for a detailed explanation of the dependency ratio.

7. See Chapter 1 for a detailed explanation of annualized growth rates.

8. See Chapter 1 for a detailed explanation of C_{65+}.

9. For a full development of the model and associated notation, see Appendix 3.1.

10. This classification extends the work of McCarthy (1983) and Bekkering (1990). McCarthy focused primarily on the role of migration, while Bekkering added an aging-in-place component as a single category.

11. The terms "congregation," "recomposition" and "accumulation" were provided by McCarthy (1983).

12. The combined effects of net migration for the elderly and non-elderly is greater than 3.5%.

13. The index is the ratio of the number of areas with a given scenario to the number that would be expected given identical distributions within each region.

CHAPTER

4

THE HEALTH
OF AN AGING POPULATION

Conventional wisdom suggests that older people suffer more health problems than younger people and that, as the ranks of the elderly continue to swell in the coming decades, this could have wide public policy implications. But how accurate is the conventional wisdom? In this chapter we will test the conventional wisdom, and sharpen the focus of the picture with empirical observations.

Measuring the health status of an individual or a population is far from straightforward. External measures might gauge an individual's health from a medical perspective—the presence of specific illness or disease. However, diagnosis and prognosis are often difficult and uncertain, and the individual might have several conditions at the same time.

Another approach is to measure an individual's degree of functioning in regard to the activities of daily living, such as walking a given distance, climbing stairs, reading a newspaper, hearing a voice on the telephone and cutting up food. One might also measure an individual's ability to accomplish the instrumental activities of daily living such as shopping, meal preparation and housework, each of which are derivative of more basic activities but which contribute to the quality of daily life. This approach is a weaker prognostic tool, but it defines more accurately an individual's ability to cope with daily living.

Health status is not a purely physical condition. Different individuals cope with similar physical conditions with differing degrees of success. The way people feel about themselves—their self-definition of health—plays a critical role in an their ability to function independently. As they age, people expect their ability to perform certain activities to decline, but as long as this decline does not seriously hamper them in the activities they want to pursue, it may have little or no effect on how they feel about their health.

The health status of the population as a whole can be viewed in terms of outcomes that impact on delivery of services such as hospitalization and use of formal and informal support services. While factors other than individuals' health affect utilization, such as availability of resources, cost of access and structure of referral mechanisms, it is an important outcome measure for planning and policy that is sensitive to the elderly's changing health status.

A series of national surveys conducted between 1985 and 1991 enables us to examine the health status of the population from different perspectives. The two major resources for analysis of health and social supports are the General Social Survey (GSS), Cycles 1 (1985) and 6 (1991) and the Health and Activity Limitation Survey (HALS), a post-censal survey conducted in 1986 and 1991. Because the two surveys were each repeated five years apart with virtually the same set of questions in each cycle, we can assess how the characteristics they measured were changing at the end of the 1980s.

The GSS is conducted annually with approximately 11,000 respondents. It focuses on different social policy issues each year, and re-examines selected issues every five years. The first and sixth surveys contain external, self-evaluative and utilization-based measures of health status.

The HALS is much larger—there were 175,000 respondents in 1986 and 105,000 in 1991. The survey is linked to the census through responses to questions on the long census form (sent to 20% of Canadian households) about activity limitations and disabilities. The responses to the census questions provide the survey's sampling frame. The HALS is also more focused; it stresses the measurement of activity limitation, as well as the broad range of socio-economic and demographic conditions that influence each activity limitation's prevalence and impact. The survey measures health status based on functioning in activities of daily living and instrumental activities of daily living, and sheds light on how people use both formal and informal supports. The HALS also has an important separate component that examines health-related institutions. This component is the only data source available that allows the health status of all elderly, including those in institutions, to be estimated.

Another valuable source for examining aspects of social support and independent living is the Survey on Ageing and Independence. Conducted in September 1991, this survey measures factors that contribute to elderly people's quality of life and independent living. It examines many characteristics of both the elderly and those approaching their senior years. Specifically, the survey provides national-level estimates concerning the health, social and economic situation of the population 65 and over. The survey also provides national-level data on the population between 45 and 64 concerning their planning choices and preparations for their senior years.

4.1 HEALTH STATUS IN 1991

4.1.1 Health status and activity limitation

Our first attempt to define health status relies on the definitions used in the HALS, which focuses on the definition of disability and its relationship to the concept of activity limitation. The definition of disability used in the HALS is based on the World Health Organization's International Classification of Impairments, Disabilities and Handicaps:[1]

> In the context of health experience, a disability is any restriction or
> lack (resulting from an impairment) of ability to perform an activity in
> the manner or within the range considered normal for a human being.

The HALS disability score is a summary indicator of the degree of limitation in a person's activities of daily living. Each of 23 questions describing a basic daily activity is formulated as "Do you have any trouble with…?" and is answered by one of the following:

  i) no trouble;
  ii) yes, (I have) trouble, but am not completely unable (to function);
  iii) completely unable (to function).

Based on a total score derived from the responses across all areas, each person is assigned a disability rating of:

  i) "minor disability" (the lowest 45% of the disabled);
  ii) "moderate disability" (the middle 35% of the disabled);
  iii) "severe disability" (the 20% with the highest total scores).

The breakdown by severity only refers to an individual's overall condition. For specific functional areas such as mobility, degree of severity is not defined. (For more details, see McDowell 1988.)

Disability measured by functional limitation is widely accepted as a very good indicator when the data are derived from survey responses from the disabled person. It is wide-ranging and grounded in everyday tasks. Its limitation is that it is based on the perceptions of the affected person, and such perceptions often differ from direct measurements on physical limitation such as those, for example, obtained from audiological hearing tests.

It is also important to note what the disability score does not measure. In addition to the activities-of-daily-living measure, professional groups, consumer groups, academics from various disciplines, and public and private agencies place different weights on many overlapping dimensions of disability: the underlying causes of disability; the effects on the individual's quality of life; the degree of social stigma; and the duration of the condition. Clearly, some of these dimensions are best assessed from sources other than the "disabled" person, and some are difficult to assess under any circumstances. Other views that combine these dimensions in different ways are the traditional medical model, the health sciences/

chronic conditions models (Nolan and Pless 1986), and the World Health Organization's continuum model (WHO 1980).

The types of disability defined in the HALS are grouped into five major categories: mobility, agility, seeing, hearing and speaking. An additional category, "other," represents positive responses to a series of questions about learning, developmental and mental disabilities. The prevalence of each condition, as well as the number of different types of limitation, is given in Figures 4.1 and 4.2.[2] In every case the rates of prevalence saw a non-linear increase moving up the age scale. However, the rates of those more severely limited increased more rapidly at higher ages; this pattern was repeated in the distribution of those with three or more limitations.[3] Mobility and agility limitations were the most common and, in fact, almost all those who were severely limited and had three or more limitations had a mobility limitation. This finding most directly affects service delivery, as many with severe limitations would have difficulty reaching service locations without special transportation. The alternative, of course, would be to provide services at home, which may cost service agencies more in the short term, but may cost relatively less than providing special transportation services.

It is tempting to conclude that disability is widespread, particularly among the elderly, and that this indicates poor health status for this population. However, it is important to remember that the measures of disability are sensitive to the slightest limitations on individual functional ability. Even among the young elderly— those between 65 and 74—almost half of those classified as disabled fall into the "mild" category, reflecting a disability that may have little impact on their daily lives.

Wilkins (1991) argues that more sensitive health status indicators would link the measurement of disability with the degree of individuals' independence, and thereby better measure what services the community needs to help those individuals to function. He suggests the following classification:

- not disabled

- disabled but independent (no help needed)

- somewhat dependent (for instrumental activities of daily living such as shopping or housework only)

- heavily dependent (for activities of daily living such as personal care and getting around the home)

- institutionalized

The HALS permits such a classification because it asks a range of questions about whether the respondent obtains help for a wide range of instrumental activities of daily living and activities of daily living, and because it allows estimation of the numbers who are institutionalized in given age and gender categories. The distribution of this classification by age and gender, using data from the survey's 1986 micro-data file, is shown in Table 4.1 and Figure 4.3.[4]

FIGURE 4.1A: DISABILITY RATES, BY AGE, SEX AND DEGREE, 1991

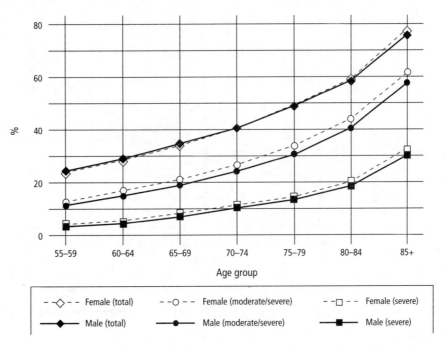

FIGURE 4.1B: INDIVIDUALS WITH THREE OR MORE LIMITATIONS, BY AGE AND SEX, 1991

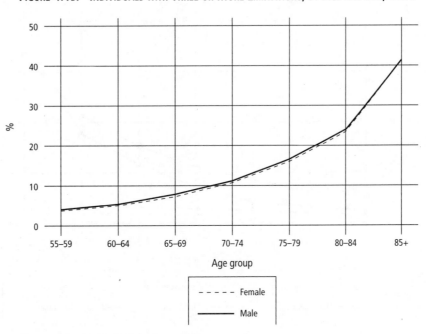

Source: Health and Activity Limitation Survey, 1991.

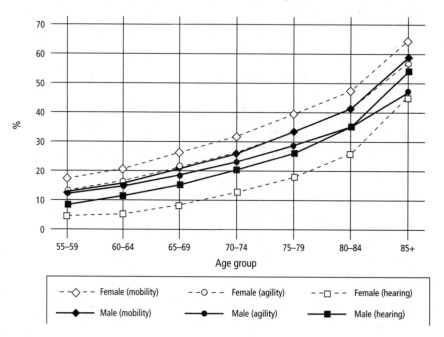

FIGURE 4.2A: DISABILITY RATES, BY AGE, SEX AND TYPE, 1991

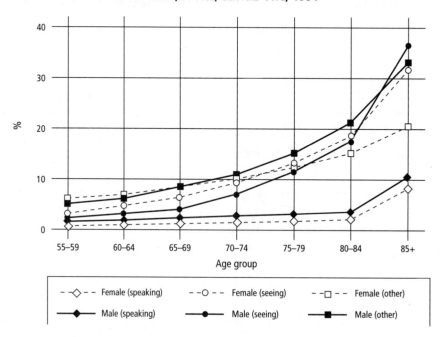

FIGURE 4.2B: DISABILITY RATES, BY AGE, SEX AND TYPE, 1991

Source: Health and Activity Limitation Survey, 1991.

Health status	AGE GROUP							
	15–24	25–34	35–44	45–54	55–64	65–74	75–84	85+
	Females (%)							
Not disabled	95.7[1]	93.8	90.5	85.7	74.2	65.7	42.9	15.2
Disabled: no help with IADL[2] or ADL[3]	3.5	4.6	6.4	8.6	15.7	18.8	21.2	12.4
Disabled: help with IADL	0.5	1.3	2.6	4.6	8.2	10.9	19.3	23.4
Disabled: help with ADL	0.3	0.3	0.4	0.8	1.5	2.7	5.6	11.9
Institutionalized	0.0	0.0	0.1	0.2	0.4	1.8	11.0	37.1
	Males (%)							
Not disabled	95.4	93.1	90.8	84.4	73.9	61.0	52.5	25.1
Disabled: no help with IADL or ADL	3.9	5.7	7.8	12.5	20.0	29.4	25.5	19.0
Disabled: help with IADL	0.3	0.7	0.9	2.0	4.2	5.4	10.0	18.8
Disabled: help with ADL	0.3	0.4	0.4	0.9	1.4	2.5	5.3	13.3
Institutionalized	0.0	0.1	0.1	0.2	0.5	1.6	6.7	23.9

1. Percentage of females aged 15 to 24 who report no disability.
2. Instrumental activities of daily living.
3. Activities of daily living.
Source: Statistics Canada, Health and Activity Limitation Survey, 1986.

This classification is much richer than the simple classification by disability. It demonstrates clearly that, even into the middle range of the elderly population (those aged 75 to 84), most were independent. Seventy-eight percent of men in that age group were either not disabled or were classified as disabled but needed no help with instrumental activities of daily living or activities of daily living. Sixty-four percent of women were in the same categories, but among the 19.3% who needed help with instrumental activities of daily living, a significant component needed help with heavy housework (including exterior yard work). For men, in fact, much of the increase in reported disability from age 55 to 75 involved conditions that did not seem to cause increased demands for support. The changes in the likelihood of being "heavily dependent" were similar for both men and women; the likelihood approximately doubled from the 65-to-74 age range to the 75-to-84 age range, and then doubled again for the group 85 and over. It is the latter age group that creates the greatest pressure not only on public systems but, more importantly, on caregivers—particularly close family members—who often bear the greatest burden helping with the more personal aspects of daily life.

4.1.2 Subjective views of health status

The population's health can also be assessed by how individuals perceive their own health and their ability to conduct specific types of daily activities. Individuals might expect that their functional abilities will decline with age; but if they are

FIGURE 4.3A: FEMALE POPULATION, LEVEL OF DISABILITY/SUPPORT, 1986

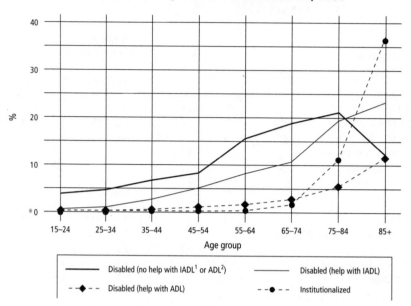

FIGURE 4.3B: MALE POPULATION, LEVEL OF DISABILITY/SUPPORT, 1986

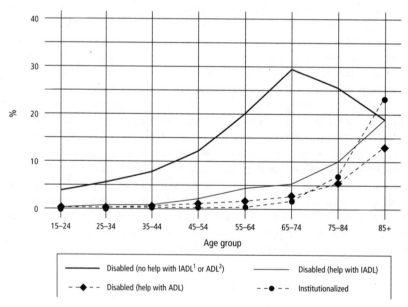

1. Instrumental Activities of daily living.
2. Activities of daily living.

Source: Health and Activity Limitation Survey, 1986.

coping with such changes, they may be satisfied with their health despite minor deterioration.

In Cycle 6 of the GSS in 1991, respondents were asked, "Are you satisfied or dissatisfied with your health?" Their answers (see Figure 4.4) hold different information from that in the HALS. First, although there was a small but steady increase with age in the proportion that claimed dissatisfaction with their own health, there was no dramatic increase among the elderly to mirror the physical assessments. It suggests very strongly, as others have indicated (Rosenthal and Gladstone 1994), that most elderly people accept their declining health and find ways to cope with the impact on their daily lives. Even among the non-institutional population who were 80 and over, the proportion expressing dissatisfaction with their health was barely 20%.

However, women were more likely to express dissatisfaction with their health than were men; this contrasts with the data on activity limitation. This dissatisfaction appeared in almost every age group, and was particularly noticeable among those between 35 and 60, and among those 70 and over. Although the survey contains little that may explain this phenomenon, it is reasonable to suggest that the dissatisfaction may stem from women's growing awareness that their health

FIGURE 4.4:   DISSATISFACTION WITH HEALTH STATUS, MALES AND FEMALES, 1991

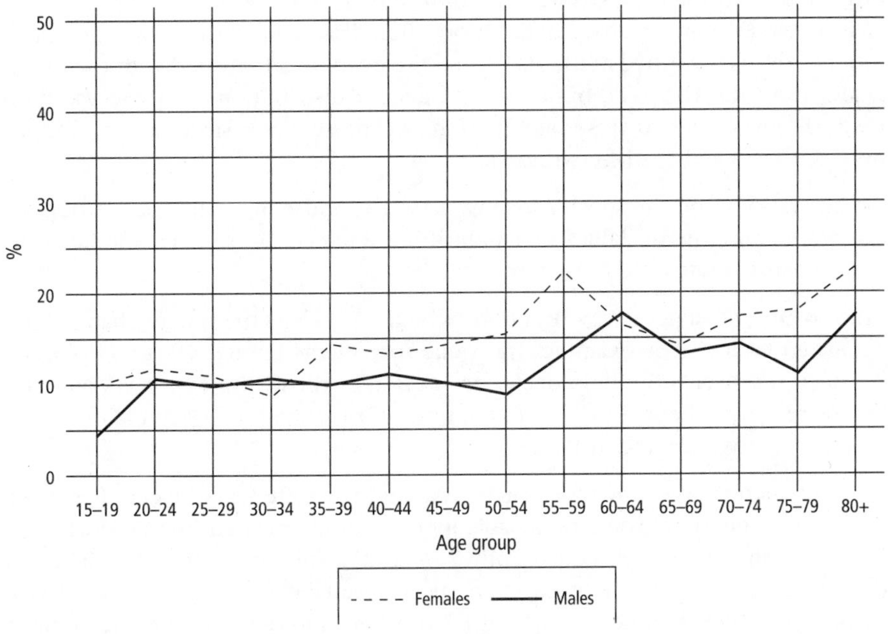

Source: General Social Survey, 1991.

issues have not received the attention from the medical profession that their prevalence and significance justifies. In particular, the relative lack of progress in the diagnosis and treatment of breast cancer has been the subject of much debate (Ross, Rosenberg and Pross 1994a; Ross, Rosenberg, Pross and Bass 1994b), and has particular salience for the group of women in late middle age (45 to 64) that expressed greatest dissatisfaction relative to men.

These findings suggest that pressures to improve the quality and extent of women's health services will likely continue, and that there will be a demand that more priority be given to conditions that afflict women exclusively or mostly, such as osteoporosis. It is not clear, however, how these efforts will fare in a climate of increasing fiscal constraint.

4.1.3 Changes in health status from 1986 to 1991

The population's health status changes constantly. As medical knowledge increases, as the delivery of health care and social services evolves, and as elderly people's attitudes and expectations change, so both external and self-evaluative measures of health status change. Measuring these changes is difficult; comparable data are needed on the same variables measured at two different points in time. Fortunately, the HALS, taken in 1986 and 1991, and the health-related components of the GSS, taken in 1985 and 1991, help us document changes in both physical and attitudinal measures of health status.

Here we examine changes in the proportion disabled and the proportion institutionalized as identified in the HALS, and the proportion satisfied with their own health from the GSS. The basic age and gender distributions of these variables were shown earlier in this chapter. Here we present the structure of changes between 1986 and 1991 in two ways:

i) the ratio of the age-specific values in 1991 to those in 1986 by age group for women and men. Values of 1 indicate no change; those over 1 indicate an increase in rates and those under 1 a decrease;

ii) the ratio of values by 1991 cohort, which represents the rate of change for a given cohort. For example, the value for activity-limited 70- to 74-year-old men represents the ratio of the proportion of those 70 to 74 years old who were activity-limited in 1991 to the proportion of 65- to 69-year-old men who were activity-limited in 1986.

The structure of change for activity limitation is quite pronounced. For those of working age, there was a noticeable increase in the propensity to report activity limitation—rates were consistently 20% to 25% higher in 1991 than in 1986. (The progression by cohort is even more dramatic; see Figure 4.5). These increases, however, almost disappear for those 55 and over. In those age groups there is only the normal increase in the likelihood of disability with age. However, Chen, Verma, George and Dai (1993) show that the primary source of increase lies in the mild disability category. Age- and sex-specific work-disability rates remained fairly stable, as the disabilities that tend to limit people in their work are usually moderate or severe. The implications of this situation are unclear, and beg a better understanding of the dynamics of individual disability. This would reveal whether those with mild disability are more likely to suffer moderate or severe disability and associated levels of dependence in later years than those classified as not disabled. Those with mild disability are more likely to return to good health; Crimmins and Saito (1990) report that up to 30% of the mildly disabled elderly population returned to good health in a two-year period. On the other hand, the stabilization of disability rates at older ages is encouraging, and holds promise that future rates will also remain stable.

The likelihood that an individual of any given age would be institutionalized remained stable between 1986 and 1991. Rates for older people tended to edge upward relative to those for younger people (see Figure 4.6). The cohort measure saw a dramatic increase between 1986 and 1991 such that all ratios exceeded 2 for ages 70 to 74 and over. This indicates that for every five-year cohort 65 and over, the likelihood of being institutionalized at least doubled in each successive five-year period. Whether this trend has continued—and will—depends much on the nature of long-term care and the availability of places in health-related institutions as the number of older elderly grows rapidly. This question does draw attention to anticipated growth in demand for institutional spaces as the elderly population grows (see Chapter 5).

Another issue that may draw attention to the need for institutional spaces is people's perceptions about their own health. Canadians' dissatisfaction with their health has shown an erratic pattern over time (see Figure 4.7), partly because the numbers of dissatisfied respondents were small in both 1986 and 1991. Over 80% of each population sub-group and over 90% of many sub-groups said they were either "satisfied" or "very satisfied" with their health. However, the ratios tended to be less than 1 for both men and women 65 and over, indicating rising levels of satisfaction. In contrast, the majority of values for younger age groups were over 1; this is almost uniformly the case for women. In other words, middle-aged women were much more likely to be dissatisfied with their health than before. The implication is perhaps not so much that their health was deteriorating but that they were becoming more aware of health issues, and that they believed the health care they received was not as good as it might have been.

The problem posed by elderly people's greater satisfaction is that it may represent a perception that care for the elderly has improved and that this greater satisfaction may also represent an expectation that the same level of service will be maintained. With the significant increase in absolute numbers of elderly—and consequently in those in need of support—over the next two decades, this high satisfaction rate may prove fragile if service cannot be maintained under the increasing fiscal pressures faced by all levels of government.

While the evidence on recent changes both in disability rates and satisfaction with health for the elderly gives some cause for optimism, what is happening at younger ages does not. Changes both in the prevalence of disability and satisfaction with health suggest that increased pressures on health care and social

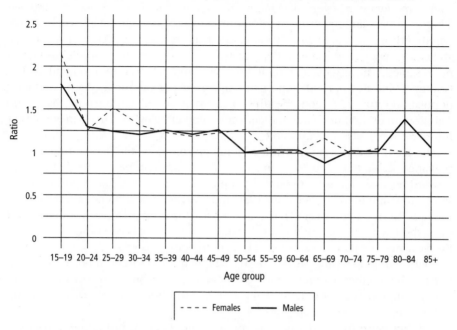

Age group

Females — Males

FIGURE 4.5B: PERCENTAGE DISABLED, RATIO 1991/1986, BY SEX AND AGE GROUP, 1991 COHORT

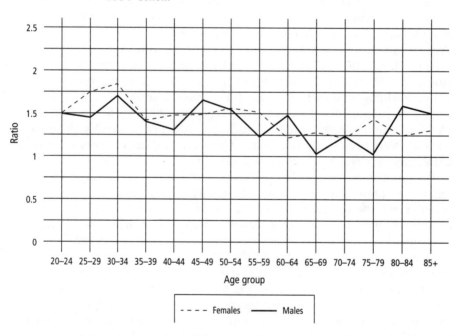

Age group

Females — Males

Source: Health and Activity Limitation Survey, 1986 and 1991.

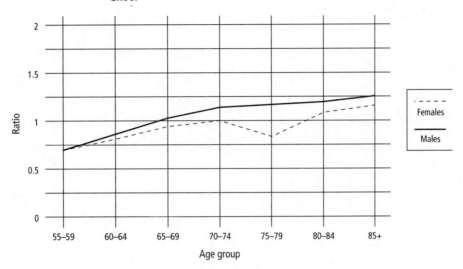

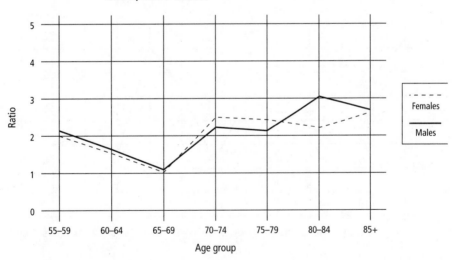

Source: Health and Activity Limitation Survey, 1986 and 1991.

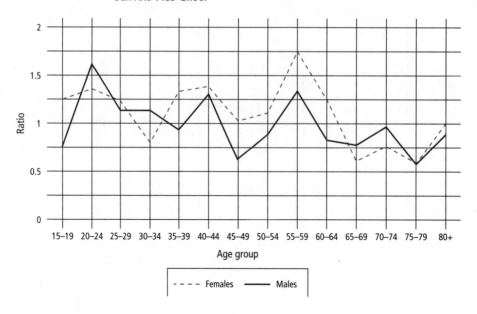

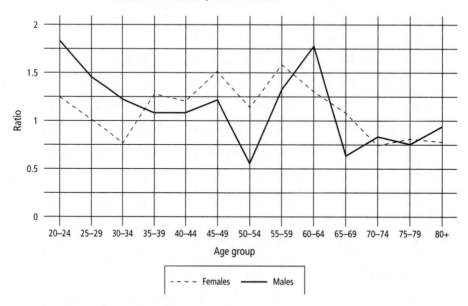

Source: General Social Survey, 1985 and 1991.

support may come from younger people and contribute to future growth in demand among the elderly while, at the same time, competing for current resources. A real need exists to monitor both changing attitudes and changing behaviours to better understand how cohorts' current attributes may be linked to their future attributes.

4.1.4 Measures of service utilization

Who uses what health-related services is a function of many social, economic and political influences that determine who has access to services under what circumstances. However, measures of utilization shed some light on how the health care system responds to the changing health status of an aging population. The GSS, for example, enables a measure to be constructed of the proportion of the population that has stayed in hospital for more than 7 days over the last 12 months (see Figure 4.8). This measure represents serious health conditions that impose a significant cost on the health care system. In 1991, only the 70-plus population saw the incidence of such hospitalization climb much above 5%. Even among the non-institutionalized population 80 and over, the incidence remained less than 15%.

FIGURE 4.8: PERCENTAGE STAYING IN HOSPITAL MORE THAN 7 DAYS IN THE LAST 12 MONTHS, BY SEX AND AGE, 1991

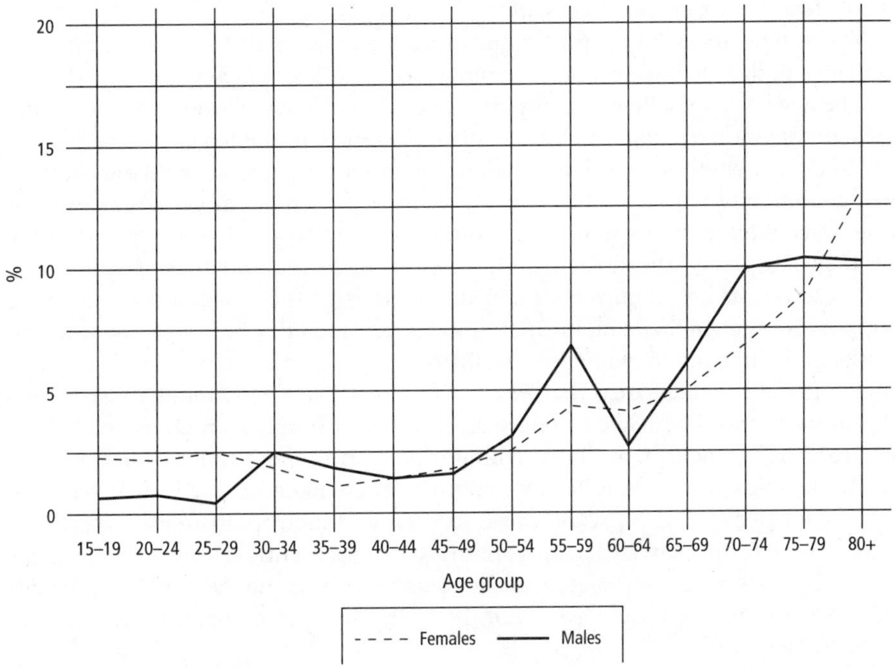

Source: General Social Survey, 1991.

The more widespread impact of aging, however, can be seen in the demand for a variety of services that support the activities of daily living. Obtaining such supports either informally from family and friends or formally through public and private agencies is critical for individuals who wish to stay in their own homes despite loss of function. With data from the HALS, we can estimate various aspects of supports for selected activities of daily living. Here we focus on the five instrumental activities of daily living—meal preparation, shopping, normal housework, heavy housework and yard work—as well as some of the activities of daily living—personal care (help with dressing, bathing and other personal functions) and moving around the home—for those who report themselves as disabled and use these services because of their condition.

Individuals' patterns of service usage should be strongly influenced by the severity of the disability that causes them to need help. In addition, we would expect those who live alone to show different usage patterns. On the one hand, those who live alone are likely to be more independent; on the other hand, once a need is expressed, those who live alone are more likely to have to rely on formal agencies for support than on family and friends.

Among those who received support for activities of daily living, those who were classified as having a severe disability showed much higher propensities to receive support (see Table 4.2). Those living alone were generally less likely to receive support. In general, women were more likely to receive support than men with similar living arrangements and severity of disability. However, because women were much more likely to live alone than were men, women were on the whole less likely to receive assistance.

Those who received support were more likely to get it for the instrumental activities of daily living, such as shopping, housework and heavy housework than for the activities of daily living of personal care and moving around in the home. Meal preparation occupied an intermediate position, although it was closer in profile to the activities of daily living than to the other instrumental activities of daily living. Difficulty with activities of daily living represents a more severe level of functional limitation; it occurred less often than the types of mobility and agility problems that cause the need for support for instrumental activities of daily living.

These results are confirmed when the analysis of the likelihood of receiving support is extended to a multivariate model that includes both age, low-income status and rural-urban status.[5] As well, utilization increased with age, and was higher in metropolitan areas than elsewhere (see Table 4.3).[6] Among those receiving support, those who lived alone were—not surprisingly—much more likely to use external agencies than those who did not: up to eight times as likely when other variables were controlled. Women were less likely to use formal services, except for personal care, while those in rural and metropolitan areas were less likely to use formal services than were those in small centres. This result suggests that access to services is easier in smaller centres, where one faces neither the distances associated with rural living nor the traffic and commuting problems found in the larger cities.

TABLE 4.2: PATTERNS OF SUPPORT, BY SEVERITY, SEX AND LIVING ARRANGEMENT, CANADIAN DISABLED POPULATION 65 AND OVER, 1986

	SEVERE DISABILITY				NOT SEVERE			
	Living alone		Not living alone		Living alone		Not living alone	
	Females	Males	Females	Males	Females	Males	Females	Males
Percentage receiving support								
Meal preparation	23.1	31.4	58.7	43.4	3.7	4.4	9.7	5.3
Shopping	66.1	50.3	83.0	57.6	27.2	12.5	27.4	9.4
Housework	53.3	59.1	79.9	54.9	15.9	14.3	28.7	10.6
Heavy housework	86.2	78.1	92.3	83.5	62.4	42.1	62.9	41.1
Personal care	16.3	14.0	33.5	38.4	2.0	0.8	4.9	2.6
Moving within residence	4.6	5.7	20.3	17.9	0.1	0.1	0.7	0.2
Percentage using external agencies (of those who receive support)								
Meal preparation	70.6	62.6	21.2	27.2	66.8	76.9	23.5	27.2
Shopping	32.3	39.2	12.8	16.5	17.0	25.4	11.1	18.8
Housework	75.2	66.7	23.0	28.2	68.5	67.7	29.1	32.0
Heavy housework	57.9	55.9	26.3	37.8	56.6	56.0	31.1	36.7
Personal care	76.8	64.2	32.9	28.7	83.4	66.6	18.1	20.6
Moving within residence	56.1	62.7	20.3	21.1	24.8	94.8	31.2	12.6
Percentage needing help or more help								
Meal preparation	19.9	23.4	28.4	20.0	4.1	5.0	5.4	2.0
Shopping	48.4	42.0	32.9	28.6	14.6	9.2	12.1	3.0
Housework	42.4	50.0	42.4	29.8	16.0	15.0	17.6	4.4
Heavy housework	60.8	61.6	54.3	54.4	35.1	31.3	37.7	23.9
Personal care	13.8	13.6	21.5	22.8	2.1	0.9	1.8	1.0
Moving within residence	5.4	6.4	12.9	13.0	0.3	0.1	2.2	0.3

Source: Health and Activity Limitation Survey, 1986.

What is also interesting about those who receive support from external agencies is that severity of disability does not appear to have made as much difference in receipt of services or need for help. For example, of those who received support for meal preparation from an external agency, a higher percentage of severely disabled women living alone used an external agency than of women living alone whose disabilities were not severe. However, a higher percentage of men living alone whose disabilities were not severe used an external agency for meal preparation than did those who were severely disabled. While this might be explained by differences in how individuals assessed their disabilities in the survey, it is likely better explained by differences in criteria used by external agencies to determine who qualifies for services. If this is indeed the case, from a policy perspective it suggests two sets of service delivery problems. First, is the geographical variation in service delivery across Canada inequitable? And, even where similar services exist in different places, are the criteria for eligibility inequitably applied?

DEPENDENT VARIABLES

Models for receipt of support services

INDEPENDENT VARIABLES[1]	MEAL PREPARATION		SHOPPING		EVERYDAY HOUSEWORK		HEAVY HOUSEWORK		PERSONAL CARE		MOVING WITHIN RESIDENCE	
	Odds ratio	Significance level	Odds ratio	Significance level	Odds ratio	Significance level	Odds ratio	Significance level	Odds ratio	Significance level	Odds ratio	Significance level
Age (5-year age groups 65+)	1.360	+++	1.416	+++	1.305	+++	1.186	+++	1.289	+++	1.193	+++
Female	1.585	+++	3.200	+++	2.612	+++	2.366	+++	0.960	NS	1.143	NS
Lives alone	0.280	---	0.692	---	0.470	---	0.937	NS	0.311	---	0.190	---
Low income	1.008	NS	1.065	NS	0.894	--	0.790	---	1.327	+++	1.021	NS
Rural area	0.876	-	0.889	--	0.891	--	1.070	NS	1.153	+	0.847	NS
Census metropolitan area	1.159	+++	1.254	+++	1.117	++	1.045	NS	1.396	+++	1.096	NS
Severe disability	11.492	+++	9.355	+++	8.131	+++	5.797	+++	12.519	+++	46.710	+++
Number of observations	25,815		25,717		25,740		23,388		25,883		25,840	

Models for use of external services by those who receive support

INDEPENDENT VARIABLES[1]	MEAL PREPARATION		SHOPPING		EVERYDAY HOUSEWORK		HEAVY HOUSEWORK		PERSONAL CARE		MOVING WITHIN RESIDENCE	
	Odds ratio	Significance level	Odds ratio	Significance level	Odds ratio	Significance level	Odds ratio	Significance level	Odds ratio	Significance level	Odds ratio	Significance level
Age (5-year age groups 65+)	1.113	+++	1.092	+++	1.135	+++	1.003	NS	1.207	+++	1.244	+++
Female	0.861	-	0.751	---	0.945	NS	0.738	---	1.166	NS	0.897	NS
Lives alone	7.841	+++	2.733	+++	7.384	+++	3.125	+++	8.000	+++	5.546	+++
Low income	1.060	NS	0.877	NS	0.749	---	0.789	---	0.916	NS	0.724	NS
Rural area	0.661	---	1.001	NS	0.803	--	0.632	---	0.509	---	0.836	NS
Census metropolitan area	0.511	---	0.774	---	0.713	---	0.954	NS	0.593	---	0.745	NS
Severe disability	1.260	++	1.642	+++	0.896	-	0.922	-	1.542	+++	0.777	NS
Number of observations	5,209		9,165		8,784		16,771		3,160		1,183	

+ + +, - - - Significant at .001
+ +, - - Significant at .01
+, - Significant at .05
The chi-square value for each model is significant for $p<.0001$
1. See Table 4.8 for definitions of variables

TABLE 4.3: LOGISTIC REGRESSION MODELS OF SUPPORT FOR DAILY LIVING FOR THOSE 65 AND OVER, 1986

DEPENDENT VARIABLES

INDEPENDENT VARIABLES[1]	MEAL PREPARATION		SHOPPING		EVERYDAY HOUSEWORK		HEAVY HOUSEWORK		PERSONAL CARE		MOVING WITHIN RESIDENCE	
	Odds ratio	Significance level	Odds ratio	Significance level	Odds ratio	Significance level	Odds ratio	Significance level	Odds ratio	Significance level	Odds ratio	Significance level
Models for need for help or additional help												
Age (5-year age groups 65+)	1.238	+++	1.231	+++	1.099	+++	1.094	+++	1.176	+++	1.228	+++
Female	1.591	+++	1.846	+++	2.077	+++	1.463	+++	1.013	NS	1.289	+++
Lives alone	0.761	---	1.642	+++	1.160	+++	1.138	+++	0.652	---	0.309	---
Low income	1.015	NS	0.891	-	0.973	NS	0.795	---	1.064	NS	0.970	NS
Rural area	0.927	NS	0.922	NS	0.830	---	0.963	NS	1.073	NS	0.740	--
Census metropolitan area	0.889	-	1.175	+++	1.190	+++	1.022	NS	1.035	NS	0.846	-
Severe disability	7.008	+++	5.160	+++	4.406	+++	2.648	+++	15.023	+++	12.124	+++
Number of observations	25,815		25,717		25,740		23,388		25,883		25,852	

+++,--- Significant at .001
++,-- Significant at .01
+,- Significant at .05
The chi-square value for each model is significant for $p<.0001$
1. See Table 4.8 for definitions of variables
Source: Health and Activity Limitation Survey, 1986.

DEPENDENT VARIABLES

INDEPENDENT VARIABLES[1]	Meal preparation		Shopping		Everyday housework		Heavy housework		Personal care		Moving within residence	
	Odds ratio	Significance level	Odds ratio	Significance level	Odds ratio	Significance level	Odds ratio	Significance level	Odds ratio	Significance level	Odds ratio	Significance level
Models for receipt of support services												
Age (5-year age groups 65+)	1.359	+ + +	1.419	+ + +	1.311	+ + +	1.188	+ + +	1.289	+ + +	1.196	+ + +
Female	1.587	+ + +	3.176	+ + +	2.647	+ + +	2.350	+ + +	0.973	NS	1.145	NS
Lives alone	0.279	– – –	0.720	– – –	0.484	– – –	0.991	NS	0.299	– – –	0.199	– – –
Low income	1.013	NS	1.013	NS	0.838	– – –	0.732	– – –	1.383	+ + +	0.952	NS
Rural area	0.857	– –	0.874	– –	0.870	– –	0.976	NS	1.166	+	0.805	–
Census metropolitan area	1.176	+ + +	1.219	+ + +	1.036	NS	0.991	NS	1.398	+ + +	1.088	NS
Severe disability	11.503	+ + +	9.473	+ + +	8.198	+ + +	5.843	+ + +	12.557	+ + +	46.647	+ + +
Atlantic provinces	1.134	NS	1.129	NS	0.642	– – –	1.427	+ + +	0.908	NS	1.162	NS
Quebec	0.907	NS	1.570	+ + +	0.975	NS	1.596	+ + +	0.813	–	1.119	NS
Ontario	0.943	NS	1.110	NS	0.586	– – –	0.841	– – –	0.963	NS	0.832	NS
Prairie provinces	0.967	NS	0.964	NS	0.613	– – –	0.929	NS	1.144	NS	0.802	NS
Number of observations	25,815		25,717		25,740		23,388		25,883		25,840	
Models for use of external services by those who receive support												
Age (5-year age groups 65+)	1.116	+ + +	1.099	+ + +	1.142	+ + +	1.008	NS	1.206	+ + +	1.276	+ + +
Female	0.885	NS	0.770	– – –	0.986	NS	0.747	– – –	1.215	+	0.993	NS
Lives alone	7.272	+ + +	2.704	+ + +	6.968	+ + +	3.185	+ + +	7.121	+ + +	4.916	+ + +
Low income	1.132	NS	0.864	–	0.787	– – –	0.750	– – –	1.003	NS	1.008	NS
Rural area	0.709	– – –	0.992	NS	0.902	NS	0.612	– – –	0.528	– – –	1.052	NS
Census metropolitan area	0.498	– – –	0.731	– – –	0.663	– – –	0.889	– – –	0.592	– – –	0.700	–
Severe disability	1.272	+ +	1.644	+ + +	0.901	–	0.927	–	1.593	+ + +	0.909	NS
Atlantic provinces	0.414	– – –	0.543	– – –	0.250	– – –	0.751	– – –	0.422	– – –	0.411	– –
Quebec	0.417	– – –	0.638	– – –	0.252	– – –	0.979	NS	0.360	– – –	0.360	– –
Ontario	0.507	– – –	0.505	– – –	0.349	– – –	0.647	– – –	0.575	– – –	1.059	NS
Prairie provinces	0.650	– – –	0.639	– – –	0.442	– – –	0.805	– – –	0.768	NS	0.584	NS
Number of observations	5,209		9,165		8,784		16,771		3,160		1,183	

+ + +, – – – Significant at .001
+ +, – – Significant at .01
+, – Significant at .05
The chi-square value for each model is significant for $p < .0001$
1. See Table 4.8 for variable definitions.

TABLE 4.4: LOGISTIC REGRESSION MODELS OF SUPPORT FOR DAILY LIVING (WITH REGIONAL VARIABLES) FOR THOSE 65 AND OVER, 1986

DEPENDENT VARIABLES

Models for need for help or additional help

INDEPENDENT VARIABLES[1]	MEAL PREPARATION Odds ratio	Significance level	SHOPPING Odds ratio	Significance level	EVERYDAY HOUSEWORK Odds ratio	Significance level	HEAVY HOUSEWORK Odds ratio	Significance level	PERSONAL CARE Odds ratio	Significance level	MOVING WITHIN RESIDENCE Odds ratio	Significance level
Age (5-year age groups 65+)	1.244	+ + +	1.235	+ + +	1.103	+ + +	1.097	+ + +	1.176	+ + +	1.227	+ + +
Female	1.633	+ + +	1.856	+ + +	2.114	+ + +	1.472	+ + +	1.025	NS	1.274	+ +
Lives alone	0.786	– – –	1.711	+ + +	1.190	+ + +	1.186	+ + +	0.650	– – –	0.303	– – –
Low income	0.945	NS	0.844	– – –	0.924	NS	0.745	– – –	1.060	NS	1.008	NS
Rural area	0.866	–	0.878	–	0.809	– – –	0.886	–	1.061	NS	0.751	–
Census metropolitan area	0.838	– – –	1.133	+ +	1.121	+ +	0.948	NS	1.016	NS	0.869	NS
Severe disability	6.980	+ + +	5.160	+ + +	4.398	+ + +	2.650	+ + +	15.021	+ + +	12.165	+ + +
Atlantic provinces	0.880	NS	1.034	NS	0.665	– – –	0.954	NS	1.000	NS	1.042	NS
Quebec	0.982	NS	1.150	+	0.868	–	1.065	NS	1.051	NS	0.871	NS
Ontario	0.593	– – –	0.771	– – –	0.571	– – –	0.584	– – –	0.976	NS	1.095	NS
Prairie provinces	0.822	–	0.815	– –	0.615	– – –	0.764	– – –	1.204	NS	0.916	NS
Number of observations	25,815		25,717		25,740		23,388		25,883		25,852	

+ + +, – – – Significant at .001
+ +, – – Significant at .01
+, – Significant at .05
The chi-square value for each model is significant for p<.0001
1. See Table 4.8 for variable definitions.
Source: Health and Activity Limitation Survey, 1986.

Regional differences were by far the strongest for the use of external agencies. Those receiving support in British Columbia were far more likely to use external agencies than were those in the other four regions; the odds ratios for the regional effects are virtually all significantly less than 1 (see Table 4.4). Part of the reason may be that services may have been more readily available in British Columbia, although we have no evidence of this. A more likely explanation is found in Chapter 2: A dramatically higher proportion of the elderly population was born outside the province than is the case anywhere else in Canada. This means that an elderly person in British Columbia is less likely to have family nearby to provide additional support when needed; that person would therefore need to seek formal sources.

Finally, among those who express a need for help (or more help), the results are similar to those for service utilization in general. Needs increased with age; those who lived alone expressed significantly greater need for help for instrumental activities of daily living (shopping and housework) but less need for help with meal preparation. The strongest overall effect is that those who were severely limited expressed much greater need, especially for personal care (see Table 4.3). Women expressed greater need for help with all services. Perhaps the most significant finding here is the overall expression of need that was particularly evident for the instrumental activities of daily living of shopping and housework: 30% to 60% of severely disabled elderly said they needed help or more help.

Although we do not have forecasts for future living arrangements and income status for the elderly, the general trends are important. The ranks of the elderly will continue to grow more rapidly than the rest of the population, and the absolute numbers of elderly women will be greater than those of elderly men for the foreseeable future. Although the increasing incidence of divorce at younger ages and the closing of the mortality gap between men and women act in opposite directions, the net effect will do little to reduce the numerical importance of older women living alone in the future. Furthermore, if the number of places in institutions fails to keep pace with the growth of the older elderly, we are likely to see a decline in institutionalization, at least for those under 80. One likely effect would be more elderly women living alone in the community with inadequate support from family and friends. We must look for alternatives to provide support for this group in particular, by providing formal home care and by encouraging greater informal support within the community.

4.2 THE SOCIO-DEMOGRAPHIC CONTEXT OF HEALTH STATUS

Age and gender differences form the core of analyses of the socio-demographic differentials of health status, but other factors are equally—if not more—important. In analysis of life expectancy, a strong argument exists for differences based on socio-economic status; those with low incomes or less education have significantly shorter life expectancies. In the United States, for example, Crimmins and Saito (1990) show that life expectancy at age 65 for white women with more than 13 years of schooling is 19.8 years, compared with 18.4 for those with less than 9 years' schooling. As well, those with more than 13 years of schooling can expect to spend 63.6% of their remaining life active and disability-free; those with less than 9 years' schooling can expect 35.6% of the rest of their lives to be active and disability-free. White men have similar education-based differentials, and black men and women have even greater ones.

Although the health care systems in the United States and Canada are different, similar arguments about life expectancy have been made by Wilkins and Adams (1992) and about health status by Roberge et al. (1993) in a study of Ontario. Consistently, lower socio-economic status is associated with poor health, whether that status is measured by education, occupation or income. The causal influences run in both directions. On the one hand, those who are poor, particularly those who have grown up poor, may lack the basic necessities of good nutrition, clothing and adequate shelter, each of which increases the likelihood of extended periods of poor health. On the other hand, poor health or disability that reduces day-to-day functioning may well influence the ability to obtain a good education or to acquire and retain a well-paying job. Whichever direction the relationship runs for a given individual—and it may well run in both directions for the same person—the aggregate association is strong, and is as evident in our data from the 1991 HALS as it is in the previous studies.

4.2.1 Low income

The effect of low income on the likelihood of being disabled is clear (see Table 4.5). Many of those with low incomes, especially younger people, were more than twice as likely to be disabled as those in higher income categories. The differences in likelihood were greater for men than for women, but they dropped for both genders at age 65 and beyond, where income differentials between individuals were smaller. However, the basic structure remains; those who were above the low-income cut-off were more likely to be classified as not disabled and less likely to fall into the other categories of dependence.

4.2.2 Education

Education has as dramatic an effect on health outcomes as it does on life expectancy (see Table 4.6). At all ages except 75 and over, the odds of being in any of the disabled/dependent categories were significantly lower for those with some postsecondary education; the differences were particularly dramatic among those who needed help with activities of daily living at younger ages. These observations reinforce the view that there is a significant population that is disadvantaged along many socio-economic, demographic and health dimensions and needs the attention of planners and policy makers.

4.2.3 Living arrangements

The degree of independence that individuals maintain is linked to their living arrangements. Those who lived alone had notably different profiles from those

TABLE 4.5: DISTRIBUTION OF HEALTH STATUS, BY AGE GROUP AND SEX RELATIVE TO LOW-INCOME CUT-OFF, FOR NON-INSTITUTIONAL POPULATION AGED 15 AND OVER, 1986

Health status	AGE GROUP							
	15–24	25–34	35–44	45–54	55–64	65–74	75–84	85+

Living above low-income cut-off

	Females (%)							
Not disabled	96.6[1]	95.0	92.2	88.0	78.9	69.3	50.4	25.6
Disabled: no help with IADL[2] or ADL[3]	2.8	3.7	5.3	7.1	12.9	16.7	22.1	18.6
Disabled: help with IADL	0.4	1.1	2.2	4.2	7.0	11.1	21.2	35.0
Disabled: help with ADL	0.2	0.2	0.4	0.6	1.2	2.8	6.3	20.8
	Males (%)							
Not disabled	96.4	94.2	92.2	87.1	77.5	63.8	56.2	36.0
Disabled: no help with IADL or ADL	3.1	5.0	6.9	10.7	18.0	28.9	28.3	22.9
Disabled: help with IADL	0.3	0.5	0.7	1.5	3.3	4.8	10.2	24.3
Disabled: help with ADL	0.2	0.2	0.2	0.7	1.2	2.5	5.3	16.8

Living below low-income cut-off

	Females (%)							
Not disabled	92.1	88.4	80.7	72.7	57.4	56.3	42.9	20.8
Disabled: no help with IADL or ADL	6.3	8.8	13.2	18.1	26.7	29.9	27.9	21.0
Disabled: help with IADL	0.9	2.4	5.3	7.4	13.5	11.3	23.3	43.5
Disabled: help with ADL	0.7	0.5	0.8	1.7	2.4	2.5	6.0	14.6
	Males (%)							
Not disabled	92.4	86.4	81.7	65.4	55.9	48.4	58.0	18.7
Disabled: no help with IADL or ADL	6.7	10.3	13.9	27.7	32.7	39.4	17.5	34.6
Disabled: help with IADL	0.4	1.8	3.0	4.7	8.5	8.9	15.3	26.8
Disabled: help with ADL	0.4	1.5	1.4	2.2	2.9	3.3	9.2	19.9

Relative odds: below low-income cut-off/above low-income cut-off

	Females (%)							
Not disabled	0.95[4]	0.93	0.87	0.83	0.73	0.81	0.85	0.81
Disabled: no help with IADL or ADL	2.24	2.38	2.49	2.53	2.07	1.78	1.26	1.13
Disabled: help with IADL	2.04	2.24	2.48	1.78	1.94	1.02	1.10	1.25
Disabled: help with ADL	4.11	2.06	2.37	2.67	1.88	0.88	0.95	0.70
	Males (%)							
Not disabled	0.96	0.92	0.89	0.75	0.72	0.76	1.03	0.52
Disabled: no help with IADL or ADL	2.15	2.05	2.00	2.60	1.82	1.37	0.62	1.51
Disabled: help with IADL	1.41	3.42	4.55	3.13	2.57	1.84	1.49	1.10
Disabled: help with ADL	1.89	7.33	5.85	3.07	2.44	1.33	1.75	1.18

1. Percentage of females aged 15 to 24 living above low-income cut-off reporting no disability.
2. Instrumental activities of daily living.
3. Activities of daily living.
4. Females 15 to 24 living below low-income cut-off are 0.95 times as likely to report no disability as those living above the low-income cut-off.

Source: Statistics Canada, Health and Activity Limitation Survey, 1986.

TABLE 4.6: DISTRIBUTION OF HEALTH STATUS, BY AGE GROUP, SEX AND LEVEL OF EDUCATION, FOR NON-INSTITUTIONAL POPULATION AGED 15 AND OVER, 1986

Health status	AGE GROUP						
	15–24	25–34	35–44	45–54	55–64	65–74	75+
No postsecondary education	Females (%)						
Not disabled	95.3	93.1	90.1	85.4	73.4	66.2	44.0
Disabled: no help with IADL[1] or ADL[2]	3.8	5.1	6.6	9.0	16.4	19.7	23.2
Disabled: help with IADL	0.6	1.5	2.8	4.8	8.7	11.3	24.3
Disabled: help with ADL	0.3	0.3	0.5	0.8	1.5	2.8	8.5
	Males (%)						
Not disabled	95.1	92.5	89.8	82.9	73.2	60.9	52.0
Disabled: no help with IADL or ADL	4.2	6.2	8.8	13.7	21.0	30.7	27.7
Disabled: help with IADL	0.4	0.9	1.1	2.4	4.3	5.7	12.9
Disabled: help with ADL	0.3	0.5	0.4	1.1	1.5	2.7	7.5
Some postsecondary education	Females (%)						
Not disabled	97.8	96.1	92.2	89.0	85.6	77.2	44.6
Disabled: no help with IADL or ADL	2.0	3.1	5.6	6.4	9.9	12.6	21.0
Disabled: help with IADL	0.2	0.7	2.0	3.8	3.7	8.0	26.2
Disabled: help with ADL	0.1	0.1	0.2	0.7	0.8	2.2	8.2
	Males (%)						
Not disabled	97.6	95.4	94.0	91.0	81.3	71.4	65.3
Disabled: no help with IADL or ADL	2.2	4.2	5.2	8.0	14.3	23.1	19.4
Disabled: help with IADL	0.1	0.3	0.6	0.8	3.3	3.7	10.4
Disabled: help with ADL	0.0	0.1	0.2	0.3	1.0	1.7	5.0
Relative odds: some postsecondary education/no postsecondary education	Females (%)						
Not disabled	1.03	1.03	1.02	1.04	1.17	1.17	1.01
Disabled: no help with IADL or ADL	0.52	0.61	0.85	0.71	0.60	0.64	0.91
Disabled: help with IADL	0.25	0.49	0.73	0.80	0.42	0.70	1.08
Disabled: help with ADL	0.23	0.36	0.33	0.89	0.54	0.77	0.97
	Males (%)						
Not disabled	1.03	1.03	1.05	1.10	1.11	1.17	1.26
Disabled: no help with IADL or ADL	0.53	0.68	0.59	0.58	0.68	0.75	0.70
Disabled: help with IADL	0.24	0.34	0.58	0.33	0.77	0.66	0.81
Disabled: help with ADL	0.12	0.20	0.48	0.25	0.67	0.65	0.67

1. Instrumental activities of daily living.
2. Activities of daily living.
Source: Health and Activity Limitation Survey, 1986.

who lived with others, whether they live with their spouse, children or non-family household members (see Table 4.7). Those living alone had a lower propensity to be "not disabled" than those who lived with others. Those living alone—women and men—were also more prone than those living with others to report a functional limitation but not to need help. They were also on the whole more likely to report receiving help only for instrumental activities of daily living.

This latter observation casts some light on the way in which questions are perceived. When an individual lives with others, especially a spouse or other partner, the instrumental activities of daily living are often shared unequally. One partner may do all the meal preparation or shopping, for example, while the other may do much of the heavy housework, but neither partner may declare that they receive help or need help with the other's tasks. The potentially misleading aspect of these responses is that one clearly cannot infer that those who need no help when living with others would also need no help if they lived alone.

As one might expect, those who live alone are less likely to need help with activities of daily living, since, if one needs help, one is more likely to live with someone who can provide such support. However, it is important to note the large absolute number of people 65 and over estimated to live alone and need support for activities of daily living; there were an estimated 33,000 women and 3,700 men in this situation in 1991. It is this group, which is much more likely to put pressure on formal support services, that will both grow significantly in the next two decades and pose the greatest concern for long-term care.

4.2.4 Mobility

Elderly people's lives are subject to many changes not only in health and in family characteristics but also in the local environments in which they live. Chapter 3 showed that changes of residence resulting from migration are often a major event in the lives of the elderly, even if they do not occur as often as at younger ages.

Health status is important in understanding elderly people's mobility behaviour. Litwak and Longino (1987) argue that elderly life experiences are associated with three dominant types of moves at different stages, the first two of which were discussed in Chapter 2. Amenity-oriented moves are most common at or around retirement time, and are most common among affluent, intact and healthy couples. As ability to maintain complete independence declines, reflecting deteriorating health of the individual or spouse or even the loss of a spouse, a support-oriented move takes place; the individual moves to live with or near family members who can offer support. A final institutional-oriented move occurs when the individual is unable to live independently in the community, either for health reasons or for a lack of adequate social support.

While this model clearly has empirical validity (Zimmerman, Jackson, Longino and Bradsher 1993), the import of its predictions for planning has still to be fully developed. It is clear that those who were activity-limited were more likely to have moved and less likely to have migrated between 1986 and 1991 than were

Health status	AGE GROUP							
	15–24	25–34	35–44	45–54	55–64	65–74	75–84	85+
Not living alone	Females (%)							
Not disabled	95.9	93.9	91.1	86.7	76.0	68.7	47.2	27.7
Disabled: no help with IADL[1] or ADL[2]	3.3	4.5	5.8	7.8	14.1	15.8	22.3	14.3
Disabled: help with IADL	0.5	1.3	2.6	4.6	8.2	12.1	21.0	32.6
Disabled: help with ADL	0.2	0.3	0.4	0.8	1.6	3.4	9.6	25.3
	Males (%)							
Not disabled	95.4	93.7	91.2	85.1	74.6	61.9	55.7	35.7
Disabled: no help with IADL or ADL	4.0	5.2	7.6	11.9	19.8	30.2	26.9	24.8
Disabled: help with IADL	0.3	0.7	0.9	2.0	4.0	5.1	10.9	19.9
Disabled: help with ADL	0.3	0.4	0.4	0.9	1.5	2.8	6.6	19.7
Living alone	Females (%)							
Not disabled	90.5	92.7	80.3	73.0	66.2	63.0	49.3	19.2
Disabled: no help with IADL or ADL	7.9	6.3	17.6	21.0	24.5	26.5	25.4	27.1
Disabled: help with IADL	0.6	0.9	1.9	4.9	8.7	9.0	22.5	43.3
Disabled: help with ADL	1.0	0.0	0.2	1.1	0.6	1.5	2.8	10.4
	Males (%)							
Not disabled	97.1	89.5	88.4	75.6	70.8	63.4	58.7	19.7
Disabled: no help with IADL or ADL	2.8	9.5	10.0	21.8	22.7	28.0	29.3	25.5
Disabled: help with IADL	0.1	0.7	1.3	2.3	5.8	7.8	10.2	47.9
Disabled: help with ADL	0.0	0.3	0.3	0.3	0.6	0.8	1.8	6.9
Relative odds: living alone/not living alone	Females (%)							
Not disabled	0.94	0.99	0.88	0.84	0.87	0.92	1.05	0.69
Disabled: no help with IADL or ADL	2.40	1.41	3.02	2.69	1.73	1.68	1.14	1.89
Disabled: help with IADL	1.05	0.70	0.72	1.06	1.06	0.74	1.07	1.33
Disabled: help with ADL	4.28	0.11	0.55	1.32	0.35	0.44	0.30	0.41
	Males (%)							
Not disabled	1.02	0.96	0.97	0.89	0.95	1.03	1.05	0.55
Disabled: no help with IADL or ADL	0.72	1.82	1.32	1.83	1.15	0.93	1.09	1.03
Disabled: help with IADL	0.30	0.96	1.45	1.16	1.45	1.51	0.94	2.41
Disabled: help with ADL	0.00	0.68	0.78	0.34	0.39	0.27	0.27	0.35

1. Instrumental activities of daily living.
2. Activities of daily living.
Source: Health and Activity Limitation Survey, 1986.

able-bodied elderly. Among those who moved, the likelihood of having moved to be nearer support increased dramatically with age (see Chapter 2, Table 2.16). However, even among the population 75 and over, less than 10% moved for support reasons between 1986 and 1991.

The role of housing-related adjustments is also sustained at higher ages; over 25% of those 75 and over moved for this reason. In part, the difficulty of looking after larger homes when mobility and agility decline makes moves to smaller units a practical solution. While we are aware of the importance of this adjustment, we do not know the extent to which such adjustments are blocked by a lack of opportunity or financial means. If a larger home is owned outright but is in an undesirable location or is in poor condition, it may be difficult to sell, and the equity realized may not be enough to afford adequate rental accommodation in a tight market. Particularly in larger cities with older suburbs built in the 1940s and 1950s, where the quality of construction was often poor and the current population is aging (see Chapter 3), this scenario describes a potentially serious problem. If the elderly find it difficult to move from these locations, providing support services would become more difficult, compounded by today's financial constraints and the higher unit costs of delivering services to a dispersed population.

The consequences of moving at older ages need more critical assessment. Moving for support reasons, particularly for those who are no longer married, increases the likelihood of close proximity to a family member. At the same time, however, it is much less likely that the friend to which the individual feels closest will be nearby. Those who make a support move are more likely to leave this friend behind than are individuals who did not engage in this type of move. Support moves have a significant negative association with general measures of life satisfaction, although this is also related to the loss of control over the pattern of daily life as well as to access to long-time social networks (McGuinness 1996). Clearly, family support may be a significant positive impact of the move, especially if it reduces the need for help from external agencies. At the same time, the loss of access to friends and attendant loss of life satisfaction may well have the effect of speeding up the individual's deterioration. It is also important to note that the increasing pressures on family caregivers arising from the move often produces its own set of consequences both for the individual and for public agencies (Rosenthal and Gladstone 1994).

4.3   A MULTIVARIATE MODEL OF HEALTH STATUS

The socio-economic, demographic and locational effects discussed above certainly interact with health status. In this section, we examine these combined effects using a series of logistic regression models, which focus on both the basic categorizations of the population by severity of disability and on the more rigorous classification based on dependence level (see Tables 4.9 and 4.10). For each case, we also analyse separately those aged 65 to 74 and 75 and over, since the incidence and severity of functional limitation increases rapidly with age. As well, the relationships between socio-economic attributes and health may themselves vary with age. Table 4.8 provides a list of the variables used in these analyses.

DEPENDENT VARIABLES

1. Meal preparation	1 = Respondent receives help with meal preparation; 0 otherwise
2. Shopping	1 = Respondent receives help with shopping; 0 otherwise
3. Heavy housework	1 = Respondent receives help with heavy housework; 0 otherwise
4. Everyday housework	1 = Respondent receives help with everyday housework; 0 otherwise
5. Personal care	1 = Respondent receives help with personal care; 0 otherwise
6. Moving within residence	1 = Respondent receives help moving within residence; 0 otherwise
7. Disabled	1 = Respondent is disabled; 0 otherwise
8. Severely disabled	1 = Respondent is severely disabled; 0 otherwise
9. Activities of daily living	1 = Respondent receives help with activities of daily living; 0 otherwise
10. Activities of daily living or instrumental activities of daily living	1 = Respondent receives help with activities of daily living or instrumental activities of daily living; 0 otherwise

INDEPENDENT VARIABLES

Socio-demographic indicators

Age variables:

1. Age grouping 1	1 = Respondent is between 65 and 69
	2 = Respondent is between 70 and 74
2. Age grouping 2	1 = Respondent is between 75 and 79
	2 = Respondent is between 80 and 84
	3 = Respondent is 85 or older
3. Female	1 = Respondent is female; 0 otherwise
4. Lives alone	1 = Respondent lives alone; 0 otherwise
5. Low income	1 = Respondent lives below the low-income cut-off; 0 otherwise
6. Postsecondary education	1 = Respondent has received Bachelor's or first professional degree; 0 otherwise

Residential mobility indicators: reference catergory = respondent did not move in previous five years

7. Local mover	1 = Respondent moved within the same census subdivision in the previous five years; 0 otherwise
8. Migrant	1 = Respondent moved from a different census subdivision in the previous five years; 0 otherwise

Size-of-place indicators: reference category = respondent lives in an "other urban" location

9. Census metropolitan area	1 = Respondent lives in a metropolitan area; 0 otherwise
10. Rural area	1 = Respondent lives in a rural area; 0 otherwise

Regional indicators: reference category = respondent lives in British Columbia

11. Atlantic provinces	1 = Respondent lives in Newfoundland, Prince Edward Island, Nova Scotia or New Brunswick; 0 otherwise
12. Quebec	1 = Respondent lives in Quebec; 0 otherwise
13. Ontario	1 = Respondent lives in Ontario; 0 otherwise
14. Prairie provinces	1 = Respondent lives in Manitoba, Saskatchewan, or Alberta

TABLE 4.9: LOGISTIC REGRESSION MODELS OF THE CORRELATES OF DISABILITY

DEPENDENT VARIABLE = DISABLED

Independent variables[1]	65 to 74 years Odds ratio	Significance level[2]	Independent variables	75 years and over Odds ratio	Significance level
Without regional variables					
Age Grouping 1	1.309	+++	Age Grouping 2	1.693	+++
Female	0.767	---	Female	1.416	+++
Lives alone	0.949	NS[3]	Lives alone	0.829	---
Low income	1.881	+++	Low income	1.347	+++
Postsecondary education	0.669	---	Postsecondary education	0.804	---
Local move	1.103	+	Local move	1.503	+++
Migrant	1.194	+++	Migrant	1.712	+++
Census metropolitan area	0.708	---	Census metropolitan area	0.979	NS
Rural area	1.032	NS	Rural area	0.980	NS
With regional variables					
Age Grouping 1	1.306	+++	Age Grouping 2	1.703	+++
Female	0.767	NS	Female	1.428	+++
Lives alone	0.950	NS	Lives alone	0.795	---
Low income	1.954	+++	Low income	1.391	+++
Postsecondary education	0.668	---	Postsecondary education	0.814	---
Local move	1.125	+	Local move	1.550	+++
Migrant	1.198	+++	Migrant	1.762	+++
Census metropolitan area	0.758	---	Census metropolitan area	1.043	NS
Rural area	1.050	NS	Rural area	0.949	NS
Atlantic provinces	1.370	+++	Atlantic provinces	1.562	+++
Quebec	0.786	---	Quebec	0.823	---
Ontario	1.162	++	Ontario	1.177	++
Prairie provinces	1.124	+	Prairie provinces	1.427	+++
Number of observations	19,912		Number of observations	14,253	

DEPENDENT VARIABLE = SEVERELY DISABLED

Independent variables	65 to 74 years Odds ratio	Significance level	Independent variables	75 years and over Odds ratio	Significance level
Without regional variables					
Age Grouping 1	1.444	+++	Age Grouping 2	1.967	+++
Female	1.172	++	Female	1.717	+++
Lives alone	0.713	---	Lives alone	0.502	---
Low income	1.591	+++	Low income	1.319	+++
Postsecondary education	0.539	---	Postsecondary education	0.800	-
Local move	1.621	+++	Local move	1.458	+++
Migrant	1.125	NS	Migrant	1.066	NS
Census metropolitan area	0.833	---	Census metropolitan area	0.918	NS
Rural area	0.866	NS	Rural area	1.057	NS
With regional variables					
Age Grouping 1	1.442	+++	Age Grouping 2	1.965	+++
Female	1.173	++	Female	1.725	+++
Lives alone	0.713	---	Lives alone	0.491	---
Low income	1.607	+++	Low income	1.341	+++
Postsecondary education	0.534	---	Postsecondary education	0.798	-
Local move	1.635	+++	Local move	1.452	+++
Migrant	1.119	NS	Migrant	1.065	NS
Census metropolitan area	0.851	-	Census metropolitan area	0.939	NS
Rural area	0.853	-	Rural area	1.038	NS
Atlantic provinces	1.148	NS	Atlantic provinces	1.128	NS
Quebec	0.807	-	Quebec	0.835	-
Ontario	0.902	NS	Ontario	0.987	NS
Prairie provinces	0.954	NS	Prairie provinces	1.138	NS
Number of observations	19,912		Number of observations	14,253	

+++, --- Significant at .001
++, -- Significant at .01
+,- Significant at .05
1. See Table 4.8 for variable definitions.
2. Significance level.
3. Not significant.
The chi-square value for each model is significant for $p<.0001$
Source: Health and Activity Limitation Survey, 1986.

TABLE 4.10: LOGISTIC REGRESSION MODELS: THE RECEIPT OF ASSISTANCE FOR ACTIVITIES OF DAILY LIVING AND INSTRUMENTAL ACTIVITIES OF DAILY LIVING

DEPENDENT VARIABLE = ACTIVITIES OF DAILY LIVING

Independent variables[1]	65 to 74 years Odds ratio	65 to 74 years Significance level[2]	75 years and over Odds ratio	75 years and over Significance level
Without regional variables				
Age Grouping 1	1.741	+ + +	2.018	+ + +
Female	1.206	+	1.441	+ + +
Lives alone	0.308	– – –	0.222	– – –
Low income	1.407	+	1.823	+ + +
Postsecondary education	0.702	NS	0.839	NS
Local move	1.725	+ + +	1.508	+ + +
Migrant	1.044	NS	1.243	NS
Census metropolitan area	1.168	NS	1.109	NS
Rural area	0.956	NS	1.181	NS
With regional variables				
Age Grouping 1	1.731	+ + +	2.008	+ + +
Female	1.208	+	1.465	+ + +
Lives alone	0.310	– – –	0.216	– – –
Low income	1.436	+ +	1.852	+ + +
Postsecondary education	0.701	NS	0.813	NS
Local move	1.745	+ + +	1.454	+ + +
Migrant	1.045	NS	1.237	NS
Census metropolitan area	1.213	NS	1.111	NS
Rural area	0.959	NS	1.129	NS
Atlantic provinces	1.255	NS	1.095	NS
Quebec	0.883	NS	0.875	NS
Ontario	1.128	NS	0.879	NS
Prairie provinces	1.163	NS	1.268	+
Number of observations	19,912		14,253	

DEPENDENT VARIABLE = ACTIVITIES OF DAILY LIVING OR INSTRUMENTAL ACTIVITIES OF DAILY LIVING

Independent variables	65 to 74 years Odds ratio	65 to 74 years Significance level	75 years and over Odds ratio	75 years and over Significance level
Age Grouping 2	1.508	+ + +	1.999	+ + +
Female	1.981	+ + +	2.074	+ + +
Lives alone	0.602	– – –	0.663	– – –
Low income	1.332	+ + +	1.391	+ + +
Postsecondary education	0.680	– – –	0.961	NS
Local move	1.416	+ + +	1.524	+ + +
Migrant	1.161	NS	1.161	NS
Census metropolitan area	0.937	NS	1.089	NS
Rural area	0.889	NS	1.092	NS
Age Grouping 2	1.511	+ + +	1.998	+ + +
Female	1.979	+ + +	2.085	+ + +
Lives alone	0.603	– – –	0.656	– – –
Low income	1.317	+ + +	1.397	+ + +
Postsecondary education	0.675	– – –	0.951	NS
Local move	1.417	+ + +	1.510	+ + +
Migrant	1.173	+	1.151	NS
Census metropolitan area	0.938	NS	1.102	+
Rural area	0.858	–	1.068	NS
Atlantic provinces	1.227	+	1.059	NS
Quebec	1.020	NS	0.791	– – –
Ontario	0.943	NS	0.865	–
Prairie provinces	1.000	NS	0.961	NS
Number of observations	19,912		14,253	

+ + +, – – – Significant at .001
+ +, – – Significant at .01
+, – Significant at .05
1. See Table 4.8 for variable definitions.
2. Significance level.
The chi-square value for each model is significant for $p < .0001$
Source: Health and Activity Limitation Survey, 1986.

First, we will consider the relationships with disability. The analyses distinguish between those who reported any level of disability and those whose functional limitations were defined as severe (see Table 4.9). Among both groups the role of age is strong; the coefficient for the 75-plus age group is larger, indicating that the propensity to be disabled increases at a rising rate moving up the age scale.

The role of gender is instructive; it emphasizes the importance of the separate analyses for the two age groups. For all degrees of disability, women aged 65 to 74 were less likely to be disabled, but the relationship was reversed for those 75 and over (see Table 4.9). Among severely disabled individuals, women 65 to 74 were slightly more likely to be in this category (the odds ratio is 1.17); among women 75 and over the odds ratio is 1.72. Part of the reason for these differences may be the incidence among women of serious illnesses such as osteoporosis, but part of the explanation is also women's longer lives, which means women live in disabled states for a longer period (Chapter 2; Wilkins and Adams 1992).

It is important to appreciate the meaning of these odds ratios. The odds ratio of being classified low income for those who were 75 and over is 1.35. For two individuals of that age group who are identical in all respects other than low income status, the relative odds of being disabled for someone below the low-income cut-off compared with someone above it is 1.35. If we combine the attributes of *female, low income* and *living alone* we get an odds ratio of (1.416*1.347*.829), or 1.58. Thus, a low-income man 75 or over is just more than one-and-a-half times as likely to be disabled as a non–low-income man living with his spouse or with others, assuming that the men's other attributes are the same. Also, a low-income woman living alone is 1.35 times as likely to be disabled as a non–low-income woman living alone. These significant odds ratios tell us about the strength of socio-demographic variables in differentiating the odds of being disabled.

The effects of living alone increase both with severity of the disability and with age. Those living alone were much less likely to be disabled than those living with others, and those living alone at older ages were less likely to be disabled than their peers who lived with others. The effects of being female and living alone offset each other in this analysis; a woman 75 or over living alone had greater odds of being disabled than a man of that age living alone and lower odds than a woman living with others. However, that woman 75 or over living alone had slightly higher odds of being disabled but lower odds of being severely disabled than a man living with others (the odds ratios for *female* and *alone* can be multiplied together to achieve the latter results).

For both degrees of disability, the impact of the socio-economic variables are as expected. Those classified as *low income* had significantly higher chances of being disabled or severely disabled; the opposite was true for those with some level of postsecondary education. The effects weaken with age; those aged 65 to 74 with some postsecondary education were barely half as likely to be severely disabled as those who had no postsecondary education.

Local moves and migration are particularly influential in these analyses. Those who moved locally between 1986 and 1991 were much more likely to be disabled, whether this is defined as severe or includes all degrees of disability. The effects were as strong or stronger for the older age group. They stress the importance of moves within the local community in later life, many of which are associated with the loss or anticipated loss of some degree of functional independence. While these moves do not affect the characteristics of the local population, they often lead to better access to social supports, especially family (see Table 4.10).

Migration plays a different role. Although all of the coefficients for *migrant* are positive—they produce odds ratios greater than 1—those associated with the severely disabled are not significant (see Table 4.9). However, when all degrees of disability are considered, the odds ratios are significantly greater than 1, and the odds ratios for those 75 and over are dramatically higher (1.71). This is strong, though indirect, evidence for the claim by Litwak and Longino (1987) of the importance of support-related moves among the older elderly. The implication is that many elderly migrate back to areas where they spent a large part of childhood or working life after they have lost some ability and independence, but before they are too limited by any disabling conditions. As well, the coefficients for migration do not become negative (the odds ratios do not fall below 1), which suggests that severe disability is not a widespread deterrent to migration, although it may be for specific individuals.

The locational variables show some general differences. Metropolitan residents were a little less likely to be either disabled or severely disabled at younger ages—65 to 74. Among older residents, however, these differences are not significant. Strong regional differences occur primarily when all degrees of disability are included in the analysis. Quebec has significantly lower incidence of disability than does British Columbia, which is the reference category (i.e., the coefficients for the other regions are each compared with British Columbia); the other regions have higher rates. Among the severely disabled, these differences disappear—except in Quebec, which has lower rates to begin with. Given the detailed nature of the questions on functional problems that underlie the definition of disability, it is difficult to explain these differences. One argument might be that the flows of pre-retirement and younger elderly populations to British Columbia have been made up of more affluent healthy individuals, and that those who are left behind are slightly more prone to disability. There could also be a process of support-oriented return migration among the older elderly; these moves would be mostly to provinces other than British Columbia. However, this does not explain the Quebec figures. One might argue that differences in local culture lead to different propensities to report mild disabling conditions as problems, but there is no supporting evidence for such a claim. The same lower incidence of disability did exist in Quebec in 1991 (see Chapter 3), although the data do not support the same level of detailed analysis as is possible for 1986.

Classifying health status based on the level of dependency involves two sets of analyses. The first considers the likelihood of receiving help with the activities of daily living of personal care and moving around the home. The second looks at the probability of receiving help for either activities of daily living or instrumental activities of daily living. These results are similar to those for the severely disabled. The effects of age and of being female are strongly positive, and they increase among the older age group. The effects of being alone are negative, and are strongest, for the 75-plus cohort, for activities of daily living support. In other words, people in this age group who live alone were much less likely to receive support for activities of daily living than were those living with others (see Tables 4.7 and 4.10). The low income and postsecondary education variables have the same signs as do the disability measures, although the low income effect is much stronger, especially among those receiving activities of daily living support.

Because the support conditions for activities of daily living and instrumental activities of daily living identify the severely limited individuals, only the local move variable is significant in the equations; being a local mover increases the likelihood of receiving such support by 40% to 70% across all the equations in Table 4.9, and confirms the importance of local moves in the lives of elderly with declining abilities. When we consider these support conditions, the role of the locational variables is not significant for the activities of daily living or instrumental activities of daily living of the groups aged 75 and over, except in Quebec.

4.4 REGIONAL VARIATIONS IN THE INCIDENCE OF DISABILITY

The regression analyses above demonstrated general location effects on the likelihood of individuals having various levels of functional limitation. In particular, likelihoods in each analysis were lower for Quebec respondents to the HALS, even when a broad range of socio-economic and demographic variables were controlled. Two questions arise: Can these regional effects be defined in greater geographic detail? How would spatial differences affect the potential loads on health care and social services?

Two elements underlie the spatial distribution of the disabled elderly population. The first is the distribution of the elderly themselves. Where local populations have significantly higher proportions 65 and over, a relatively higher proportion of the population could be both elderly and disabled. The geographical nature of the distribution of the elderly was discussed at length in Chapter 3.

The second element is the spatial variation in the propensity to be disabled. In other words, are some local areas associated with higher likelihoods of being disabled than others, and can such variations be the result of differences in the attributes of local communities? The product of the local elderly population and the age- and sex-specific local rates will be the number of elderly disabled people in the local population.

The ability to pursue such an analysis is limited by the data available for small areas on a national scale. The HALS itself is not suitable, as its sample size does not permit small-area estimates. However, a screening question was asked in the 1991 Census itself, which asked whether the respondent had experienced a long-term condition causing a functional limitation at home, work or school. Although data from the question are not considered reliable estimates of the actual numbers of functionally limited people in the community,[7] the data arguably serve as a sound indicator of *relative* incidence of functional limitation—provided we assume that the way in which the question was interpreted and answered did not vary significantly from one place to another.

For each census division the number of people who are and are not functionally limited are given by gender for six age groups. If D_{ki} is the number of disabled individuals in age group k in area i and P_{ki} is the population of that age group in that census division, then

$$r_{ki} = \frac{D_{ki}}{P_{ki}}$$

is the age-specific rate of disability for age group k in area i. Furthermore, if p_k is the proportion of the Canadian population in age group k, then

$$L_i = \Sigma_k p_k \cdot r_{ki}$$

is the age-standardized rate of disability for area i. We can construct a second measure $L_i(65)$ by standardizing on just the age groups 65 and over.[8]

The proportion of the population in area i that is elderly and has a long-term condition associated with functional limitation is given by

$$G_i = \frac{\Sigma_{k>65} D_{ki}}{\Sigma_k P_{ki}}$$

The distributions of $L_i(65)$ and G_i are mapped in Figures 4.9 and 4.10. The age-standardized rates have a strong regional structure. They were relatively high (consistently over 22%) in British Columbia, northern parts of the Prairies, Northern Ontario, the territories and in Nova Scotia (most census divisions in the province were over 26%) and New Brunswick. Lower rates (under 22% and often under 18%) predominated in Quebec, and were also prevalent in the southern Prairies and, to a lesser extent, in Newfoundland.

Attempts to determine whether additional community characteristics were associated with these age-standardized rates were unsuccessful (see Table 4.11). Although a significant amount of the variation in these rates can be accounted for, the primary source of variation is the set of regional dummy variables. The same analysis for the values of L_i does indicate an association between higher rates of disability and low-income areas, but this does not sustain itself for the elderly alone. We do know that higher mortality levels are associated with low income, both at the individual scale and at the small area level. However, when individuals do survive to older ages, differences cannot be detected in the propensity to report disability as a function of the affluence of the local community.

The interaction between the regionally structured disability rates and the strong geographic patterns of the elderly distribution produce a strongly differentiated pattern of proportions of the population who are both elderly and disabled (see Figure 4.10). Four distinct regions of high concentration are found: the interior of southern British Columbia, the central Prairies, central Ontario from Prince Edward County on Lake Ontario north to the Muskokas, Nova Scotia, and southwestern New Brunswick. In each of these regions, more than 3% of the population is so classified, and in many areas the proportion exceeds 4%. These rates are

FIGURE 4.9:   AGE-STANDARDIZED RATES OF DISABILITY AMONG THE POPULATION AGED 65 AND OVER AND DISABLED, BY CENSUS DIVISION, CANADA, 1991

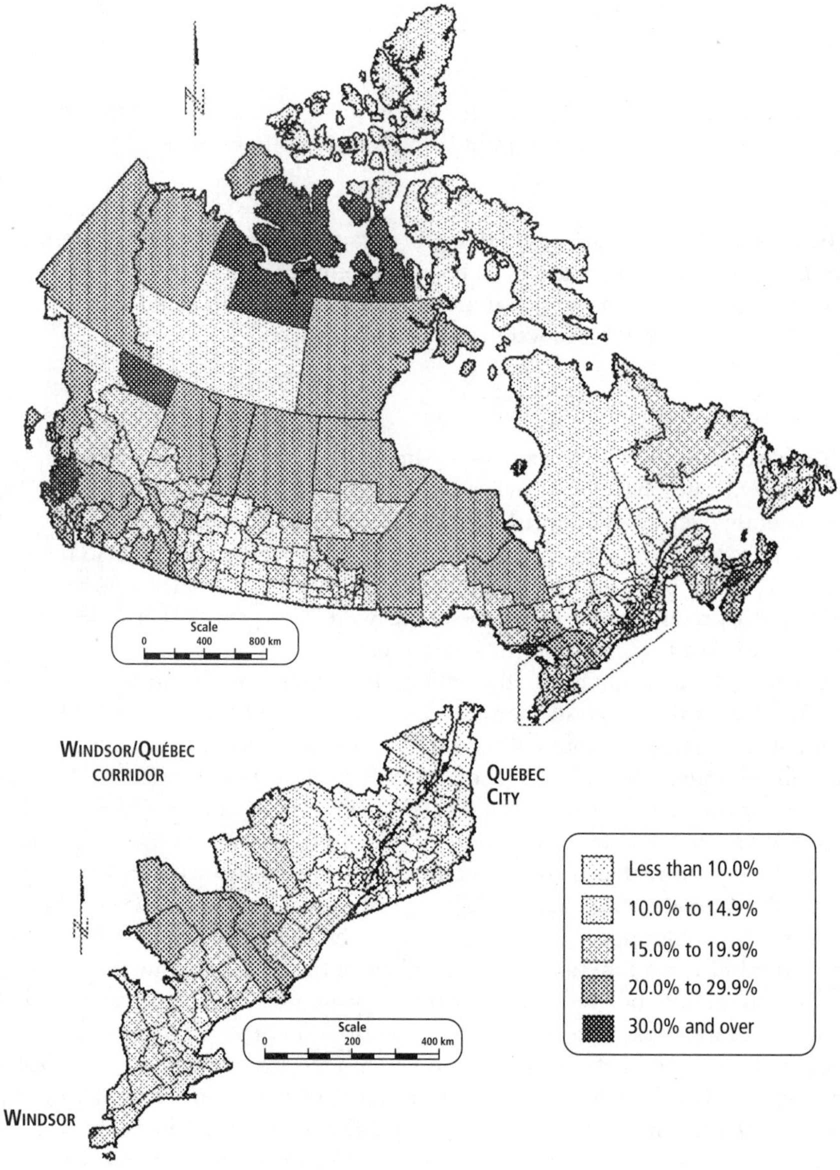

Scale
0   400   800 km

WINDSOR/QUÉBEC
CORRIDOR

QUÉBEC CITY

Scale
0   200   400 km

WINDSOR

Less than 10.0%
10.0% to 14.9%
15.0% to 19.9%
20.0% to 29.9%
30.0% and over

Source: Census of Canada, 1991

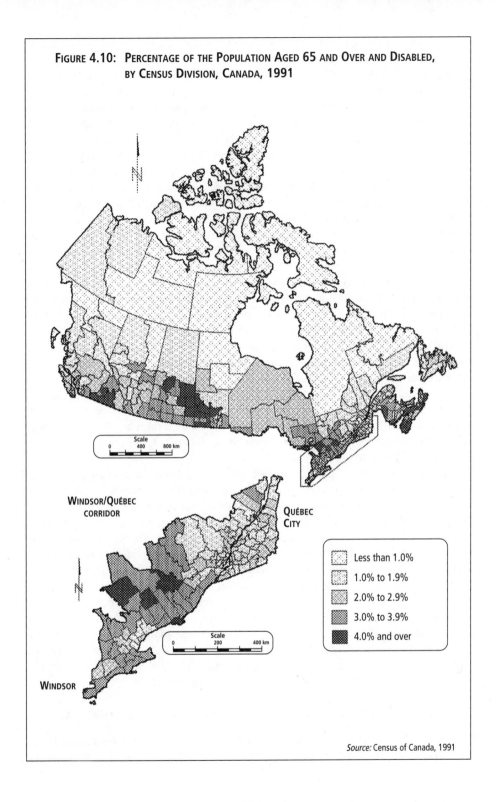

FIGURE 4.10: PERCENTAGE OF THE POPULATION AGED 65 AND OVER AND DISABLED, BY CENSUS DIVISION, CANADA, 1991

WINDSOR/QUÉBEC CORRIDOR

QUÉBEC CITY

WINDSOR

Less than 1.0%
1.0% to 1.9%
2.0% to 2.9%
3.0% to 3.9%
4.0% and over

Source: Census of Canada, 1991

twice as high as those in Quebec and much of northern Canada and, significantly, in virtually all the major metropolitan areas.

An analysis of the correlates of this distribution focuses on many of the factors underlying the population distribution itself. The high values are associated with stable, lower income communities. The association with the distribution of health service workers is interesting. The two associations emphasize the importance of smaller, relatively stable communities such as London and Kingston, Ontario, Sherbrooke, Quebec and the metropolitan areas of the Prairies, that have relatively well-educated populations and, in many cases, strong tertiary-care medical centres or university teaching hospitals. While the sheer numbers of potential clients are greater in the major metropolitan areas of Toronto, Montréal and Vancouver, the relative burden of providing health care and social services is heavier in smaller communities. Furthermore, the elderly population is relatively less mobile than its younger counterpart; it is unreasonable to think that this population can readily move to where the resources are. High house prices and rents in larger cities are a considerable deterrent for those wanting to move from smaller to larger centres. It is not unusual for the children of those living in smaller urban and rural areas to have migrated to larger urban centres in previous years. Higher housing costs may make it difficult for parents to move closer to their children.

The disabled elderly did not strongly tend to congregate where there were high concentrations of services (measured by physicians per thousand and hospital beds per thousand). The exception found was the similar distributions of the elderly disabled population and health service workers in smaller communities with well-educated populations. Physicians were concentrated more in larger cities and on the West Coast than were the elderly disabled population. The distribution of hospital beds reflected decisions made when the population was more dispersed and less urbanized.

Clearly, these simple associations are not a good basis for allocating services. The organization of health services with more specialized services assigned to tertiary care centres implies the concentration of both health service workers and doctors in tertiary care centres in a way that does not necessarily reflect the population distribution. Furthermore, the delivery of services in areas of sparse population cannot be based on the simple ratio of doctors to population, since the time required to reach patients may vary greatly from one community to another.

The core point is that the elderly population is a major component of the future demand for health care and social services. Elderly people are concentrated *relatively* in many of the less economically advantaged parts of the country, and they are not particularly mobile. If they are to be given adequate basic services, a suitable delivery mechanism must exist where they live, which must be ensured by public agencies; we cannot assume the elderly can simply adjust to where the resources are, either by moving or travelling greater distances.

4.4.1 Spatial variation in health status in Toronto, Montréal and Vancouver

In this section we will repeat the analysis in the previous section for census tracts in Toronto, Montréal and Vancouver, Canada's three largest metropolitan areas.

TABLE 4.11: REGRESSION MODELS OF LONG-TERM DISABILITY RATES, BY CENSUS DIVISION, 1991

DEPENDENT VARIABLES

Independent variables	Total population % with long-term disability	Population 65+ % with long-term disability	Total population Age-standardized long-term disability	Population 65+ Age-standardized long-term disability
Intercept	14.794***	5.863***	13.771***	44.130***
% population urban	-0.004	-0.001	-0.000	0.012
Metropolitan area	0.079	-0.079	0.124	-0.240
% population immigrants 1986–1991	-0.103	-0.022	-0.106	-0.207
Sex ratio over 65	-2.252**	-0.827*	-1.617*	-2.719
% households below low-income cut-off	0.157***	0.025	0.138***	0.130
Average income	-0.151***	-0.085***	-0.074***	-0.120
Population growth 1986–1991	0.110*	0.017	0.138**	0.244
% with university degree	-0.027	0.012	-0.030	0.086
Physicians per thousand	0.185	0.061	0.111	-0.111
Hospital beds per thousand	0.017	-0.002	0.037	0.098
Health service workers per thousand	0.016	0.019*	-0.016	-0.045
Mean July temperature	-0.037	-0.008	-0.040	-0.025
Mean January temperature	0.037*	0.040***	-0.026	-0.082
Number of hours of sunshine per year	0.077	0.037	-0.029	-0.525**
Atlantic	0.171	0.017	0.010	-1.663
Quebec	-2.370***	-1.145***	-2.609***	-10.250***
Ontario	1.266***	0.327*	0.632*	-1.553
Prairies	-1.772***	-0.597***	-1.622***	-4.262***
% elderly 80 and over	0.062*	0.054**	0.026	0.020
% with less than Grade 9 education	-0.053**	-0.006	-0.053**	-0.086
% unemployed	-0.178***	-0.096***	-0.098***	-0.191*
Degrees of freedom	268	268	268	268
R-square	0.750	0.765	0.657	0.641

Source: Census of Canada, 1991.

Similar data to those for census divisions allow us to construct measures of the proportion of each census tract's population with long-term disabilities (both for all ages and those 65 and over) and age-standardized measures of the proportion with long-term disability. The proportions of the population that are both elderly and disabled is again a function of two variables: the distribution of the proportion of the population that is elderly and the age-standardized disability rates for those 65 and over.

The variable of primary interest here is the proportion of each area's population that is 65 and over; it is the most direct indicator of the potential demand for health care and social services from the elderly. These values vary strongly across metropolitan areas, as Figures 4.11, 4.12 and 4.13 show. In both Toronto and Montréal, the census tracts with high proportions of elderly and disabled individuals were concentrated in the central part of the city and the older suburbs built in the 1940s and 1950s. In Toronto, much more than in the other two cities, the core of the central city had much lower concentrations of both elderly and disabled elderly. This reflects the effect of high levels of immigration in the past decade. Immigrants have significantly younger age distributions than non-immigrants (see Chapter 1, Table 1.4) and they are much less likely to report disability than non-immigrants (see Table 4.12).

Vancouver presents a different picture than Toronto and Montréal; the high concentrations of disabled elderly are much more dispersed throughout the region. This is partly because Vancouver's suburban communities have substantial working class populations, and more areas outside the core have concentrations of low income populations than is the case in the two largest metropolitan areas.

In each city the distribution of the proportion that is elderly and disabled closely follows the distribution of the elderly simply because the age-standardized rates of long-term disability for those 65 and over do not vary much, nor do they correlate highly with other socio-demographic variables (see Table 4.12). In fact, a series of regression analyses that examines the relations between selected socio-economic and demographic variables and health status measures shows remarkably consistent results in all three metropolitan areas (see Table 4.12), both according to their overall performance measured by the R-square values and by the patterns of significant coefficients. The models for the proportion of the population with long-term disability and the age-standardized rates for the total population generally perform best. Models for the proportion that are elderly and disabled still illustrate strong links between areas with high concentrations to those with low levels of academic achievement, high unemployment and high proportions of elderly living alone. The models for age-standardized rates for those 65 and over are generally much weaker; the primary correlates are areas with high proportions speaking neither English nor French and with low levels of education. The analyses for the total disabled population consistently confirm that the presence of recent immigrants reduces the incidence of reporting long-term disability. As well, the concentration of higher rates occurs in more disadvantaged areas with high proportions of unemployed and high proportions of households that fall below the low-income cut-off. As in the case of the census division analysis,

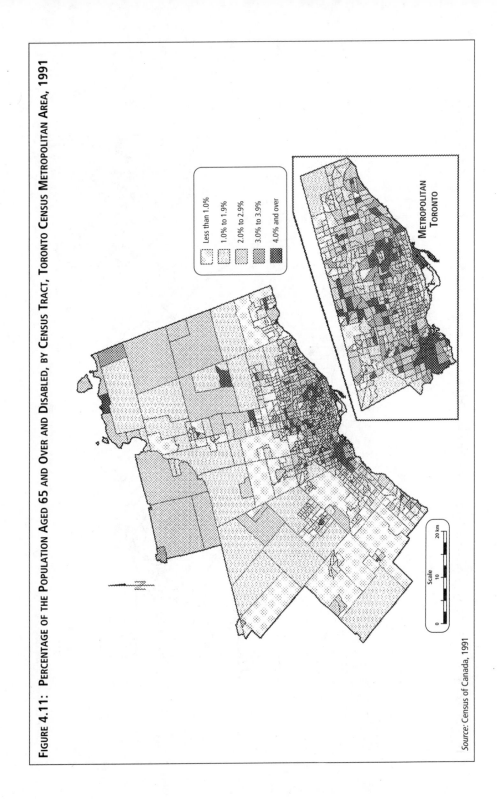

FIGURE 4.11: PERCENTAGE OF THE POPULATION AGED 65 AND OVER AND DISABLED, BY CENSUS TRACT, TORONTO CENSUS METROPOLITAN AREA, 1991

Less than 1.0%
1.0% to 1.9%
2.0% to 2.9%
3.0% to 3.9%
4.0% and over

METROPOLITAN TORONTO

Scale
0   10   20 km

Source: Census of Canada, 1991

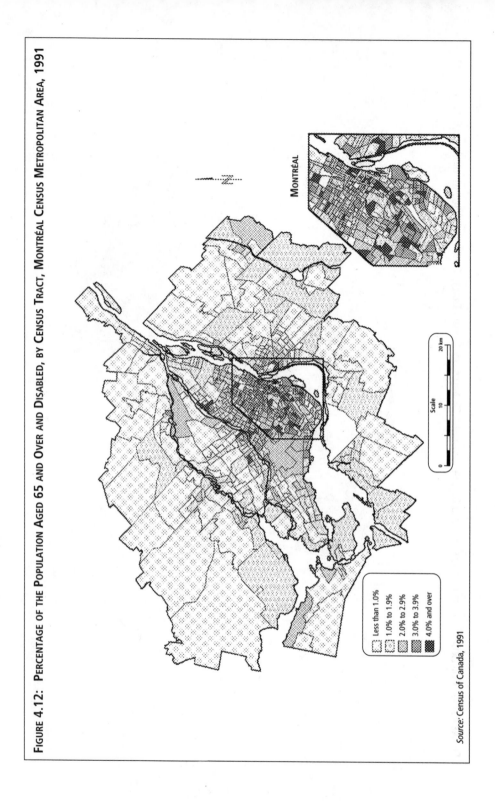

FIGURE 4.12: PERCENTAGE OF THE POPULATION AGED 65 AND OVER AND DISABLED, BY CENSUS TRACT, MONTRÉAL CENSUS METROPOLITAN AREA, 1991

MONTRÉAL

Scale

0   10   20 km

Less than 1.0%
1.0% to 1.9%
2.0% to 2.9%
3.0% to 3.9%
4.0% and over

Source: Census of Canada, 1991

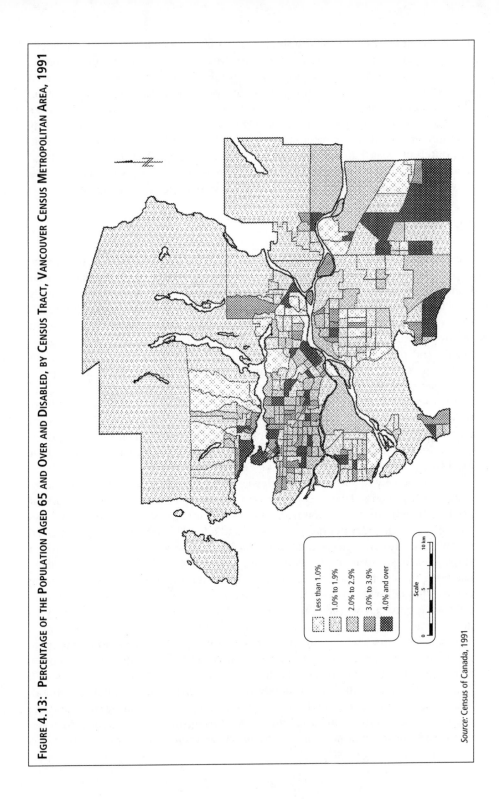

FIGURE 4.13: PERCENTAGE OF THE POPULATION AGED 65 AND OVER AND DISABLED, BY CENSUS TRACT, VANCOUVER CENSUS METROPOLITAN AREA, 1991

Less than 1.0%
1.0% to 1.9%
2.0% to 2.9%
3.0% to 3.9%
4.0% and over

Scale

0   5   10 km

Source: Census of Canada, 1991

the strong message is that the distribution of communities with high concentrations of elderly and disabled individuals reflects the distribution of economic disadvantage.

The implications of this analysis for future demand for health care and social services are that those areas with growing proportions of elderly, particularly the older suburbs of the major cities, are likely to be the site of growing concentrations of those with long-term disability. The age-specific rates are not sufficiently differentiated spatially to suggest that disabled people will concentrate in markedly different areas than will the elderly themselves. Although those with mild and moderate disability do move in considerable numbers (see Chapter 2), their moves do not significantly affect the distribution between census tracts.

4.5 CONCLUSION

The core issues that arise from analysis of elderly Canadians' health status are the importance of age, gender, living alone and poverty. The elderly population is far from homogeneous, and each of these socio-demographic variables is strongly associated with different experiences with personal health and with the health care and social service systems. Perhaps the most important observation is that the overwhelming majority of the younger elderly (those under 80) enjoy good health, and pursue active lives with little dependence on external agencies for health care or social support. It is only among those of more advanced age that the incidence of severe functional limitations that affect the ability to live independently rises substantially. Among those 85 and over, the likelihood of being institutionalized is a major factor in the accounting of health status in any local population. Given the high proportions in this category, a major public policy issue arises when institutional spaces are cut—which causes greater demand for local community services.

The propensity to suffer different levels of functional limitation is highly associated with poverty. There are consistent associations between higher odds of poor health and the proportion falling below low income standards or having less education. While older people's economic and educational background improved notably over the previous two decades, recent economic trends have indicated a slowing of these advances. Particularly important to this analysis of disadvantage has been the continued increase in the concentration of elderly women living alone. Although widowhood rates have declined among the younger elderly, the imbalance between women and men at older ages remains, and is unlikely to decline much in the coming decades. This concentration of women living alone is significant because, while this group has relatively greater functional independence, it also makes much more use of formal agencies than do other groups. A significant proportion of those who live alone have limited social networks, and relatively few have either close family or friends living in the neighbourhood. Again, there is little prospect of this situation changing significantly soon, and the growth in the elderly population will continue to push up demand for formal services from those without family or friends near them. Furthermore, given this

Census metropolitan area	Independent variables	Total population % with long-term disability	Population 65+ % with long-term disability	Total population Age-standardized long-term disability	Population 65+ Age-standardized long-term disability
Toronto	Intercept	2.239***	0.842***	0.033***	0.174***
	% with less than Grade 9	0.116***	0.068***	0.000***	0.001*
	% elderly living alone	0.079***	0.052***	0.000***	0.000*
	% dwellings needing major repairs	0.042**	0.012	0.000*	-0.000
	% unemployed (age over 15)	0.050*	-0.076***	0.001***	-0.001
	% households below low-income cut-off	0.024**	-0.004	0.000***	0.001***
	% speaking neither English nor French	-0.141***	-0.076***	-0.001***	-0.004**
	% immigrants 1986–1991	-0.078***	0.007	-0.001***	-0.001***
	Degrees of freedom	789	789	729	729
	R-square	0.530	0.404	0.347	0.051
Montréal	Intercept	0.319***	0.098	0.014***	0.105***
	% with less than Grade 9	0.090***	0.022***	0.001***	0.000
	% elderly living alone	0.074***	0.044***	0.000***	0.000
	% dwellings needing major repairs	0.032*	-0.005	0.000**	0.001
	% unemployed (age over 15)	0.060***	-0.015	0.001***	0.002*
	% households below low-income cut-off	0.011*	0.006	0.000**	0.000
	% speaking neither English nor French	-0.240***	-0.048*	-0.003***	-0.005***
	% immigrants 1986–1991	-0.006	0.020	-0.000	0.000
	Degrees of freedom	723	723	723	723
	R-square	0.598	0.324	0.442	0.061
Vancouver	Intercept	2.507***	1.509***	0.036***	0.204
	% with less than Grade 9	0.335***	0.182***	0.002***	0.003
	% elderly living alone	0.098***	0.071***	0.000***	0.000
	% dwellings needing major repairs	-0.085*	-0.079**	-0.000	-0.003
	% unemployed (age over 15)	0.126***	-0.150***	0.002***	0.001
	% households below low-income cut-off	-0.051***	-0.014	0.000	0.001
	% speaking neither English nor French	-0.285***	-0.089*	-0.003***	-0.005
	% immigrants 1986–1991	-0.106**	-0.020	-0.001***	-0.003
	Degrees of freedom	289	289	289	289
	R-square	0.694	0.455	0.614	0.114

DEPENDENT VARIABLES

Source: Census of Canada, 1991.

group's relative lack of financial resources, the public funding of services for its members should assume a high priority.

Recent writings have stressed migration and moves within the local community by the older elderly in response to declining functional abilities. The analysis of the HALS strongly supports this view, although it is clear that those who are less disabled are more likely to make support moves. However, there is no strong evidence that such moves significantly change the distribution of those in poorer health at a regional or metropolitan level.

The geographical analysis supports the economic relations identified in the study of individual experience. The distribution of those who are both elderly and disabled follows that of the elderly themselves, and emphasizes the concentration of these groups in communities with lower incomes, higher unemployment and slow growth. However, while there is some relation between economic disadvantage and overall age-standardized rates of long-term disability, these effects could not be detected for the population 65 and over. This is partly a problem of small numbers; but it does suggest that once people reach older ages and their health status deteriorates rapidly, there is not a great geographical variation in the odds of their being disabled. However, it is in economically disadvantaged areas that such populations accumulate.

The geographical structure at the census division scale for the country is replicated to a large degree for the three major metropolitan areas. The importance of relative poverty and low educational attainment is universal. The influence of recent immigration emerges as a significant factor in these cities. Immigration increased substantially at the end of the 1980s as national policy changed, and over 60% of the new immigration was to Toronto, Montréal and Vancouver. Immigrants have much younger age distributions than does the population as a whole; they are also much less likely to report functional limitation, at least in part because of the health screening to which they are exposed. Greater immigration thus reduces population aging and the propensity to be disabled, at least in the short run.

In the next chapter we consider some of the implications of the current structure of health status for the patterns of aging and disability over the next 20 years. Aspects of this health care future depend critically on public policy decisions regarding funding patterns for health care and social services. However, much of the future demand for such services is already set by the existing demographic structure and processes of geographic redistribution within the Canadian population.

ENDNOTES

1. World Health Organization (1980). *International Classifications of Impairments, Disabilities and Handicaps: A Manual of Classification Relating to the Consequences of Disease*, p. 143.

2. Because of the small numbers in the 1991 sample that are associated with high coefficients of variation, Figures 4.1 and 4.2 are fitted curves of the form $y = ae^{-bx}$, where y is the age-specific rate, x is age and a,b are constants.

3. This means that an individual has at least one functional problem in each of the six categories of disability: mobility, agility, seeing, hearing, speaking and other.

4. The 1991 file was not designed to permit a breakdown of the population 65 and over by age. The sampling design for the 1986 file had a much larger number of elderly observations, which supports this more detailed analysis. The general structure of aging and health status is very similar for the two years, and there is no reason to believe that the inferences drawn here are compromised by using the earlier data.

5. The age-related data are from 1986. Individuals were identified as living in rural, other urban or metropolitan areas. The reference category in the logistic regressions in Table 4.3 is "other urban."

6. See Chapter 3, section 3.2 for an illustration of the interpretation of odds ratios.

7. For example, the 1991 Census question provides an estimate that 19.5% of the population has a long-term disability, whereas the final 1991 HALS estimates that 25.8% had a moderate or severe disability.

8. In this case we standardize on the age groups 65 and over. p_k is the proportion of the Canadian population in age group k where $k>65$ and

$$L_i (65) = \Sigma_{k>65} p_k \cdot r_{ki}$$

CHAPTER

THE NEXT 20 YEARS

In Chapters 1 to 4, we set out the basic demographic structure of Canada's elderly population, its health status and its pattern of geographic concentration in 1991. In this chapter, we project these three themes into the future. In the next section, paralleling Chapter 1, the demographic characteristics of the elderly population of 2011 are described. The second section parallels Chapter 3: A series of measures are generated at the census division level to examine the elderly population's future geographic distribution. In the third section, age- and gender-specific rates of activity limitation are used to estimate the future health of Canada's elderly population.

Population projections at any geographic scale directly reflect the assumptions underlying them. Projection Series Number 2 from the Population Projections Section, Demography Division, Statistics Canada (1994) is used throughout this chapter to provide the base values presented. The assumptions underlying Projection Series Number 2 are:

- that life expectancy will continue to improve from 74.6 years for men and 80.9 years for women in 1991 to 78.5 years for men and 84.0 years for women in 2016;

- that the fertility rate will remain constant at 1.70 (the medium natural increase assumption);

- that immigration will increase from 219,300 in 1991 to 250,000 in 2016 (the medium immigration assumption);

- that emigration will increase from 43,700 in 1991 to 53,790 in 2016;

- that the number of returning Canadians will increase from 18,500 in 1991 to 25,630 in 2016;

- that the number of non-permanent residents will decrease from 381,000 to 149,600; and

- that net interprovincial migration will be based on the "medium" scenario— an average of the west scenario (which favours British Columbia as the main destination for interprovincial migrants) and the central scenario (which favours Ontario as the main destination for interprovincial migrants).[1]

The assumptions about mortality and fertility directly affect the size of the elderly population. The medium mortality assumption calls for improved life expectancy. Given continual technological innovation and greater attention to women's health issues, greater rather than smaller improvements are more likely. No changes are assumed in the fertility rate, but should it decline to even lower levels in the next 20 years, any combination of improved life expectancy and lower fertility rates will increase the size of the future elderly population even more than what is projected here.

While life expectancy and fertility behaviour are relatively insensitive to changing public policy (for example, the effect of "baby bonus" grants on long-term fertility rates is highly debatable), the magnitude and demographic composition of assumptions about immigration, emigration, returning Canadians and non-permanent residents are very sensitive to changing public policy. On the one hand, future Canadian governments might reduce immigration levels significantly or change the conditions for being a non-permanent resident, which will almost immediately affect the numbers in these categories. Reducing immigration will increase the rate of population aging in the short run, since most immigrants are not elderly, but increasing immigration will reduce the rate of population aging. As long as annual net immigration levels remain less than 1.0% of the total population, immigration's impact on the size of the future elderly population, however, is likely to be minimal (Mitra 1992).

The implications of the above assumptions mainly affect the size of the future elderly population, but the implications of net interprovincial migration will be felt more keenly at the local level. Either a west or central interprovincial migration assumption significantly affects the size of the future elderly population at the local level in many places. For example, the west interprovincial migration assumption calls for British Columbia to continue to be the major destination for interprovincial migrants—both young and old. (However, different age groups will be attracted to different parts of the province, as was demonstrated in Chapter 3.) What also makes the net interprovincial migration assumption different from other assumptions is its greater sensitivity to short-term changes in local economies and relative insensitivity to public policy changes. For example, resource-based communities in Western Canada saw both intense population growth from interprovincial migration during boom periods and population decline during bust periods in the 1970s and 1980s.

TABLE 5.1: PROJECTED CANADIAN POPULATION, 1991 TO 2011

POPULATION COUNTS (THOUSANDS)

YEAR	FEMALES				MALES				TOTAL POPULATION			
	Total population	Population 65+	Population 80+	% 65+ who are 80+	Total population	Population 65+	Population 80+	% 65+ who are 80+	Total population	Population 65+	Population 80+	% 65+ who are 80+
1991	13,730.0	1,834.0	432.0	23.6	13,344.0	1,327.0	226.0	17.0	27,073.0	3,161.0	657.0	20.8
1996	15,126.9	2,116.2	558.6	26.4	14,836.8	1,541.9	284.4	18.4	29,963.7	3,657.9	842.9	23.0
2001	16,096.1	2,320.7	678.3	29.2	15,781.2	1,710.1	339.4	19.8	31,877.3	4,030.8	1,017.7	25.2
2006	17,003.2	2,519.5	811.1	32.2	16,674.3	1,879.8	412.4	21.9	33,677.5	4,399.3	1,223.5	27.8
2011	17,878.5	2,824.9	906.4	32.1	17,541.8	2,156.2	481.7	22.3	35,420.3	4,981.1	1,388.1	27.9

PERCENTAGES

Year	FEMALES		MALES		TOTAL POPULATION	
	% 65+	% 80+	% 65+	% 80+	% 65+	% 80+
1991	13.4	3.1	9.9	1.7	11.7	2.4
1996	14.0	3.7	10.4	1.9	12.2	2.8
2001	14.4	4.2	10.8	2.2	12.6	3.2
2006	14.8	4.8	11.3	2.5	13.1	3.6
2011	15.8	5.1	12.3	2.7	14.1	3.9

Sources: Statistics Canada Projection Series No. 2, 1994; Census of Canada, 1991.

We have seen that the rate of population aging is particularly sensitive to the economic underpinnings of migration flows, particularly for the working-age population. If there was any major shift away from the pattern of in-migration to British Columbia and Ontario, the effect on the rate of population aging would be rapid. In both provinces, migration moderates a significant aging momentum in the current demographic structure.

In sum, Projection Series Number 2 is based on a set of "middle of the road" assumptions. Only dramatic declines in life expectancy or increases in fertility and immigration will lead to a smaller future elderly population than that discussed in the remainder of this chapter. At the local level, the future size of the elderly population might be significantly greater or smaller than what is projected here, depending on local economic performance.

5.1 CANADA'S ELDERLY POPULATION IN 2011

In the projection to 2011, Canada's population will reach 35.4 million and the elderly population will grow to almost 5 million, or 14.1% of the total population (see Table 5.1). Almost 1.4 million Canadians will be 80 or over, representing 27.9% of the population aged 65 and over. While the overall population will be fairly well-balanced between males and females, older women will continue to outnumber older men in 2011. Over 12% of men will be 65 and over compared with 15.8% of women. The gender gap among the elderly will be even more marked for those 80 and over. Men 80 and over will make up 22.3% of the male elderly population. Women 80 and over will be almost one-third (32.1%) of the elderly female population.

Only examining the percentages at different points in time masks the subtler trends that are projected to take place in the coming decades. While the elderly gender gap will continue, the sex ratios will gradually converge (see Table 5.2).

Different ways of measuring the trends lead to different perspectives on the future elderly population. Depending on how we calculate the change in the size of the elderly population between 1991 and some future time period, we may conclude that the elderly population will grow at an astronomic rate, or that it will

TABLE 5.2: RATIO OF MALES PER 100 FEMALES BY AGE, CANADA, 1991 TO 2011

| Year | AGE GROUP | | | |
	55–64	65–74	75–84	85+
1991	96.8	81.7	65.6	43.8
1996	97.7	84.8	65.0	41.9
2001	97.4	88.6	66.2	40.9
2006	97.4	89.7	69.7	40.9
2011	96.5	90.2	73.3	42.2

Sources: Statistics Canada Projection Series No. 2, 1994; Census of Canada, 1991.

grow faster than the total population but at a less-than-alarming rate. The projected change between 1991 and 2011 is an increase of 58% in the elderly population compared with an increase of 31% in the total population. Annualized growth rates, however, show a different picture of the period 1991 to 2011 (see Figure 5.1). The annualized growth rate is projected to slow to about 1.0% for the total population. For the elderly female population it will fall to less than 2.0% before increasing to 2.5% in 2011. For the elderly male population, the pattern is similar, except in 2011 when the annualized growth rate will be closer to 3.0%. This is consistent with the widely held view that the gap in life expectancy between Canadian women and men will narrow in the coming decades. The annualized growth rates for women and men aged 80 and over are projected to slow between 1991 and 2011 as well. In sum, the elderly population will continue to grow at a faster rate than the Canadian population as a whole, but the differences will not be so great that we should fall into the ageist trap of assuming a larger future elderly population will bankrupt our health and social service systems.

The rate of population aging for the population aged 65 and over is projected to remain relatively flat until 2001; after the turn of the century it will begin to increase (see Figure 5.2). For the population 80 and over, the rate of population aging is projected to decline modestly for women and remain virtually unchanged for men.

At the provincial level, Quebec, Manitoba, Saskatchewan and the Atlantic provinces are projected to see their elderly female populations grow to over 17% of the total female population by 2011 (see Figure 5.3). The Ontario and British Columbia elderly female populations will be close to the national proportion of 15.8%; Alberta and the territories will have elderly female populations well below the national proportion. For elderly men a similar pattern can be seen, although the proportions are consistently lower than those for elderly women. Among the female population aged 80 and over, Saskatchewan stands well above the national average proportion, but the Maritime provinces, Quebec, Manitoba and British Columbia also have proportions above the national proportion. The provincial breakdown is similar for men 80 and over, but again the proportions are consistently smaller compared with those for women 80 and over.

When considering the rates of population aging until 2011, it is useful to consider the decades 1991 to 2001 and 2001 to 2011 separately. While the rates for the latter decade are projected to be higher than those for the current decade, the gender differences are important. After 2001, the male population will begin to age significantly faster; the rate for the female population will stay relatively constant over the two decades. With the exception of Newfoundland and the territories, the female rates will be between 5% and 15%, while some of the male rates will exceed 20% in the latter decade. This is clearly a catch-up period, as men's mortality rates are projected to continue to approach those of women.

5.2 AGING ACROSS CANADA

While the growth of the elderly population between 1991 and 2011 will pose fiscal challenges for the federal and provincial governments, providing services

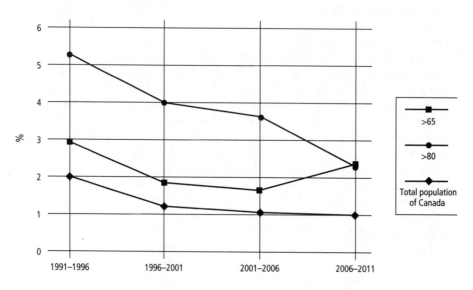

FIGURE 5.1A: ANNUALIZED GROWTH RATES FOR FEMALES, BY AGE, CANADA, 1991 TO 2011

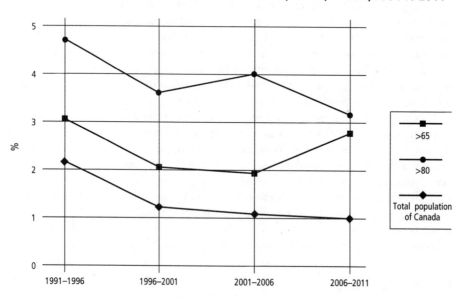

FIGURE 5.1B: ANNUALIZED GROWTH RATES FOR MALES, BY AGE, CANADA, 1991 TO 2011

Source: Statistics Canada Projection Series No. 2, 1994.

FIGURE 5.2A: C_{65+} BY SEX, FOR CANADA, 1991 TO 2011

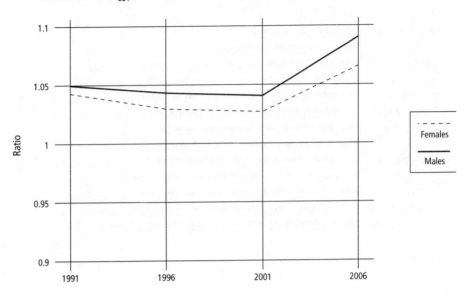

FIGURE 5.2B: C_{80+} BY SEX, FOR CANADA, 1991 TO 2011

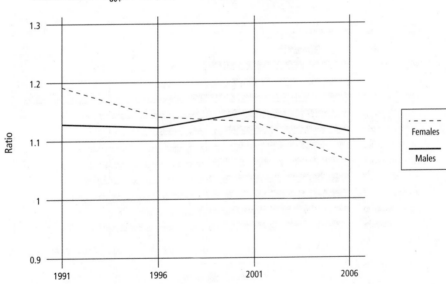

Source: Statistics Canada Projection Series No. 2, 1994.

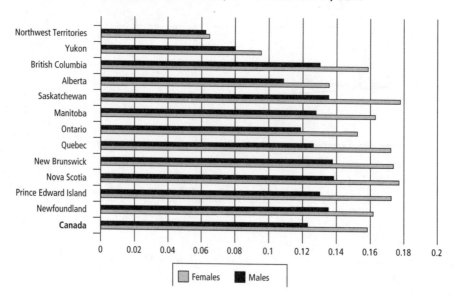

FIGURE 5.3A: PROPORTION 65 AND OVER, BY PROVINCE AND SEX, 2011

FIGURE 5.3B: PROPORTION 80 AND OVER, BY PROVINCE AND SEX, 2011

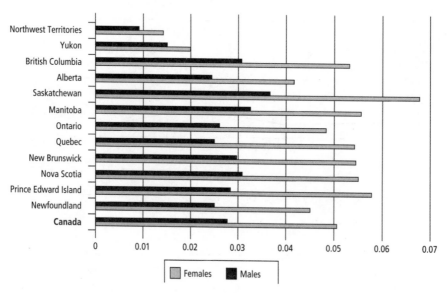

Source: Statistics Canada Projection Series No. 2, 1994.

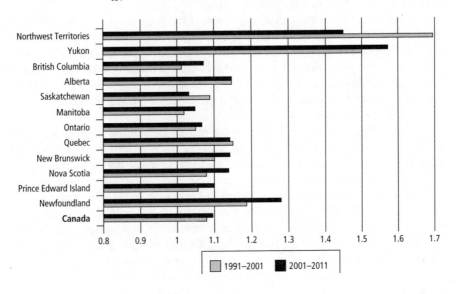

FIGURE 5.4A: C_{65+} VALUES FOR FEMALES, BY PROVINCE, 1991 TO 2011

1991–2001   2001–2011

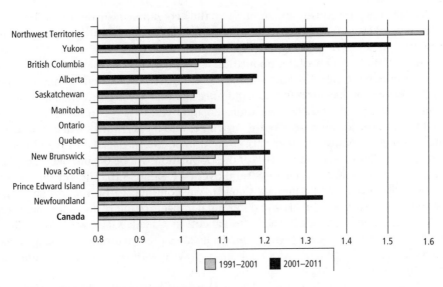

FIGURE 5.4B: C_{65+} VALUES FOR MALES, BY PROVINCE, 1991 TO 2011

1991–2001   2001–2011

Source: Statistics Canada Projection Series No. 2, 1994.

either in homes or in institutions will fall to local governments, agencies and the communities in which elderly people reside.

As a first step in describing the challenge at the local level, an adaptation of a standard cohort survival model for five-year age groups and five-year projection periods is applied to each census division in Canada for the period 1991 to 2011 (Figure 5.4). An option is used to make the cumulative age–gender distribution of the projected populations over the census divisions in a province for each five-year period consistent with the provincial projection from Statistics Canada's Projection Series Number 2.

One way of interpreting the geographic distribution of the elderly population in 2011 is to see Figure 5.5 as a *deepening* of the distribution of the elderly population in 1991 (see Figure 3.1). Most of Nova Scotia, Cape Breton and the Gaspé Peninsula will have census divisions where, by 2011, over 18% of the population is projected to be aged 65 and over. With the exception of Montréal and the census divisions surrounding it, most of the census divisions in West Quebec and many of the census divisions in the Eastern Townships of Quebec will also have populations where more than 18% are aged 65 and over. The elderly population will grow more slowly around Ottawa and Metropolitan Toronto but, in many census divisions throughout the rest of southern Ontario the proportion of the population 65 and over will grow to over 14%, and the census divisions along the shores of Lake Huron will see their elderly proportions grow to over 18%. The core of census divisions in southern Manitoba and Saskatchewan with large elderly populations, first identified in Chapter 3, will increasingly appear as a belt of census divisions spreading from the Manitoba–Ontario border to the edges of British Columbia.

The changes are equally apparent when the geographic distribution of the population aged 80 and over in 2011 (see Figure 5.6) is compared with the geographic distribution in 1991 (see Figure 3.2). In most of Atlantic and Central Canada, between 2.0% and 4.0% of the population in most census divisions will be 80 and over. A core of census divisions will have more than 8.0% of their populations 80 and over. In south-central British Columbia, another cluster of census divisions will have over 6.0% of their populations 80 and over.

In 2011, the northern parts of the provinces and the territories will continue to have younger populations than those found in Southern Canada. In many northern census divisions, less than 10% of the population will be 65 and over (see Figure 5.5) and less than 4% will be 80 and over (see Figure 5.6). The key difference between Northern and Southern Canada will continue to be the younger age structure of Northern Canada and differential impacts of interprovincial migration and immigration, especially in and adjacent to Canada's largest metropolitan areas. The only change that will dramatically alter these patterns will be a fundamental shift in the geography of economic growth, with resulting shifts in migration; this is highly unlikely.

Almost everywhere in Southern Canada, the sex ratios of the elderly population are projected to continue to favour elderly women over elderly men in the year 2011 (see Figure 5.7). However, the gender gap in many census divisions will

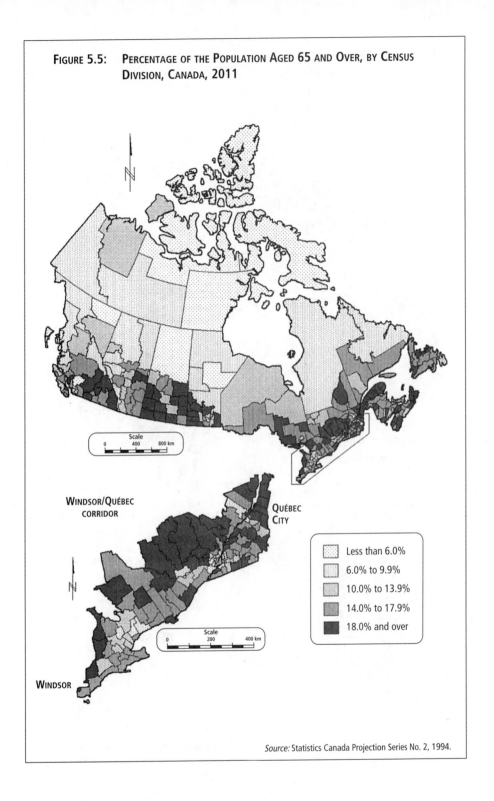

FIGURE 5.5:   PERCENTAGE OF THE POPULATION AGED 65 AND OVER, BY CENSUS
DIVISION, CANADA, 2011

Scale
0   400   800 km

WINDSOR/QUÉBEC
CORRIDOR

QUÉBEC
CITY

Less than 6.0%
6.0% to 9.9%
10.0% to 13.9%
14.0% to 17.9%
18.0% and over

Scale
0   200   400 km

WINDSOR

Source: Statistics Canada Projection Series No. 2, 1994.

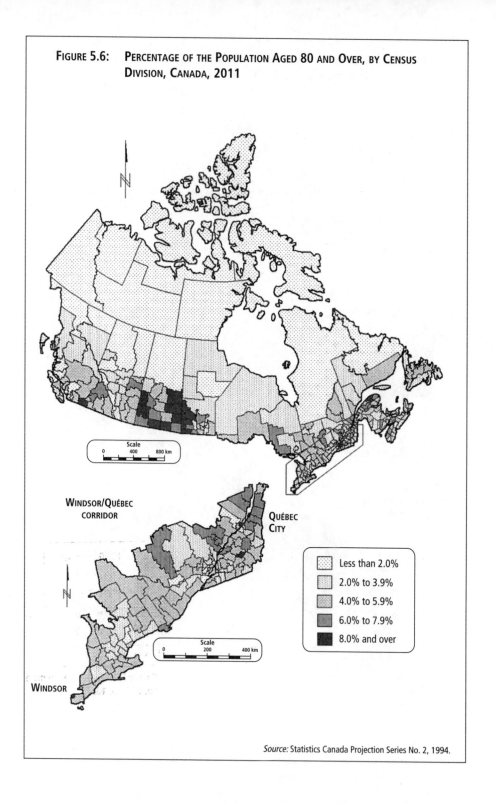

FIGURE 5.6: PERCENTAGE OF THE POPULATION AGED 80 AND OVER, BY CENSUS DIVISION, CANADA, 2011

Scale
0   400   800 km

WINDSOR/QUÉBEC
CORRIDOR

QUÉBEC
CITY

Less than 2.0%
2.0% to 3.9%
4.0% to 5.9%
6.0% to 7.9%
8.0% and over

Scale
0   200   400 km

WINDSOR

Source: Statistics Canada Projection Series No. 2, 1994.

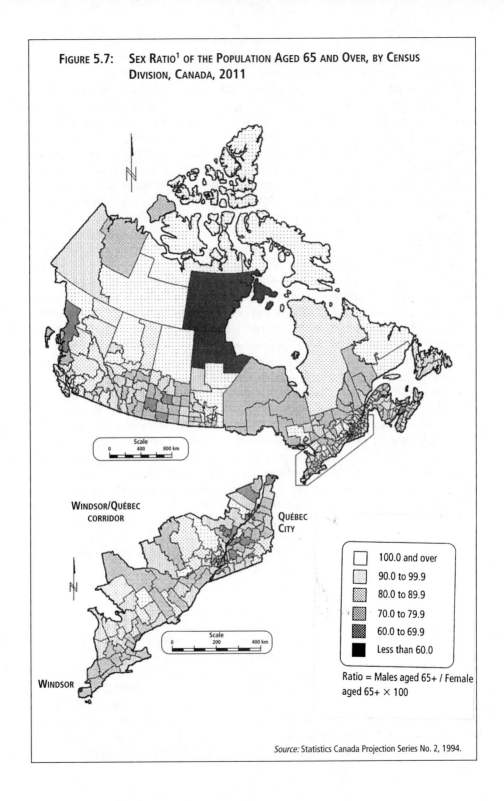

FIGURE 5.7: SEX RATIO[1] OF THE POPULATION AGED 65 AND OVER, BY CENSUS DIVISION, CANADA, 2011

Scale
0 400 800 km

WINDSOR/QUÉBEC CORRIDOR

QUÉBEC CITY

Scale
0 200 400 km

WINDSOR

	100.0 and over
	90.0 to 99.9
	80.0 to 89.9
	70.0 to 79.9
	60.0 to 69.9
	Less than 60.0

Ratio = Males aged 65+ / Female aged 65+ × 100

Source: Statistics Canada Projection Series No. 2, 1994.

decline by 2011 (compare Figure 3.3). In Northern Canada, the opposite will take place. In 2011, the sex ratios will be even lower than they were in 1991 (i.e., the imbalance between elderly women and elderly men will increase).

Across Southern Canada the sex ratios for the population aged 80 and over are projected to be even lower in 2011 (see Figure 5.8) than they were in 1991 (see Figure 3.4). They will also be lower in much of Northern Canada. The different direction in the trends for the population 65 and over (see Figure 5.7) and the population 80 and over is at least partly explained by the narrowing of the gap in life expectancy between males and females taking place in non-elderly age cohorts now; those cohorts will become the young elderly in the early decades of the next century. However, the ratios will increase again in later decades as the younger elderly age according to convergent mortality schedules.

Low fertility rates and increasing growth of the elderly population will mean that, by 2011, many of the census divisions of Southern Canada will have older dependency ratios (ODRs) above 30% (see Figure 5.9). Clusters of census divisions previously mentioned in Nova Scotia, the Gaspé, West Quebec, in southern Manitoba and Saskatchewan, and in the interior of British Columbia particularly stand out in this respect. As might be expected, the census divisions in the northern parts of the provinces and the territories will continue to have lower ODRs than census divisions in the south. These high ODRs do not, however, mean that these communities will need to provide high levels of service for *all* of their elderly populations. As we demonstrated in Chapter 4 and discuss below, most of the elderly population will be disability-free or will not need any help with activities of daily living or instrumental activities of daily living until they are 80 and over.

In 1991, the absolute distribution of the elderly population as a share of the total population by census division favoured Canada's largest metropolitan areas (see Figures 3.6, 5.10). Metropolitan Toronto, Montréal, Vancouver, Calgary and Edmonton each had 2% or more of Canada's elderly population. In 2011, the concentration of the elderly population in the metropolitan areas of Canada is projected to be even greater; many of the largest cities will contain more than 5% of the elderly population. What is also noticeable, particularly in southern Ontario, is the number of census divisions surrounding Metropolitan Toronto that will contain large absolute numbers of elderly. This will represent the third stage in the greying of Canadian cities.[2]

5.3   DISABILITY IN 2011

To create projections of disability in 2011 for Canada and the provinces, disability rates by age and sex from the 1986 Health and Activity Limitation Survey (HALS) were applied to the 1991 Census counts and the projections for 2011. The assumptions underlying this method are that age- and sex-specific disability rates remain constant over time, and that provincial disability rates can be applied to their respective census divisions. Overall disability rates, it is generally believed, will not likely fall in the future. However, one hypothesis suggests that as life expectancy increases, the number of years of disability-free life expectancy will

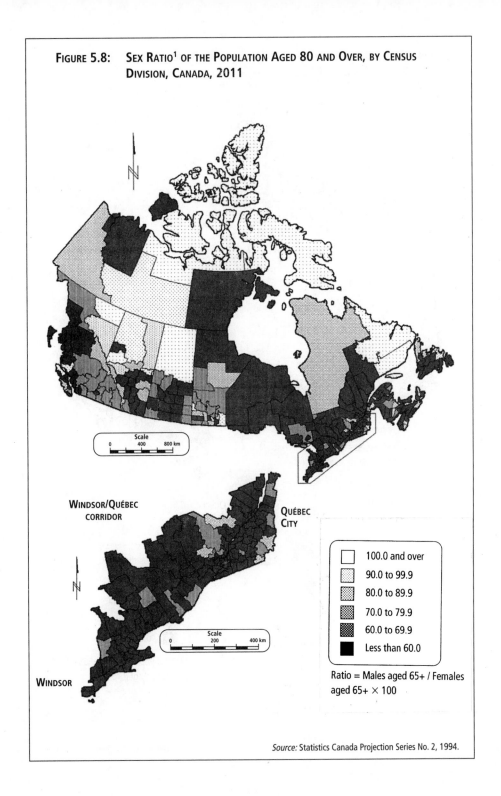

FIGURE 5.8:   SEX RATIO[1] OF THE POPULATION AGED 80 AND OVER, BY CENSUS
DIVISION, CANADA, 2011

WINDSOR/QUÉBEC
CORRIDOR

QUÉBEC
CITY

WINDSOR

Scale
0   200   400 km

Scale
0   400   800 km

	100.0 and over
	90.0 to 99.9
	80.0 to 89.9
	70.0 to 79.9
	60.0 to 69.9
	Less than 60.0

Ratio = Males aged 65+ / Females
aged 65+ × 100

Source: Statistics Canada Projection Series No. 2, 1994.

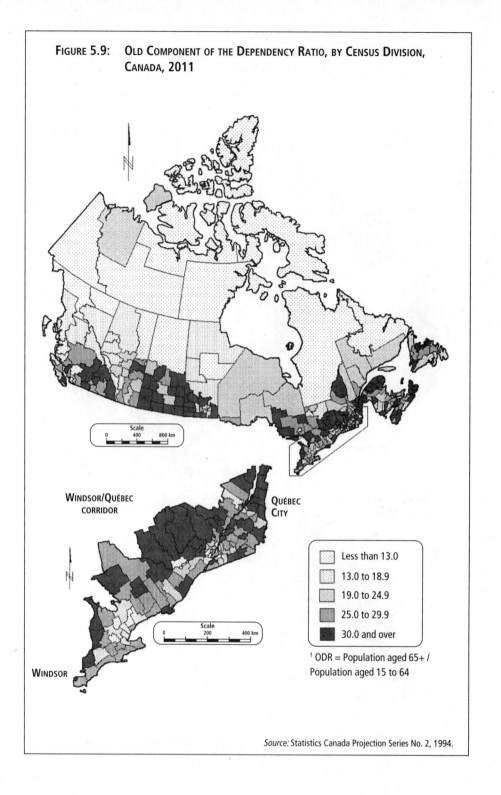

FIGURE 5.9: OLD COMPONENT OF THE DEPENDENCY RATIO, BY CENSUS DIVISION, CANADA, 2011

WINDSOR/QUÉBEC CORRIDOR

QUÉBEC CITY

WINDSOR

Scale
0   400   800 km

Scale
0   200   400 km

Less than 13.0

13.0 to 18.9

19.0 to 24.9

25.0 to 29.9

30.0 and over

[1] ODR = Population aged 65+ / Population aged 15 to 64

Source: Statistics Canada Projection Series No. 2, 1994.

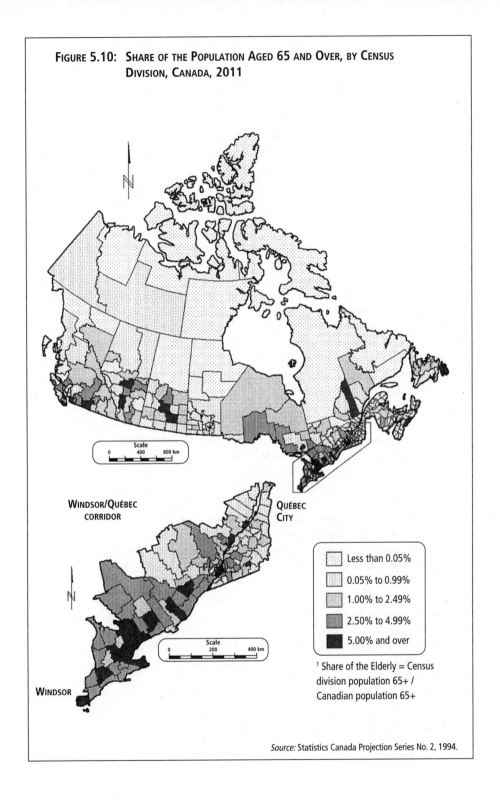

FIGURE 5.10: SHARE OF THE POPULATION AGED 65 AND OVER, BY CENSUS DIVISION, CANADA, 2011

Scale
0   400   800 km

WINDSOR/QUÉBEC CORRIDOR

QUÉBEC CITY

WINDSOR

Scale
0   200   400 km

Less than 0.05%
0.05% to 0.99%
1.00% to 2.49%
2.50% to 4.99%
5.00% and over

[1] Share of the Elderly = Census division population 65+ / Canadian population 65+

Source: Statistics Canada Projection Series No. 2, 1994.

also increase (Wilkins and Adams 1992). This will leave fewer disabled people in younger age cohorts, but many more older disabled people, especially among the old elderly.

Of the 4.98 million people aged 65 and over in 2011, about 1.04 million living outside institutions are projected to have some level of disability. Almost 300,000 are projected to have a severe disability. Using rates based on activities of daily living and instrumental activities of daily living, 100,000 people 65 and over will need help with activities of daily living and 300,000 will need help with instrumental activities of daily living. Given the way the projections have been done, as their age increases the percentage of elderly with severe disabilities will increase, as will the percentage who need help with activities of daily living or instrumental activities of daily living.

At the provincial level, the size of the disabled elderly population will vary significantly because of the differences in age-specific 1986 disability rates and the differences assumed in the population projections by province. However, the proportions of disabled in each province are projected to be the same as they were in 1986 (see Tables 5.3 and 5.4). Provinces where the elderly population is projected to grow most in absolute terms will also experience the greatest growth in their elderly disabled populations. The magnitude of these changes is summarized in Table 5.5 for each province by gender, level of severity, activities of daily living, and instrumental activities of daily living. In every province, the percentage increase will be substantial both in the number of severely disabled elderly and the number who need help with activities of daily living or instrumental activities of daily living. In provinces with small populations, such as Newfoundland and the territories, the percentage increases are partly a result of the small numbers involved in the calculations; but even in these places the absolute number of elderly living outside institutions will pose a great challenge to their communities. In Newfoundland, for example, about 13,000 elderly people living in the community are projected to have severe disabilities. In Ontario, this number will top 207,000.

In projecting the size of the elderly population living in institutional settings in 2011, the rates of institutionalization are assumed to remain constant based on 1986 rates. This assumption needs to be treated with special care, because institutionalization rates are highly dependent on the number of institutional places available in a jurisdiction. Any change in supply would change institutionalization rates.

Given current trends, such high rates of institutionalization may not occur, but this would mean a significant increase in the percentage of the elderly population with severe disabilities living outside institutions who would need a great deal of support for activities of daily living and instrumental activities of daily living. Many would be women 85 and over, without a spouse and with incomes below the low-income cut-off. It will take an enormous commitment of either voluntary support from other elderly people or a mixture of publicly and privately funded formal support services to maintain this part of the elderly population in the community, should institutionalization rates be much lower in the future.

TABLE 5.3: PROJECTED ELDERLY POPULATION, BY DISABILITY STATUS, 2011

Province	Age group	WOMEN						MEN					
		Total population	Not disabled	Mild	Moderate	Severe	Total in institutions	Total population	Not disabled	Mild	Moderate	Severe	Total in institutions
Newfoundland	65–74	24,100	14,000	3,107	3,994	2,537	463	23,500	13,779	3,476	4,473	1,435	338
	75–84	13,800	4,426	1,986	2,300	3,907	1,181	10,700	4,476	1,446	2,403	1,674	702
	85+	6,600	412	872	1,345	2,147	1,824	2,900	497	311	232	1,419	441
Prince Edward Island	65–74	6,100	3,504	1,222	903	387	84	5,500	2,888	1,200	947	419	46
	75–84	4,100	1,602	836	908	508	247	2,800	1,265	596	612	210	117
	85+	2,400	350	246	537	658	607	900	253	66	142	226	213
Nova Scotia	65–74	43,900	24,337	8,366	6,789	3,886	522	39,600	21,746	7,027	6,484	3,878	465
	75–84	27,600	11,777	4,293	5,390	4,062	2,077	20,100	10,016	3,370	3,650	2,201	863
	85+	15,100	1,742	512	4,007	4,871	3,968	6,800	952	563	1,927	2,288	1,070
New Brunswick	65–74	34,100	20,097	5,307	5,526	2,549	621	31,600	17,061	5,154	6,051	2,830	505
	75–84	22,000	8,944	3,187	3,916	3,855	2,097	15,600	6,223	3,597	3,312	1,562	905
	85+	11,700	1,918	1,273	1,484	3,419	3,606	5,100	870	855	752	1,614	1,008
Quebec	65–74	363,400	253,730	35,596	38,168	26,011	9,895	319,100	217,103	45,285	31,879	16,676	8,157
	75–84	233,600	108,529	27,524	35,255	30,822	31,470	154,500	88,520	18,200	16,445	17,513	13,822
	85+	121,200	25,946	3,759	21,747	23,523	46,225	43,800	10,894	6,039	7,728	9,276	9,862
Ontario	65–74	544,800	348,114	72,763	69,382	42,039	12,501	487,000	279,684	106,913	59,890	29,109	11,404
	75–84	355,500	147,167	49,560	67,690	47,813	43,270	263,800	142,104	42,510	36,925	22,481	19,779
	85+	185,700	19,438	12,355	26,476	52,443	74,987	81,000	28,623	4,338	11,489	13,706	22,843

+ + +, – – – Significant at .001
+ +, – – Significant at .01
+, – Significant at .05

(...continued)

Province	Age group	WOMEN						MEN					
		Total population	Not disabled	Mild	Moderate	Severe	Total in institutions	Total population	Not disabled	Mild	Moderate	Severe	Total in institutions
Manitoba	65–74	48,200	29,371	6,935	6,885	4,216	793	42,900	25,134	7,916	5,828	3,458	564
	75–84	32,600	12,056	3,984	8,185	5,348	3,025	24,500	10,731	4,888	3,856	3,242	1,784
	85+	19,000	4,062	895	3,470	4,731	5,842	9,300	706	2,057	3,018	2,303	1,216
Saskatchewan	65–74	40,000	26,771	4,680	5,420	2,385	744	36,400	22,197	5,892	5,317	2,220	773
	75–84	30,100	11,289	3,539	7,531	4,791	2,950	22,800	11,069	2,061	4,969	3,099	1,602
	85+	20,600	4,110	2,404	2,150	4,638	7,298	8,800	1,356	1,595	1,265	2,102	2,482
Alberta	65–74	116,200	76,464	13,550	14,946	8,587	2,653	106,100	62,682	19,906	13,396	7,381	2,734
	75–84	73,100	29,391	7,230	13,451	12,710	10,318	57,600	24,930	8,733	10,043	7,867	6,026
	85+	37,800	5,045	3,301	3,383	4,829	21,242	16,800	2,657	2,749	2,611	3,282	5,500
British Columbia	65–74	188,600	128,396	18,865	24,641	13,969	2,730	180,000	111,736	30,450	22,503	13,022	2,288
	75–84	124,500	56,397	10,380	26,326	17,582	13,815	99,400	52,916	14,385	12,582	13,038	6,480
	85+	73,700	10,666	10,066	9,340	12,908	30,719	33,200	6,395	2,425	3,519	8,747	12,115
Yukon	65–74	1,200	462	522	125	91	– – –	1,100	607	185	268	40	– – –
	75–84	500	30	53	300	117	– – –	400	225	22	51	102	– – –
	85+	200	– – –	66	34	100	– – –	100	– – –	– – –	26	74	– – –
Northwest Territories	65–74	1,700	891	127	139	543	– – –	1,800	616	912	157	116	– – –
	75–84	800	19	148	172	462	– – –	800	80	23	369	327	– – –
	85+	300	– – –	– – –	125	175	– – –	97	43	– – –	54	– – –	– – –

+ + +, – – – Significant at .001
+ +, – – Significant at .01
+, – Significant at .05
Sources: Statistics Canada Projection Series No. 2, 1994; Health and Activity Limitation Survey, 1986.

TABLE 5.4: PROJECTED ELDERLY POPULATION, BY HEALTH STATUS, 2011

Province	Age group	FEMALES Total population	Not disabled	No help with IADL[1] or ADL[2]	Help with IADL	Help with ADL	Total in institutions	MALES Total population	Not disabled	No help with IADL or ADL	Help with IADL	Help with ADL	Total in institutions
Newfoundland	65–74	24,100	14,000	5,522	3,210	906	463	23,500	13,779	7,273	1,428	683	338
	75–84	13,800	4,426	3,637	3,125	1,432	1,181	10,700	4,476	3,150	1,566	806	702
	85+	6,600	412	592	1,487	2,285	1,824	2,900	497	889	423	650	441
Prince Edward Island	65–74	6,100	3,504	1,896	460	156	84	5,500	2,888	2,147	243	175	46
	75–84	4,100	1,602	1,199	769	283	247	2,800	1,265	945	356	118	117
	85+	2,400	350	284	875	283	607	900	253	235	88	111	213
Nova Scotia	65–74	43,900	24,337	12,210	5,901	929	522	39,600	21,746	12,954	2,910	1,525	465
	75–84	27,600	11,777	6,619	5,539	1,587	2,077	20,100	10,016	6,245	2,272	705	863
	85+	15,100	1,742	868	5,167	3,355	3,968	6,800	952	1,982	1,753	1,043	1,070
New Brunswick	65–74	34,100	20,097	8,947	3,745	690	621	31,600	17,061	10,577	2,243	1,214	505
	75–84	22,000	8,944	5,627	4,102	1,230	2,097	15,600	6,223	5,856	1,873	743	905
	85+	11,700	1,918	1,387	3,474	1,315	3,606	5,100	870	650	1,646	926	1,008
Quebec	65–74	363,400	253,729	50,455	41,478	7,843	9,895	319,100	217,104	68,394	18,017	7,429	8,157
	75–84	233,600	108,529	39,089	38,626	15,886	31,470	154,500	88,520	28,002	17,328	6,827	13,822
	85+	121,200	25,946	11,341	26,722	10,966	46,225	43,800	10,894	8,972	7,026	7,045	9,862
Ontario	65–74	544,800	348,115	111,429	55,289	17,466	12,501	487,000	279,684	159,279	25,672	10,961	11,404
	75–84	355,500	147,166	83,487	65,182	16,395	43,270	263,800	142,104	68,506	20,956	12,454	19,779
	85+	185,700	19,438	24,879	49,831	16,565	74,987	81,000	28,623	8,655	12,720	8,159	22,843

+ + +, – – – Significant at .001
+ +, – – Significant at .01
+, – Significant at .05
1. Instrumental activities of daily living.
2. Activities of daily living.

(...continued)

TABLE 5.4: PROJECTED ELDERLY POPULATION, BY HEALTH STATUS, 2011 (CONTINUED)

FEMALES

Province	Age group	Total population	Not disabled	No help with IADL[1] or ADL[2]	Help with IADL	Help with ADL	Total in institutions
Manitoba	65–74	48,200	29,371	9,923	6,606	1,506	793
	75–84	32,600	12,056	9,694	5,115	2,709	3,025
	85+	19,000	4,062	1,095	2,706	5,295	5,842
Saskatchewan	65–74	40,000	26,771	7,699	3,789	997	744
	75–84	30,100	11,289	7,163	7,016	1,683	2,950
	85+	20,600	4,110	2,345	4,373	2,474	7,298
Alberta	65–74	116,200	76,464	21,226	11,831	4,026	2,653
	75–84	73,100	29,391	13,305	16,661	3,424	10,318
	85+	37,800	5,045	4,280	4,310	2,923	21,242
British Columbia	65–74	188,600	128,396	33,523	19,813	4,139	2,730
	75–84	124,500	56,397	18,726	29,808	5,754	13,815
	85+	73,700	10,666	13,016	10,474	8,824	30,720
Yukon	65–74	1,200	462	606	105	27	– – –
	75–84	500	30	83	327	60	– – –
	85+	200	– – –	100	33	67	– – –
Northwest Territories	65–74	1,700	891	180	464	165	– – –
	75–84	800	19	7	594	181	– – –
	85+	262	– – –	– – –	166	96	– – –

MALES

Province	Age group	Total population	Not disabled	No help with IADL or ADL	Help with IADL	Help with ADL	Total in institutions
Manitoba	65–74	42,900	25,134	13,323	2,237	1,642	564
	75–84	24,500	10,731	7,833	2,879	1,273	1,784
	85+	9,300	706	3,353	2,295	1,730	1,216
Saskatchewan	65–74	36,400	22,197	11,036	1,442	951	773
	75–84	22,800	11,069	6,182	2,163	1,784	1,602
	85+	8,800	1,356	2,271	1,512	1,179	2,482
Alberta	65–74	106,100	62,682	34,795	4,054	1,835	2,734
	75–84	57,600	24,930	19,019	4,476	3,149	6,026
	85+	16,800	2,657	4,149	2,975	1,518	5,500
British Columbia	65–74	180,000	111,737	51,386	9,718	4,871	2,288
	75–84	99,400	52,916	21,147	12,060	6,797	6,480
	85+	33,200	6,395	3,862	7,670	3,158	12,115
Yukon	65–74	1,100	607	262	65	166	– – –
	75–84	400	225	88	46	41	– – –
	85+	100	– – –	14	86	– – –	– – –
Northwest Territories	65–74	1,800	616	1,024	103	57	– – –
	75–84	800	80	644	46	30	– – –
	85+	100	43	25	33	– – –	– – –

+ + +, – – – Significant at .001
+ +, – – Significant at .01
+, – Significant at .05
1. Instrumental activities of daily living.
2. Activities of daily living.
Sources: Statistics Canada Projection Series No. 2,1994; Health and Activity Limitation Survey, 1986.

TABLE 5.5: PERCENTAGE INCREASE IN POPULATION 65 AND OVER, BY DISABILITY STATUS AND HEALTH STATUS, FOR PROVINCES, 2011

Province	PERCENTAGE INCREASE BY DISABILITY STATUS					PERCENTAGE INCREASE BY HEALTH STATUS				
	Not disabled	Mild	Moderate	Severe	Total in institutions	Not disabled	No help with IADL[1] or ADL[2]	Help with IADL	Help with ADL	Total in institutions
Females (%)										
Newfoundland	40.0	47.0	49.0	53.2	75.0	40.0	41.7	49.5	72.4	75.0
Prince Edward Island	23.6	25.2	30.9	41.6	56.3	23.6	24.2	40.9	39.4	56.3
Nova Scotia	25.4	25.1	36.2	44.3	60.5	25.4	25.4	40.0	57.7	60.5
New Brunswick	27.6	31.7	32.3	46.0	62.6	27.6	29.5	42.9	50.1	62.6
Quebec	47.3	49.3	63.7	70.6	99.0	47.3	53.5	65.6	75.4	99.0
Ontario	47.4	53.1	59.6	75.2	96.9	47.4	55.0	69.7	71.2	96.9
Manitoba	12.0	11.8	18.4	26.4	45.7	12.0	11.6	17.7	41.5	45.7
Saskatchewan	6.2	16.3	12.6	32.4	62.6	6.2	10.9	23.7	40.0	62.6
Alberta	64.6	72.1	71.9	79.5	121.6	64.6	70.8	75.4	85.0	121.6
British Columbia	48.6	67.4	61.0	74.7	125.8	48.6	62.1	64.4	96.0	125.8
Yukon	243.0	257.8	254.6	295.1	— —	243.0	261.4	254.4	316.0	— —
Northwest Territories	294.8	282.5	266.7	275.8	— —	294.8	282.5	274.6	270.8	— —
Males (%)										
Newfoundland	47.1	48.4	46.9	60.2	58.8	47.1	49.2	50.4	59.6	58.8
Prince Edward Island	25.6	24.8	24.9	29.5	33.4	25.6	25.8	23.2	28.9	33.4
Nova Scotia	35.5	36.7	42.7	49.5	61.1	35.5	39.0	48.2	52.5	61.1
New Brunswick	37.2	39.4	38.8	48.1	55.8	37.2	37.2	48.9	50.8	55.8
Quebec	62.4	65.5	69.7	77.9	86.6	62.4	65.4	74.5	85.1	86.6
Ontario	66.4	62.5	70.6	79.6	102.0	66.4	63.5	80.3	86.0	102.0
Manitoba	19.1	25.7	31.2	32.9	40.0	19.1	25.5	36.6	39.5	40.0
Saskatchewan	5.9	10.5	10.4	19.1	31.4	5.9	9.4	19.8	20.6	31.4
Alberta	76.1	78.9	82.6	87.7	99.3	76.1	79.6	91.0	92.6	99.3
British Columbia	66.7	67.6	71.0	85.3	118.0	66.7	67.0	87.0	83.9	118.0
Yukon	177.9	174.1	179.0	202.7	— —	177.9	179.2	201.9	176.2	— —
Northwest Territories	205.2	215.6	208.7	233.6	— —	205.2	221.1	183.6	223.9	— —

+ + +, - - -   Significant at .001
+ +, - -   Significant at .01
+, -   Significant at .05
1. Instrumental activities of daily living.
2. Activities of daily living.
Sources: Statistics Canada Projection Series No. 2, 1994; Census of Canada, 1991.

Without a significant public commitment to support elderly people in the community, the prospect arises of a market-driven system that creates service-rich and service-poor elderly individuals and, just as problematic, service-rich and service-poor areas. If the provision of services is a function of the ability to pay, those communities with greater individual and aggregate resources will tend to provide more and better services. The enhanced service infrastructure will be more attractive to those who can afford to move, with consequences in both origin and destination areas. Sustained over one or two decades, the aggregate resources of the service-rich will tend to increase and those of the service-poor decrease in a manner anticipated by Tiebout's (1956) model of local services. The outcome will be a significant widening of the gap in service access between rich and poor communities.

5.4 CONCLUSION

Almost 5 million people, or 14.1% of the population, are projected to be 65 or over in 2011. Demographically, there will still be more elderly women than men, more of the elderly population will be 80 or over, and dependency ratios will be higher than they were in 1991. Geographically, the patterns that existed in 1991 will likely become more defined, accentuating the relative concentration of elderly in high-amenity areas in southern British Columbia and Ontario as the result of growth trends, and in Saskatchewan and Manitoba as the result of shrinking trends, particularly in younger age cohorts. In absolute terms, the spatial distribution of the elderly population will continue to reflect the concentration of Canada's population in its largest metropolitan areas. As the result of the dominance of aging in place, some of the fastest-growing outer suburbs around Canada's largest cities will likely show early signs of growing elderly populations.

Using disability rates from the 1986 HALS to project the health status of the elderly population in 2011 suggests that most of the future elderly population will be disability-free or only mildly disabled. It is also apparent, however, that there will be a large percentage of people on both the national and provincial scales, particularly among those 85 and over, with severe disabilities or who will need help with either activities of daily living or instrumental activities of daily living. There will also be a substantial institutional population, especially aged 85 and over and female.

Estimating the future institutional population at the local level is particularly problematic. We know very little about the dynamics of moves into and out of institutions, or even about the differential mortality experience of the institutional and non-institutional populations (see Chapter 4). However, what proportions of moves to and from institutions are local as opposed to migrations will affect demand at the local level. Clearly, this is an area that deserves much more attention by researchers using a longitudinal approach to data collection and analysis.

Even if governments were to maintain their transfers to the elderly, public pension plans and the current number of institutional places, the size of the elderly population suffering severe disabilities and living outside institutions will present a major service-delivery challenge to communities across Canada. This challenge becomes even greater should the deinstitutionalization trend of the 1970s and 1980s continue, with the concomitant increase in the number of elderly who are severely disabled, in need of help and living outside institutions. The risk is that the failure to recognize the magnitude of these changes will shift the responsibility for support to the informal sector or private sector, creating service-rich and service-poor elderly individuals drawing on their own resources and networks, and service-rich and service-poor communities drawing on the organizational abilities of non-profit groups and the commitment of local governments.

ENDNOTES

1. For more detailed information on the assumptions underlying the Projections Series, see Statistics Canada (1994).

2. The first stage of the greying of Canadian cities was the concentration of the elderly population near the central business districts. The second stage, now taking place, is the growing concentration of the elderly population in the older suburban areas. The third stage, which will begin in the next century, will see the outer suburbs begin to grey as working-age people living there today age in place.

CHAPTER

6

CONCLUSIONS

The 1991 Census and surveys such as the Health and Activity Limitation Survey, the Survey on Ageing and Independence and the General Social Survey have allowed us to draw a portrait of Canada's elderly population that illustrates its demographic structure, geographical variation, socio-economic characteristics and health status. The ground floor of the analysis was the description of demographic structure and change in the elderly population at the national and provincial levels in Chapter 1. The second storey was the interplay among some basic socio-economic characteristics of the elderly population and mobility, migration and location (Chapter 2). How the elderly population is geographically distributed across Canada at the census division level, and the different impacts that aging in place and migration have on where the elderly population is concentrated, was the third storey of our analysis (Chapter 3). The fourth storey was a profile of the health status of the elderly population (Chapter 4). In the penultimate chapter— the attic—projections of the elderly population and its health status to the year 2011 were undertaken to demonstrate what the future geography of the elderly population might look like under a specific set of assumptions.

The current policy discussion about the elderly is infused with misconceptions and misapprehensions (McDaniel 1987; Northcott 1994). Perhaps the most serious of these misconceptions is that the great increases in benefits to the elderly over the last four decades mean there is no longer a significant portion living below the poverty line. Among the more widespread misapprehensions is that the elderly population will be so large in the future that it will require many more supporting resources. It is such misconceptions and misapprehensions that have led many policy makers and members of the public to believe that the elderly no longer need public programs, or that the growth of the elderly population under-lies many of our current or future public policy dilemmas.

In 1991, Canada's elderly population reached 3.2 million, or 12.0% of the total population. The population 80 and over reached 657,000, or 2.4% of the population. The sex ratio for the elderly population was 72 men for every 100 women and the older dependency ratio was 17.2% compared with 30.1% for the population under 15. In other words, the population under 15 (5.7 million people) is still 80% larger than the population 65 and over (3.2 million). The geographical distribution of the elderly population in general reflects the distribution of the total population; most of the elderly population now live in urban areas and many of them live in the largest metropolitan areas.

We showed that when the elderly population is disaggregated by age cohort, women predominate among those 75 and over; many such women are widowed and live alone. An astonishing 40% of these women live below the low-income cut-off defined by Statistics Canada. While there is debate over the accuracy of the low-income cut-off for defining poverty among the elderly, it nevertheless stresses the concentration of economic vulnerability within a particular but substantial sub-group of Canada's elderly population. In this age cohort, only a small percentage of women or men who live alone have close family members or friends living nearby. While we are also able to show that migration and local moves allow some elderly to move nearer to family or friends either in anticipation of declining health status or as a response to a major life course event (such as the death of a spouse), elderly who live in lower-priced housing markets or have limited financial resources often cannot make such moves; this restricts their independence. There is clearly a significant and predominately female segment of the elderly population made up of people who have neither the personal means nor the informal networks to support themselves, but who live independently in their later years (see Chapter 2). These findings alone should give pause to those intent on reforming the social safety net for Canada's seniors based on the assumption that there is no longer an economically vulnerable elderly population.

Within this demographic context, the health status of Canada's elderly population was examined. The overwhelming majority of the young elderly are disability-free or their disabilities are so mild that they need no support. However, after age 80 the prevalence and severity of disability increases rapidly, significantly affecting the need for support for both activities of daily living and instrumental activities of daily living. When analysed in a multivariate framework, we show that the likelihood of severe disability is associated with being part of the old elderly population as well as having a low income and less education. Those who are more likely to seek help from formal agencies are older females who live alone. Furthermore, among the severely disabled population, a significant proportion—20% to 50% depending on the type of service—reported either that they needed help and were not getting it or that they needed more help.

We have tried to avoid imputing causality to the correlates among the elderly population's demographic, socio-economic and health characteristics. However, from a policy perspective we cannot ignore the fact that many who are least able to maintain their economic and social independence are likely to, as a result of severe disability or the need for help with activities of daily living or instrumental activities of daily living, place the greatest pressures on public agencies.

While population aging and its consequences are national phenomena, we also emphasize that the geography of Canada's elderly population is far from uniform. The total population is highly concentrated in major urban areas, but there are clearly parts of British Columbia, Saskatchewan, Manitoba, Ontario and the Atlantic provinces where, in *relative* terms, the elderly population has concentrated in a different pattern from that of the total population. In Chapter 3, we showed that the relative concentration of the elderly population is the result of the differential impacts that aging in place and migration are having on local communities. Although aging in place is the dominant process in much of the country—implying that the shape of tomorrow's elderly population is largely a function of today's age structure—net migration remains an important influence in many areas. In fact, it is dominant in much of the Prairie and Atlantic provinces. Aging is also dependent on the migration patterns of working-age people—strong outflows from many rural areas and small towns, and concentrations in the areas of economic growth in British Columbia and Ontario. It is the communities whose younger members are leaving in substantial numbers that are aging fastest. These are also the census divisions that tend to comprise smaller towns and rural areas, that are poorer, and that have populations that are growing little or are actually shrinking. The geography of disability mirrors the geography of the elderly population. This combination of characteristics suggests that these poorer, small-town or rural places are where the relative demand for services by the elderly will be greatest, and where the communities themselves will be least able to provide services because they will likely have shrinking tax bases.

There is some shift in the momentum of population aging in Canada's largest cities. Their age structure is now generating significant proportionate growth of young elderly, particularly in suburban areas. The concentration of the old elderly in the largest cities, and the high proportion of women in this group, will continue through 2011. After that the growth in the proportion of those 80 and over will also be increasingly apparent in the rest of urban Canada.

In Canada's largest metropolitan areas, relative concentrations of the elderly population can be found increasingly in the older suburbs and in those parts of the region whose residents are poorer and less educated. What distinguishes the geographical pattern of the elderly and the disabled at the census tract level in Toronto, Montréal and Vancouver is the moderating effect that immigration plays. Immigrants' younger age distribution and lower likelihood of disability have reduced population aging in Canada's largest cities. This moderating effect will continue at least into the early part of the next century.

It is also important to note that one segment of the elderly and disabled population lives under much different conditions than those discussed above. Despite the deinstitutionalization trend in the 1970s and 1980s, the absolute size of Canada's institutional population has continued to increase. In 1991, most of the 260,000 people in institutions were elderly; the highest proportions were very old and female. The age-specific rates of institutionalization have changed little in the last decade so that, as the elderly population grows over the next 20 years, keeping up with the demand for institutional space will be the crucial issue. If the number of spaces does not keep pace, who will be accommodated and who will continue to live in the community? While family supports may absorb some of the need, our research suggests that many of those eligible for institutional support are women with few family and friends available to help them manage in the community. This suggests there will be greater demand for public and private agencies to provide long-term care and in-home services in the community. Because older women living alone are economically vulnerable, they are not likely to have the resources to buy services they need from the private sector, and the voluntary and public sectors may not have the capacity to offer the services without more resources from higher levels of government.

The penultimate chapter of this study shows projections of demographic trends for the elderly population to the year 2011. By the very nature of the cohort survival model and its built-in assumptions, the geographical patterns of those demographic trends represent a deepening of the trends apparent in 1991. Amenity-rich areas in British Columbia, southern Ontario and the Atlantic provinces will continue to see their elderly populations grow. The elderly population will also continue to grow in rural Canada, especially in Saskatchewan and Manitoba, but for different reasons—the loss of younger people and aging in place of the older population. There will be some shifts in momentum as aging in place in predominantly urban Canada drives the growth of the elderly population. Aging of the younger elderly will accelerate in the cities and decline somewhat in rural and small-town Canada, although rates of aging for the oldest groups will continue to be highest in the Prairie and Atlantic provinces. The geographical pattern of the disabled elderly population will mirror the geographical pattern of the entire elderly population. This will mean that communities where the elderly are likely to concentrate will face even greater challenges to provide support in the next century than those already described.

These challenges will be compounded by how governments choose to alter transfer payments and public pensions to the elderly, governments' direct and indirect support of community services to help the elderly remain independent, and governments' institutionalization policies. Much of the current policy debate about reforming Canada's system of transfer payments to the elderly assumes that the conditions of the elderly population in 1991 will be the conditions of the elderly population in 2011 or into the future. But we saw that even in 1991 a substantial part of the elderly population lived below low-income cut-off lines and had limited informal support networks. Although it was beyond the scope of this book, the future elderly are in the labour force today. Someone who was 35 in 1991 will be 65 in 2021. He or she is likely to have experienced more unemployment, under-employment and part-time employment than someone who turned 65 in 1991 or even 2011. People turning 65 in 2021 are less likely to have built up as large an asset base as today's elderly have, and will therefore probably live less comfortably than do today's elderly.

A larger elderly population in 2011 will also mean greater need for support in the community. As Canadian society becomes increasingly mobile and the economic demands on the working-age population—especially women—grow, informal support networks of family and friends of elderly individuals will shrink. One possibility is that the younger elderly, who already play a major role in supporting their older relatives and friends, will be called upon to increase that role given their growing numbers. Alternatively, local governments, non-profit organizations and private agencies may increase their role in supporting the elderly population in the community.

Without strong public policies to ensure uniform levels of community support for the elderly, the quantity and quality of support will vary as a function of the economic resources, organizational abilities and commitment of individuals and their communities. The outcome would likely be a patchwork of service-rich and service-poor places for the elderly across Canada; if government transfers are reduced, leaving the elderly to pay for their services, then the service-rich communities would likely attract those who can afford to move there, exacerbating the difficulties of service-poor communities that would be increasingly populated by poorer elderly with greater needs for services.

The final issue that needs to be considered for its policy implications is the future of the institutionalized elderly. The size of the institutionalized elderly population projected to the year 2011 is dependent on governments' willingness to create publicly funded institutional spaces. If an effective policy of deinstitutionalization is in place, or if the number of institutional spaces grows more slowly than the elderly population, then the increased number of elderly with severe and multiple disabilities living in the community will put even more pressure on them and on their families, friends and communities to support them.

From today into the next century, most of Canada's elderly will be active and independent, and will have the social and economic means to maintain themselves. A significant portion of them, however, will not have adequate financial and social supports in their latter years; their numbers will continue to grow up to and beyond 2011. The question we must face today is whether the public policies adopted now will create equality of services or service-rich and service-poor elderly and communities in the future.

REFERENCES

Adams, O. 1990. "Life expectancy in Canada—an overview." *Health Reports.* 2,4: 361–376. Statistics Canada Catalogue no. 82-003.

Angus, D. 1984. "The long-term budgetary problem." *Report of the Policy Forum on Medicare in an Age of Restraint.* Kingston, Ontario: John Deutsch Institute.

Aronson, J. 1994. "Women's sense of responsibility for the care of old people: 'But who else is going to do it?'" In V. Marshall and B. McPherson, eds. *Aging Canadian Perspectives.* Peterborough, Ontario: Broadview Press. 175–194.

Auditor General of Canada. 1993. *Report of the Auditor General of Canada to the House of Commons.* Ottawa: Minister of Supply and Services Canada.

Barer, M.L., R.G. Evans and C. Hertzman. 1995. "Avalanche or glacier? Health care and the demographic rhetoric." *Canadian Journal on Aging.* 14, 2: 193–224.

Barer, M.L., R.G. Evans, C. Hertzman and J. Lomas. 1987. "Aging and health care utilization: new evidence on old fallacies." *Social Science and Medicine.* 24, 10: 851–862.

Beaujot, R. 1991. *Population change in Canada: the challenges of policy adaptation.* Toronto: McClelland and Stewart.

Bekkering, M. 1990. *Patterns of change in the spatial distribution of the elderly, 1966–1986.* Unpublished MA Thesis, Department of Geography, Queen's University, Kingston, Ontario.

Bergob, M. 1995. "Destination preferences and motives of senior and non-senior interprovincial migrants in Canada." *Canadian Studies in Population.* 22, 1: 31–48.

Boyd, M. 1989. "Immigration and income security policies in Canada: implications for elderly immigrant women." *Population Research and Policy Review.* 8, 1: 5–24.

Chen, J.G., R. Verma, M.V. George and S.Y. Dai. 1993. *The demography of disability in Canada: current trends and projections among the working-age population.* Paper presented at the Conference of the International Union for the Scientific Study of Population, Montréal.

Connidis, I.A. 1994. "Growing up and old together: some observations on families in later life." In V. Marshall and B. McPherson, eds. *Aging Canadian Perspectives.* Peterborough, Ontario: Broadview Press. 195–205.

Crimmins, E.M. and Y. Saito. 1990. *Getting better and getting worse: transitions in functional status among older Americans.* Paper presented at the Annual Meeting of the Population Association of America, Toronto.

Denton, F.T., and B.G. Spencer. 1995. "Demographic change and the cost of publicly funded health care." *Canadian Journal on Aging.* 14, 2: 174-192.

Denton, F.T., S.N. Li and B.G. Spencer. 1987. "How will population aging affect the future costs of maintaining health-care standards?" In V.W. Marshall, ed. *Aging in Canada: Social Perspectives,* Second Edition. Toronto: Fitzhenry and Whiteside.

Desjardins, B. 1993. *Population Ageing and the Elderly.* Ottawa: Minister of Industry, Science and Technology Canada. Statistics Canada Catalogue no. 91-533E.

Dooley, M. 1994. "Women, children and poverty in Canada." *Canadian Public Policy.* 20, 4: 430-443.

Dunn, P.A. 1990. *Barriers confronting seniors with disabilities in Canada.* Ottawa: Minister of Regional Industrial Expansion Canada. Statistics Canada Catalogue no. 82-615, Vol. 1.

Evans, R.G. 1987. "Hang together or hang separately: the viability of a universal health care system in an aging society." *Canadian Public Policy.* 13, 2: 165-180.

Foot, D.K. 1982. *Canada's Population Outlook: Demographic Futures and Economic Challenges.* Ottawa: Canadian Institute for Economic Policy.

Foot, D.K. 1989. "Public expenditures, population aging and economic dependency in Canada, 1921-2021." *Population Research and Policy Review.* 8, 1: 97-117.

Fournier, G.M., D. Rasmussen and W. Serow. 1988. "Elderly migration: for sun and money." *Population Research and Public Policy.* 7,2: 189-199.

Frey, W.H. 1986. "Lifecourse migration and redistribution of the elderly across U.S. regions and metropolitan areas." *Economic Outlook USA.* 1986 2nd quarter: 10-16.

Frey, W.H. 1992. "Metropolitan redistribution of the U.S. elderly, 1960-70, 1970-80, 1980-90." In A. Rogers, ed. *Elderly migration and population redistribution: A comparative study.* London: Belhaven.

Frey, W.H. 1995. "Elderly demographic profiles of U.S. states: impacts of 'new elderly births,' migration and immigration." *The Gerontologist.* 35: 6.

Gee, E.M. and M.M. Kimball. 1987. *Women and Aging.* Toronto: Butterworths.

Gee, E.M. and S.A. McDaniel. 1994. "Social policy for an aging society." In V. Marshall and B. McPherson, eds. *Aging Canadian Perspectives.* Peterborough, Ontario: Broadview Press. 219-231.

George, M.V., A. Romaniuc and F. Nault. 1990. *Effects of fertility and international migration on the changing age composition in Canada.* Paper presented at the Conference of European Statisticians, Ottawa.

Gibson, D.M., and D.T. Rowland. 1984. "Community vs. institutional care: the case of the Australian aged." *Social Science and Medicine.* 18, 11: 997–1004.

Golant, S. 1992. "The suburbanization of the U.S. elderly." In A. Rogers, ed. *Elderly migration and population redistribution: A comparative study.* London: Belhaven. 163–180.

Grant, P.R. and B. Rice. 1983. "Transportation problems of the rural elderly: a needs assessment." *Canadian Journal on Aging.* 2, 3: 107–124.

Havens, B. 1995. "Long-term care diversity within the care continuum." *Canadian Journal on Aging.* 14, 2: 245–262.

Health and Welfare Canada. 1989. *Charting Canada's Future: A Report of the Demographic Review.* Ottawa: Minister of Supply and Services Canada.

Henripin, J. 1994. "The financial consequences of population aging." *Canadian Public Policy.* 20, 1: 78–94.

Kalbach, W.E., and W.W. McVey. 1971. *The Demographic Bases of Canadian Society.* Toronto: McGraw-Hill Ryerson.

Kalbach, W.E., and W.W. McVey. 1979. *The Demographic Bases of Canadian Society,* Second Edition. Toronto: McGraw-Hill Ryerson.

Kleinbaum, D.G. 1994. *Logistic Regression: A Self-learning Text.* New York: Springer.

Litwak, E. and C.F. Longino. 1987. "Migration patterns among the elderly: a developmental perspective." *The Gerontologist.* 27: 266–272.

Marshall, V. 1994. "A critique of Canadian aging and health policy." In V. Marshall and B. McPherson, eds. *Aging: Canadian Perspectives.* Peterborough, Ontario: Broadview Press. 232–244.

McCarthy, K. 1983. *The Elderly Population's Changing Spatial Distribution: Patterns of Change since 1960.* Santa Monica: The Rand Corporation.

McDaniel, S.A. 1986. *Canada's Aging Population.* Toronto: Butterworths.

McDaniel, S.A. 1987. "Demographic aging as a guiding paradigm in Canada's welfare state." *Canadian Public Policy.* 13, 3: 330–36.

McDowell, I. 1988. *A Disability Score for the Health and Activity Limitation Survey.* Ottawa: Statistics Canada. Staff paper STC2204.

McGuinness, D. 1996. Unpublished MA Thesis, Department of Geography, Queen's University, Kingston, Ontario.

McKeown, T. 1988. *The Origins of Human Disease.* Oxford: Basil Blackwell.

McVey, W.W. and W.E. Kalbach. 1995. *Canadian Population.* Toronto: Nelson.

Menken, J.L. 1985. "Age and fertility: how late can you wait?" *Demography.* 22, 4: 469–484.

Mitra, S. 1992. "Below replacement fertility, net international migration and Canada's future population." *Canadian Studies in Population.* 19, 1: 27–46.

Moore, E.G. 1992. *A geographic perspective on the demography of disability.* Paper presented at the annual meetings of the Association of American Geographers, San Diego.

Moore, E.G. 1993. *What questions shall we ask? Data availability and analytic strategies in population geography.* Annual lecture on new directions in population geography, presented at the annual meetings of the Association of American Geographers, Atlanta.

Moore, E.G. and W.A.V. Clark. 1987. "Stable structure and local variation: a comparison of household flows in four metropolitan areas." *Urban Studies.* 23, 3: 185-196.

Moore, E.G., and M.W. Rosenberg. 1988. *Population Redistribution of the Elderly and Its Impact on Government Services and Government Financing.* For the Review of Demography. Kingston, Ontario: Department of Geography, Queen's University.

Moore, E.G., and M.W. Rosenberg. 1991. *Disabled Adults in Ontario Institutions.* For the Ontario Ministry of Community and Social Services. Kingston, Ontario: Department of Geography, Queen's University.

Moore, E.G., and M.W. Rosenberg. 1992. *A Review of Demographic Studies of Persons with Disabilities.* For Mainstream 1992. Kingston, Ontario: Department of Geography, Queen's University.

Moore, E.G., and M.W., Rosenberg. 1993. "Measurement of disability at different geographic scales in Canada—local area estimation using microdata from a national disability survey with aggregate census data for local areas." *Proceedings of the International Population Conference.* Montréal: International Union for the Scientific Study of Population Congress, Vol. 1: 553-568.

Moore, E.G., M.W. Rosenberg, and M. Bekkering. 1989. *An Atlas of the Elderly Population of Atlantic Canada.* For the Review of Demography. Kingston, Ontario: Department of Geography, Queen's University.

Moore, E.G., M.W. Rosenberg, and M. Bekkering. 1989. *An Atlas of the Elderly Population of Québec.* For the Review of Demography. Kingston, Ontario: Department of Geography, Queen's University.

Moore, E.G., M.W. Rosenberg, and M. Bekkering. 1989. *An Atlas of the Elderly Population of Ontario.* For the Review of Demography. Kingston, Ontario: Department of Geography, Queen's University.

Moore, E.G., M.W. Rosenberg, and M. Bekkering. 1989. *An Atlas of the Elderly Population of the Prairies.* For the Review of Demography. Kingston, Ontario: Department of Geography, Queen's University.

Moore, E.G., M.W. Rosenberg, and M. Bekkering. 1989. *An Atlas of the Elderly Population of British Columbia.* For the Review of Demography. Kingston, Ontario: Department of Geography, Queen's University.

Moore, E.G., M.W. Rosenberg, and M. Bekkering. 1989. *An Atlas of the Elderly Population of the Territories*. For the Review of Demography. Kingston, Ontario: Department of Geography, Queen's University.

Moore, E.G., S.O. Burke and M.W. Rosenberg. 1990. *The Disabled Adult Residential Population*. For the Ontario Ministry of Community and Social Services. Kingston, Ontario: Department of Geography, Queen's University.

Morrison, P. 1992. *Is "aging in place" a blueprint for the future?* Invited address on major directions in population geography, presented at the annual meetings of the Association of American Geographers, San Diego, California.

Nagnur, D. 1986a. *Longevity and Historical Life Tables 1921–1981 (abridged), Canada and the Provinces*. Ottawa: Minister of Supply and Services Canada. Statistics Canada Catalogue no. 89-506.

Nagnur, D. 1986b. "Rectangularization of the survival curve and entropy: The Canadian experience, 1921–1981." *Canadian Studies in Population*, 13, 1: 83–102.

Nathanson, C. and A. Lopez. 1987. "The future of sex mortality differentials in industrialized countries: A structural hypothesis." *Population Research and Policy Review*, 6, 2: 123–136.

Newbold K.B. 1993. *Characterization and Explanation of Primary, Return and Onward Interprovincial Migration: Canada 1976–1986*. Unpublished PhD Thesis. Department of Geography, McMaster University, Hamilton, Ontario.

Newbold, K.B. and K.L. Liaw. 1990. "Characteristics of Primary, Return and Onward Inter-provincial Migration in Canada: Overall and Age-specific Patterns." *Canadian Journal of Regional Science*. 13,1: 17–34.

Nolan, T. and I.B. Pless. 1986. "Emotional correlates and consequences of birth defects." *The Journal of Pediatrics*. 109: 210–216.

Northcott, H.C. 1988. *Changing Residence: The Geographic Mobility of Elderly Canadians*. Toronto: Butterworths.

Northcott, H.C. 1994. "Public perceptions of the population aging 'crisis.'" *Canadian Public Policy*. 20, 1: 66–77.

Omran, A.R. 1971. "The epidemiological transition: a theory of epidemiology of population change." *Milbank Memorial Fund Quarterly, Health and Society*. 49: 507–537.

Péron, Y. and C. Strohmenger. 1985. *Demographic and Health Indicators: Presentation and Interpretation*. Ottawa: Minister of Supply and Services Canada. Statistics Canada Catalogue no. 82-543E.

Ram, B. 1990. *New trends in the Family: Current Demographic Analysis*. Ottawa: Minister of Regional Industrial Expansion Canada. Statistics Canada Catalogue no.91-535E.

Rees, P. and A.G.Wilson. 1977. *Spatial Population Analysis*. London: Edward Arnold.

Roberge, R., J.-M. Berthelot and M. Wolfson. 1993. *The impact of socioeconomic status on health status in Ontario.* Prepared for the 22nd International Population Conference, International Union for the Scientific Study of Population, Montréal.

Rogers, A. 1975. *Introduction to Multiregional Mathematical Demography.* New York: Wiley.

Rogers, A. 1988. "Age patterns of elderly migration: an international comparison." *Demography.* 25, 3: 355-370.

Rogers, A. 1989. "The elderly mobility transition: growth, concentration, and tempo." *Research on Aging.* 11, 1: 3-32.

Rogers, A., R. Rogers and L. Branch. 1989. "A multistate analysis of active life expectancy." *Public Health Reports.* 104, 3: 222-226.

Rogers, A., R. Rogers and A. Belanger. 1990. "Longer life but worse health? Measurement and dynamics." *The Gerontologist.* 30, 5: 640-649.

Romaniuc, A. 1994. "Fertility in Canada: retrospective and prospective." In F. Trovato and C.F. Grindstaff (eds.). *Perspectives on Canada's population: An introduction to concepts and issues.* Toronto: Oxford.

Rosenberg, M.W., E.G. Moore and S.B. Ball. 1989. "Components of change in the spatial distribution of the elderly population in Ontario, 1976-1986." *The Canadian Geographer.* 33, 3: 218-229.

Rosenberg, M. W. and E.G. Moore. 1990. "The elderly, economic dependency, and local government revenues and expenditures." *Environment and Planning C: Government and Policy.* 8: 149-165.

Rosenthal, C. and J. Gladstone. 1994. "Family relationships and support in later life." In V. Marshall and B. McPherson (eds.) *Aging Canadian Perspectives.* Peterborough, Ontario: Broadview Press. 158-174.

Ross, N.A., M.W. Rosenberg and D.C. Pross. 1994a. "Siting a women's health facility: a location-allocation study of breast cancer screening services in eastern Ontario." *The Canadian Geographer.* 38, 2: 150-161.

Ross, N.A., M.W. Rosenberg, D.C. Pross and B. Bass. 1994b. "Contradictions in women's health care provision: A case study of attendance for breast screening." *Social Science and Medicine.* 39, 8: 1015-1025.

Ruggeri, G.C., R. Howard and K. Bluck. 1994. "The incidence of low income among the elderly." *Canadian Public Policy,* 20,2: 138-151.

Sarlo, C.A. 1992. *Poverty in Canada.* Vancouver: The Fraser Institute.

Seniors Secretariat, Health and Welfare Canada. 1993. *Ageing and Independence: Overview of a National Survey.* Ottawa: Minister of Supply and Services Canada.

Shaw, R.P. 1985. *Intermetropolitan migration in Canada: Changing determinants over three decades.* Toronto: NC Press.

Simmons, J. 1991. "The urban system." In T. Bunting and P. Filion, (eds.) *Canadian Cities in Transition*. Toronto: Oxford University Press.

Stafford, J. 1992. "Welcome but why? Recent changes in Canadian immigration policy." *American Review of Canadian Studies*, 22, 2: 235-258.

Statistics Canada. 1987. *Health and Social Support, 1985*. General Social Survey Analysis Series. Ottawa: Minister of Supply and Services Canada.

Statistics Canada. 1990a. *Highlights: Disabled Persons in Canada*. Ottawa: Minister of Regional Industrial Expansion Canada.

Statistics Canada. 1990b. *A Portrait of Seniors in Canada*. Ottawa: Minister of Regional Industrial Expansion Canada.

Statistics Canada, Census Analysis Division. 1994. *Population Projections 1993-2041: Canada, Provinces and Territories*. Ottawa: Minister of Industry, Science and Technology.

Stone, L.O. 1986. "Implications of recent sharp declines in mortality rates and rapid population growth at ages 80 and above: a state of the art review." A report for Health and Welfare Canada, *Charting Canada's Future: A Report of the Demographic Review*. Ottawa: Minister of Supply and Services Canada.

Stone, L.O. 1993. Social consequences of population ageing: The human support systems dimension. *Proceedings of International Population Conference*. Montréal: International Union for the Scientific Study of Population. 3: 25-34.

Stone, L. O. and S. Fletcher. 1986. *The Seniors Boom: Dramatic Increases in Longevity and Prospects for Better Health*. Ottawa: Minister of Supply and Services Canada. Statistics Canada Catalogue no. 89-515.

Stone, L.O., and C. Marceau. 1977. *Canadian Population Trends and Public Policy through the 1980s*. Montréal: McGill-Queen's Press.

Tiebout, C. 1956. "A pure theory of local expenditures." *Journal of Political Economy*, 64: 416-424.

Todaro, M.P. 1969. "A model of labor migration and urban unemployment in less developed countries." *The American Economic Review*. 59: 138-148.

Tucker, R.D., L.C. Mullins, F. Béland, C.F. Longino, Jr. and V. Marshall. 1992. "Older Canadians in Florida: a comparison of anglophone and francophone seasonal migrants." *Canadian Journal on Aging*. 11, 3: 281-297.

Wilkins, R. 1991. "The need for population-based data on disability." Proceedings of a workshop entitled *Measuring the Health of Canadians Using Population Surveys*. Ottawa: National Health Information Council. 89-94.

Wilkins, R. and O. Adams. 1992. "Health expectancy in Canada, 1986." In Robine, J.-M., M. Blanchet and J.E. Dowd eds. *Health expectancy: First workshop of the international healthy life expectancy network* (REVES), London: HMSO. 57-60.

Wilkins, R., O. Adams and A.M. Brancker. 1989. "Changes in mortality by income in urban Canada from 1971 to 1986. *Health Reports*. 1,2: 137–175. Statistics Canada Catalogue no. 82-003.

Wiseman, R.F. 1990. "Why older people move: theoretical issues." *Research on Aging*. 2: 141–154.

Wolfson, M.C. 1989. "Divorce, homemaker pensions and lifecycle analysis." *Population Research and Policy Review*. 8, 1: 25–54.

Wolfson, M.C. and J.M. Evans. 1989. *Statistics Canada's low-income cut-offs: methodological concerns and possibilities—a discussion paper*. Ottawa. Statistics Canada Catalogue no. 72N0002.

Wright, R.E. and P.S. Maxim. 1987. Canadian fertility trends: a further test of the Easterlin hypothesis. *Canadian Review of Sociology and Anthropology*. 24, 3: 399–457.

World Health Organization. 1980. *International Classification of Impairments, Disabilities and Handicaps. A Manual of Classification Relating to the Consequences of Disease*. Geneva: World Health Organization.

Zimmerman, R.S., D.J. Jackson, C.F. Longino and J.E. Bradsher. 1993. "Interpersonal and economic resources as mediators of the effects of health decline on the geographic mobility of the elderly." *Journal of Aging and Health*. 5, 1: 37–57.

INDEX

Absolute distribution vs. relative concentration, 77
Accumulation, 101, 105
Age group, generalized births or deaths within, 17
Aging. *See* Population aging
Aging in place, 17, 20, 21, 67, 90, 93, 94, 95, 98, 189
    aging scenarios, 99–101, 102, 104, 105, 106
    decomposing the ratio of the elderly, 110
    defined, 93
    metropolitan areas, 93, 99
Aging scenarios, 99–105, 106
    index of concentration, 101, 104, 112–13
    nine scenarios, 99–101

"Baby bonus" grants, 162
Baby boom, 3, 8, 68
Birth rate. *See* Fertility rates
Breast cancer, 122

Canada and Quebec Pension Plans (CPP/QPP), 35, 36–37, 44
Census divisions, xiv, 66
    boundary changes (1986–91), 111
Children
    as dependants, 10, 11
    as support. *See* Family support
Cities
    aging of populations, 186n2, 189
    migration to. *See* Rural-urban migration
    suburbs. *See* Suburbs
    See also Metropolitan areas; Montreal; Toronto; Vancouver
Community profiles and aging, 67–70, 72, 75, 76, 89, 90, 93, 98–101, 105–7
Congregation, 101, 105

Death rates. *See* Mortality
Decomposing the ratio of the elderly, 110
Demography in population aging, 67–68, 70
    See also Sociodemographic context
Dependency, 145–46
    classification of, 116
    level of, 116, 119, 120, 145–46
Dependency ratio (DR), 10–11
    old component (ODR), 10, 11
    projections for ODRs, 174, 176
    service needs and ODRs, 75, 77, 79, 174
    young component (YDR), 10, 11
Disability
    activity limitation, 113, 115–19, 120
    changes (1986–1991), 122–27
    definition, 115
    dependency level. *See* Dependency; Dependency ratio
    geography of, 105, 142, 143, 145, 146–56, 158
    immigration and, 152, 158
    income and, 135, 144, 147, 152, 156
    institutionalization, 23–25, 33, 35, 124, 125, 178, 184, 189–90
    and local moves, 142, 144–45, 146
    measures of, 113–14
    metropolitan areas, 150, 152–56, 157, 158
    migration and, 30, 57, 58–61, 138, 140, 142, 145
    older elderly, 2, 116, 117, 118–19, 120, 146, 188, 190
    projections (for 2011), 174, 178–84
    regional differences, 142, 143, 145, 146–56
    regression models, 140–46
    service utilization. *See* Service utilization
    socio-demographic context, 134–44

subjective views, 119, 121-22, 124, 126

types measured by HALS, 115-16, 117-18, 159-3

younger elderly, xi, 2, 116, 188

See also Health; Health care institutions

Disease

chronic, 12-13

infectious, 11, 12, 13

Divorce, 31-32, 33, 134

and migration, 54, 57

Ecological correlations, 72, 112-5

Education, 42-44

by age and sex, 42, 43

future effects of higher levels, 44

health and, 29-30, 135, 137, 144

income and, 43, 44-45

life expectancy and, 134-35

migration and, 57, 58-61

Elderly population (65+)

by province, 15-18, 190

disability. *See* Disability

gender. *See* Gender

geographical distribution. *See* Geographic patterns

in metropolitan areas, 77, 80, 81, 82-87, 189

percentage of total population, 25, 188

predictors of increase in, 67

projections (to 2011), 163, 164-65, 166-69, 184-85

relative concentration vs. absolute distribution, 77

sex ratio and census division, 74, 75, 77, 78, 81, 85-87

Emigration

projections for the future, 161, 162

See also Immigration

Employment status, 41-42

and income, 42, 44, 45, 46

part-time work, 41, 42, 45

self-employment, 41, 42

Family support, 33, 46-47, 119, 190, 191

availability of, 23, 47, 48, 49, 50

effect of lower fertility rates, 25

migration and, 30, 53, 56, 62, 140, 188

regional differences, 134

Fertility rates

declines, xi, 3, 8, 10, 13, 25

effect on population aging, 66, 67, 68

migration and, 15

projections, 161, 162, 174

First World War, 3, 68

Friends, 33, 46-47, 48, 49, 50, 188, 191

and migration, 53, 56, 62, 140

Future

Canada's elderly in 2011, 163, 164-65, 166-69

disability in 2011, 174, 178-84

education levels, 44

geographic distribution in 2011, 165, 169, 170-74, 175-77

population projections, 161-64

service needs, 33, 35, 134, 156, 158, 174, 184

Gender

disability and, 119, 120, 136, 137, 139, 144, 147

geographic distribution and, 15-17, 18, 74-76, 77, 78, 81, 85-87

immigrants, 14, 15

migration and, 55, 57, 58-61

mortality and, xi, 7, 12, 30, 31, 68, 75, 165

in population aging, 3-8, 9, 26, 61

projections (for 2011), 163, 164, 165, 170, 173, 174, 175

and satisfaction with health status , 121-22

urban-rural contrasts and, 21-23

See also Men living alone; Sex ratios; Women living alone

Generalized births or deaths in an age group, 17

General Social Survey (GSS), 114, 121, 122

changes in health status, 124, 126

hospital stays, 127

Geographic patterns, xi-xii, xiii, 3, 14-23, 26, 70-81, 188, 189, 190

by census division, 71, 80

changes in, 81, 88, 89, 90, 91

disability, 105, 142, 143, 145, 146–56, 158

older elderly by census division, 72, 73, 75

projections (for 2011), 165, 168–69, 170–74, 177

provinces. *See* Provinces and territories

urban-rural contrasts, 17, 21–23

young north and old south, 70, 72, 170

Government transfers

regional payments, 107, 191

to the elderly, 35, 36–37, 38, 39, 40, 44, 190

Great Depression, 68

Growth rates for elderly population, 81, 88, 91, 93, 95, 97

models, 89, 90

Guaranteed Income Supplements (GIS), 35, 36, 37

Health

education and, 29–30, 135, 137, 144

gender and, 119, 120, 136, 137, 139, 144, 147

income and, 29, 135, 136, 144, 147, 152, 156

living arrangements and, 135, 138, 139, 140, 144

migration and, 30, 57, 58–61, 138, 140

service ratios and population growth rates, 105, 107

service utilization, 114, 127–34

sociodemographic variables and, 134–44, 156

status. *See* Disability

Health and Activity Limitation Survey (HALS), 114

changes in disability, 122–25

disability rates, 115–18

patterns of support, 128, 129

Health care

costs, 1, 2, 11

future, 156, 158

increased pressures, 124, 127

Health care institutions, 23–25, 26

health status of elderly in, 114

moves to and from, 23, 24, 54

population in, 24, 25, 119, 120, 124, 125, 178, 189–90

trends and projections, 25, 33, 35, 124, 178–84, 190, 191

Health status, as measured by disability. *See* Disability

Heart disease, 12–13

Home care, 35, 116, 134, 190

Home ownership, 39, 41

migration and, 53–54, 56, 140

Hospitals

stays by sex and age, 127

See also Health care institutions

Human capital theory, 10, 27-4

Immigration

disability and, 152, 158

effects on population aging, 13–14, 15, 26, 66, 189

projections for the future, 161, 162

Immigration Act (1976), 27-5

Income

and aging in place, 93, 99

correlates of low income, 45, 46

disability and, 29, 135, 136, 144, 147, 152, 156

education and, 43, 44–45

employment status and, 42, 44, 45, 46

low-income cut-off, 35–36, 43–44, 188, 190

marital status and, 45, 46

migration and, 57, 58–61

model of low-income status, 44–46

mortality and, 147

older elderly, 44

provinces and territories, 45, 46

service needs and, 45–46, 61–62

sources, 36–37, 38–39, 40

women living alone, 36, 37, 38, 39, 45, 46, 61, 188

Independence. *See* Dependency; Dependency ratio (DR)

Index of concentration for aging scenarios, 101, 104, 112n13

Individual aging, distinguished from population aging, 2

Infant mortality, 11

Institutional living. *See* Health care institutions